3/77

D1557441

Psychetypes

MICHAEL MALONE

Psychetypes

A New Way
of Exploring Personality

E. P. DUTTON & CO., INC. · NEW YORK

Library of Congress Cataloging in Publication Data

Malone, Michael.
   Psychetypes.

   1. Personality. 2. Typology (Psychology) I. Title.
BF698.M322 1977   155.2'6   76–42224
ISBN: 0–525–18582–8

155.2'6

MAL

*Published simultaneously in Canada by Clarke, Irwin & Company Limited,
Toronto and Vancouver*
Designed by The Etheredges

10 9 8 7 6 5 4 3 2 1

First Edition

For
Dr. Harriet Mann, whose book this is

And for
Dr. Lila Nachtigall,
who joins to great medical wisdom,
great human charity.

This book is a study of personality types based on a theory of experiential typology; in other words, a theory of how different people experience their selves and the world around them. It outlines a system for distinguishing eight basic patterns of personality and offers a vocabulary for describing these psychetypes.

This is not a how-to book. It will not give you advice or formulas on how to meditate, be more aggressive, say no, influence people, scream, gain power, save your marriage, perfect your divorce, raise your kids, or enjoy your sex. It will not tell you in sixty hours whether you're okay, not so hot, playing games, or in fear of flying.

This is a how-are book. How we are alike, and how we are different. If, as this theory assumes, each of us has a natural typological set, perhaps by coming to understand its components, we will better understand, as well, both ourselves and others. To help us communicate this knowledge, experiential typology provides a detailed descriptive vocabulary, a kind of systematic shorthand of personality traits. It offers a language for experience.

Contents

Preface

The theory of experiential typology described in this book was taught to me by Dr. Harriet Mann, whom I met in Cambridge in 1970. She was at that time practicing psychotherapy there and expanding her study of normal personality patterns, a project in which she had been engaged for some time—researching, writing, and holding seminars and group discussions. Over the next five years I became increasingly involved in Dr. Mann's work. Having learned the theory through participation in several of these sessions and having shared it with numerous friends, I was convinced of its remarkable insightfulness into the differences among basic types of people and of its efficacy as a tool for communicating those differences. I later assisted Dr. Mann in an editorial and research capacity while she was compiling extensive documentation of individual experiential worlds, behaviorial biographies of both historical persons and fictional characters.

As I understand its origins, experiential typology was first developed at Princeton by Dr. Mann, Dr. Humphry Osmond, and Mrs. Miriam Siegler. Subsequent contributions were made by Dr. Richard Smoke and by the dozens of participants in Dr. Mann's seminars. The theory's immediate source is the classification of attitude and function types created by Carl Jung in his seminal work, *Psychological Types*. Other influences include the various typological studies of Aldous Huxley, Heinrich Kluver, William Sheldon, and Bernard Aaronson. From von Uexhull's discussion of the *Umvelt*, or experiential world, came the original perception of the spatiotemporal dimensions.

Dr. Mann has not only shared with me her professional knowledge and experience; she has also most generously made available her research materials—the fruits of many years of thought and labor. With that work and my own reading in history and literature to draw on, I have tried in these pages to outline for the lay reader the system of personality patterns I learned from her. I view the relationship of this book to the theory of experiential typology as that of translation of and commentary on another's creation. The achievements of the creation belong to its originator; whatever flaws there may be in its application are entirely my responsibility.

Let me thank Dr. Mann, an intuitive oceanic, for inspiring me, and my wife, Maureen Quilligan, a thinking territorial, for her invaluable assistance in (a) theorizing, (b) organizing, and (c) structuring my time. And to my editor, William Whitehead, a feeling volcanic, my deepest gratitude for his unswerving support, unshakable patience, and unfailing critical judgment.

Psychetypes

1.
Introducing a Language for Experience

We humans have been puttering about in the universe for a few thousand years now, trying to sort out everything in it. In this perennial pastime some of us have gone in for collecting and labeling stacks of facts, while others have been more involved in defining the how, where, when, and why of things—the which of the what of it all.

Naturally, and despite the fact that astronomers have taught us better, we consider ourselves the center of this universe; after all, we seem to be the only creatures even *bothering* to sort it out, and so our favorite subject of exploration has always been "us," ourselves and our relationships to each other. We fascinate ourselves. "What a piece of work is a man ... What is this quintessence of dust?" Throughout history people have stood ready to answer Hamlet's question, often to debate or defend their answers to the death. Poets and philosophers, preachers and teachers, psychologists and songwriters, we've all been telling each other what man is ever since man was.

Probably the first thing that strikes us about the nature of human nature is its extraordinary multiplicity and diversity. You and I may both eat, sleep, dream, work, and make love, but we probably won't be alike in our ways of feeling, thinking, and acting, in our styles and our habits, our likes and dislikes. And there are still wider discrepancies among our disparate cultures and during different periods of history.

Confronted with this multiformity, the human impulse is not always to cry, *"Vive la différence!"* We are social, syncretizing creatures, and we tend to seek common denominators that will unify us as this species of featherless bipeds. So, "I think, therefore I am." "Man is the only animal who thinks, who weeps, who worships, who laughs, who kills for pleasure." This impulse to unify and define has been one of the causes of our survival, as well as one of the hopes of our salvation, for the wretched record of history reminds us that out of the Pandora's box of our differences have endlessly roared far too many horrors, from individual bigotry to international wars.

On the other hand, it is equally dangerous to deny our differences. Our insistence on uniformity can be malevolent, oppressive, and dictatorial. I insist that you be British, Buddhist, Baptist, a Communist, an anti-Communist, an achiever, a believer, a teetotaler, a meat hater, a "feminine" woman, a "masculine" man, long-haired, short-haired, a company man. In other words, insist that you be like me. Because I am right; God knows this. That's why He's on my side. The fact is, though, that people can be so different that only a leap of good will seems capable of bridging the gaps that may separate rich from poor, Westerner from Easterner, black from white, old from young, man from woman.

Our blessing (and our bane) is that we *want* to bridge these gaps. We want to understand. And we have built ourselves a miraculously complex and versatile tool with which to construct the bridge. That tool is language. With language we can create laws and mitigate individual heterogeneity for a common good. With language we can communicate how we feel, what we want, plan, hope, and need: Who we are. We can share our experiences. And we can listen.

Unfortunately, we do not always listen well, and one of the

reasons we don't is our tendency to assume that everyone must be or should be like us, that if we speak the same language, we mean the same things. That's not true. We don't always speak the same language, though we may use the same words. Words like "right," "good," "moral," "goal," or "future" can mean very different things to different people. In our efforts to communicate, we resort to analogies, examples, to inflection and volume, to "body language." And still we may throw up our hands, sighing, "You'll never understand me. Let's face it, we're in two different worlds. Either you're crazy, or I'm crazy."

The truth is probably that neither of us is crazy; the problem is that we assume we ought to be *alike*, that in the same situation our experience, our way of perceiving and reacting, will be shared by another person. If not, there's something the matter with one of us. Not necessarily so. There are a lot of different ways to be absolutely normal, and that's what this book is about.

WHAT ARE PSYCHETYPES?

There is certainly nothing new in the desire to define the differences among people. Somehow it makes us feel better when we have some handles, some categories, or a theory that will help us explain why we are who we are, and why "they" are who they are. Give us a couple who aren't getting along, and we'll come up with a system to prove why. In the Renaissance, for example, it was the humors theory: He's choleric, and she's sanguine. Or we will say they're star-crossed lovers; he's a Sagittarius, and she's a Gemini. If Jack Sprat can eat no fat, his wife can eat no lean, then he's an ectomorph, and she's an endomorph. Or they're incompatible because he's an anal compulsive and she's an oral erotic, because he's outer-directed and she's inner-directed, because she's a right-wing countess and he's a left-wing commoner, because he's square and she's hip, because he says "tomato" and she says "tomahto" and let's call the whole thing off. But whether they be physiological, morphological, psychological, economic, or sociological in focus, all these systems are attempts to classify types of people. In other words, typologies.

The theory described in this book is called experiential typology. It is a theory of psychetypes and is concerned not so much with the ways people *behave* differently in given situations as with the ways they *experience* situations differently. *Experiential typology is a descriptive theory of the different experiences that underlie behavior in normal personalities.* It assumes that if people experience things differently, their attitudes, assumptions, and actions will vary. These diverse sets of attitudes, assumptions, and actions we call psychetypes. Each individual operates, whether he is aware of it or not, out of a particular psychetype, a basic perceptual set, first for understanding and second for dealing with reality. The perception is always primary, for while two people may behave quite similarly, the texture of their experience (their own sense of what is happening) may nevertheless be worlds apart. The theory of psychetypes is a way of exploring the various experiential worlds that lie beneath, and motivate, our behavior.

Typology is not psychology. It delineates; it does not diagnose. While the theory of psychetypes developed from certain psychological assumptions of Carl Jung, it neither attempts to *assess* personalities nor to evaluate their adjustment to "reality." Instead, it offers a carefully detailed *description* of various personality types. It demonstrates that a person of a given type will have certain tendencies and potentials, certain orientations to time and space, and that these will be shared with other persons of his or her type. What that person *does* with these tendencies is a question of psychology and does not concern us here. Any psychetype can include people who are self-confident, insecure, depressed, happy, outgoing, productive, whatever. Neurosis, even psychosis, is potentially possible in all types. Nor, in a general theory, do psychetypes account for the specific facts of background and character that affect personality; people of any of the psychetypes we are going to explore may be kind or selfish, educated or not, dedicated or irresponsible, intelligent or stupid, happily or unhappily married. What this book *will* tell you is the ways in which those personal qualities are likely to function within the personality, in what directions they are likely to be oriented.

This, then, is a theory of normal personality types. Moreover, it assumes that the perimeters of human normalcy are wide, wider than we are often willing to allow. Far too many people are deemed eccentric who are functioning well within the normal boundaries of their particular type. A "neurotic" may be neurotic only insofar as we misunderstand his or her typology or choose to define that typology as variant and therefore aberrant. Of course, a theory of psychetypes neither negates abnormality nor insists that nonfunctional or destructive behavior be accepted as normal. However, one of the ways a person can become neurotic (that is, unable to realize his own potentialities) is by failing to develop his *natural* typology. (Other reasons might derive from familial, social, or intrapsychic maladjustments.) Furthermore, it is difficult for people to develop happily when their natural typology is not recognized or respected by others. By providing a language for experience, a theory of psychetypes enables us to communicate across our typological worlds and thereby come to understand and accept the validity of our differences.

THE EIGHT BASIC PSYCHETYPES

There are eight basic psychetypes, that is, normal personalities that can be distinguished from each other primarily in terms of their perceptions rather than behaviors. The combination of these perceptual sets within an individual generates one of the four Jungian *functions—thinking, feeling, sensation,* or *intuition*—as a primary experiential mode. These four experiential functions are the manifestations of two almost automatic sets of presuppositions with which we approach life. One is our sense of time. The other is our sense of space. These temporal and spatial dimensions are our *experiential areas.* In other words, the areas are those apprehensions of "reality" that lie beneath and channel our behavior. Unlike behavior, they do not seem amenable to our conscious control. Most of us, in fact, are not even aware that they are perceptions; the areas seem to us instead to be simply "the way things are." They appear so natural that we, often wrongly, assume everyone else shares them.

We have one of two basic attitudes toward the *flow of time.*

With regard to time's passage, people are either *continuous* or *discontinuous,* that is, they perceive time either as a continuous, recurrent pattern or as a discontinuous series of unique, discrete moments. Thinking and feeling types are always continuous; sensation types and intuitives are always discontinuous.

People perceive space in two different dimensions, each of which can be apprehended in one of two distinct ways. First is the internal dimension of space, what "makes up" its contents. We may assume reality to be concrete, specific, and physical *(volcanic)* or as abstract, generalized, and theoretical *(aethereal).* Second is the external dimension of space, its outer shape, so to speak. We may see the world as structured *(territorial)* or as without boundaries *(oceanic).* Our primary spatial settings depend on whether we are more concerned with the internal or the external dimension, the substance or the structure of space. When we combine a person's primary function with his primary spatial area, we have his psychetype. The eight psychetypes are:

CONTINUOUS:
{ Thinking territorial
Thinking aethereal
Feeling volcanic
Feeling oceanic

DISCONTINUOUS:
{ Sensation volcanic
Sensation territorial
Intuitive oceanic
Intuitive aethereal

THE FOUR FUNCTIONS

Thinking types are people who see time as continuously connected in a linear progression; they are analytic, theoretical, and hierarchical. Interested in ideas and goals, they structure their world and desire to understand its distinctions. As we will see, they tend to be detached, orderly, and competitive. Billie Jean King, Jimmy Carter, and Walter Cronkite are thinking types. *Feeling types* also perceive time as continuous; it is very important to them that their present life be connected with their past. But for them life is seen as merging, unified, and personal rather than bounded and abstract. Theirs is a world filled with concrete, actualized, finite things. Feeling types are generally involved, pragmatic, and receptive people. Elizabeth Taylor, Dwight D. Eisenhower, and Albert Schweitzer are examples of feeling types. *Sensation types* are people who perceive time as a series of discrete, unique moments, unlinked to the past or future. They live in a present-oriented world of immediate, specific actualities, and they tend to prefer action to theory; they structure their environment and wish to control it. Pablo Picasso, Amelia Earhart, and Robert F. Kennedy were all sensation types. *Intuitives* also see time as disconnected from the past; unlike sensation types, however, they are very involved in the future and its infinite possibilities. The world of the intuitive is unstructured, speculative, individualistic, and imaginative. Marilyn Monroe, Walt Disney, and Frank Lloyd Wright were intuitives.

We each have access to all of the four functions; each of us thinks, feels, intuits, and senses. The more we are able to realize our human potentials, the more integrated these functions are in our personalities. Yet for all of us, *one* function provides the primary avenue of contact with the outer world; we have only limited access to the others. It is on the basis of this first function that we type individuals. George Washington's first function was feeling, so we call him a feeling type. Thomas Jefferson's first function was thinking; he was, then, a thinking type. Thomas Paine, an intuitive. Benjamin Franklin, a sensation type.

Franklin was not, say, a "little bit" of a sensation type or "usually" a sensation type, for a psychetype is just that—a type. And so Franklin will consistently share more traits with other sensation types than with individuals with different first functions. Of course, he will not be *exactly* like any other sensation type. No person will ever demonstrate all of the behavioral or attitudinal traits that apply to any particular function. Our psychetype is rather the background, the stage setting on which each of our unique, personal dramas is played. Thomas A. Edison, Marlene Dietrich, and Joseph Stalin share the same typology with Franklin, and in the wide discrepancies among their values and interests we see the potential range possible within the general confines of a single typological frame.

Nor should one assume that, for example, only thinking types know how to "think" (although some thinking types may claim this is so, just as some feeling types may believe that they alone are perceptive about emotions). The point is rather that the sensation-type Franklin would not have thought in the same way as his thinking-type friend Jefferson; his thinking was more likely to be grounded, like his kite, in the actual, material, immediate, pragmatic, sensate world around him. He invented bifocals, devised almanacs, organized fire and police departments, argued politics masterfully. But it was Jefferson, not Franklin, who wrote the Declaration of Independence, with its statement of the first principles on which this country was founded.

Nor do only intuitives have imagination; nor only feeling types, profound emotions. Among the benefactors of mankind, Florence Nightingale was a thinking type; Gandhi was a sensation type, while Pope John XXIII had feeling for a first function and Mary Baker Eddy (founder of the Church of Christ, Scientist), was an intuitive. Typology never limits the awesome capacity of the human spirit nor of creative genius. Beethoven was an intuitive composer; Schubert, a feeling type; Brahms, a thinking type; and Mozart, a sensation type. Painters, too, come out of all four of the experiential worlds. Van Gogh from feeling; Joshua Reynolds from thinking; Blake from intuition; Modigliani from sensation. There are thinking-type poets like Milton; intuitives like Shelley; sensation types like Robert Frost; feeling types like Wordsworth.

Into the world arena of politics and conquest, champions of every type have charged. Intuitives from Alexander the Great to Trotsky; thinking types from Elizabeth I of England to John F. Kennedy; sensation types from Julius Caesar to Lyndon B. Johnson; feeling types from George Washington to Winston Churchill. And if we look more narrowly at a specific field of endeavor like psychology, for example, we find every function represented by seminal leaders. Thinking by Freud; intuition by Jung; sensation by Adler; and from the feeling-type world, Fritz Perl's Gestalt therapy.

As this brief sketch makes clear, no individual can be totally comprehended by a typology. It is vital to remember that when applying experiential typology to our lives. The purpose should never be to lock ourselves in separate houses but to understand better the different rooms in which we live.

THE TEMPORAL AND SPATIAL AREAS

The only absolute thing about time is that it consistently refuses to stand still for anyone; otherwise, it jerks, bolts, drags, passes, and progresses with us in a multiplicity of tempos.* While some of us are waltzing, others are doing the hustle. To type a person is automatically to categorize his or her perception of time as either *continuous* or *discontinuous.* The continuous person (thinking or feeling) experiences the passage of time in a continuum that is recurrent and patterned. Each moment is linked to what went before and what will follow. To be continuous is to believe in the evolutional nature of time, to believe that the past has created the present and the present will create the future. It is to believe in what the thinking-type philosopher Edmund Burke called "The Grand Instructor, Time." Such people are likely to believe in the importance of plans, to value consistency and temperateness, and to respect traditions.

But to the discontinuous person (sensation or intuition) "pastness" is generally far less significant. "The past is dead," as Jacques Cousteau (a sensation type) summarily put it. In this world moments of time are seen as discrete and unique. The present is existential rather than evolutional, and the innovative is likely to be valued above the "tried and true." As Henry Ford, another sensation type, said, "History is bunk."

Between these two views of time lies an enormous chasm of possible misunderstanding, a chasm into which friendships, and even marriages, can slip and fall. For as we shall see, each tends to misconstrue and to feel uncomfortable in the other's world. Each of us also has available to him the two basic modes

*Our particular *rhythm of time* defines us as more or less extraverted or introverted; for a discussion of these terms, see Chapter 10.

of perceiving space, one having to do with the internal content of space (its *substance*), the other with the external shape, or *structure*, of space. In their perceptions of the fundamental content or makeup of existence, people are either *volcanic* or *aethereal*. *Volcanics* (sensation or feeling types) perceive the world as actual, concrete, specified, and substantial. Their attitude toward it tends to be communal, active, and pragmatic. They are the people who strike us as personal, as engaged and involved in life—people like Robert F. Kennedy (a sensation volcanic) or D. H. Lawrence (a feeling volcanic).

Their polar opposites are the *aethereals* (thinking types or intuitives), whose construction of space is abstract, hypothetical, and imaginative, and whose mode of relating is theoretical, detached, and idealistic. Reality for aethereals like Virginia Woolf (a thinking aethereal) or James Joyce (an intuitive aethereal) lies in the conceptual rather than the tangible sphere. Such individuals are interested not so much in particular things, people, or events as in *ideas* about them—their symbolic meanings, their universal essences, their future significances.

As with our view of the internal substance of space, there are also diametrically opposed ways of perceiving its external structure. One is *territorial;* the other is *oceanic*. As the name suggests, *territorials* (thinking and sensation types) are very sensitive to "territory"—their own and others. They would agree with the farmer in Robert Frost's poem: "Good fences make good neighbors." Such people see reality as structured, bounded, hierarchical, and differentiated. Their attitude toward the world, then, is objective, controlled, goal-oriented, and assertive. From this world of observant, practical, and disciplined individuals have come many of our scientists, among them Madame Curie (a thinking territorial) and Louis Pasteur (a sensation territorial). For territorials everything has its proper place; objects, events, and people all exist within carefully marked boundaries that must not be muddled or overstepped.

Boundaries are largely irrelevant to *oceanics* (feeling types and intuitives), whose experiential world is unified, connected, and unstructured. Oceanics see everything in a flow in which life intermingles and merges with all other life. Their mode of dealing with the world is subjective, personal, and flexible. They "go with the flow." It was always in such imagery that feeling-oceanic novelist Thomas Wolfe spoke of the creative process—maintaining the flow, drowning in material, tapping the river or the reservoir, keeping up with the stream. People of this type tend to be receptive rather than assertive and are less interested in territorial "doing" than with the process of "being." Queen Victoria, an intuitive oceanic, relied pervasively on the territoriality of her consort Prince Albert to organize and manage not only the family but aspects of her administrative duties which she found typologically uncongenial.

The two sets of spatial dimensions contain *opposites*. We will never, therefore, find a thinking type with a volcanic sense of spatial content or an oceanic attitude toward structure. Someone who is aethereal (as thinking types are) is by definition *not* volcanic. One cannot simultaneously perceive something as concrete and not concrete. Someone who is territorial cannot, of course, like oceanics, perceive space as unbounded. Hence, there are only certain combinations possible—eight, in fact.

We accommodate all these preconscious perceptions of time and space to the outside world along certain predictable lines. For we do not live simply instinctively; instead, we attempt to control and to channel ourselves, our environment, and our situations. In so doing, we tend to act in fairly consistent, and consequently classifiable, ways. We call these individual instances of behavior *traits*. A given psychetype, then, behaves according to the personality traits belonging to his function.

TYPING A PERSON

When assigning a specific individual a psychetype, we refer to him or her not simply as an intuitive, for example, but as an intuitive oceanic or an intuitive aethereal. This distinction indicates the priority of either external spatial structure or internal spatial substance in that person's experiential world. For some people structure is primary; for others, substance. Thomas Jefferson and Woodrow Wilson were both thinking types. But for ᵀefferson the differentiated, bounded world around him (the world's structure) would have been more paramount than the hypothetical, symbolic substance of reality that is indicative of aethereality. That second world, on the other hand, took precedence in Wilson's typology. So we call Jefferson (objective, habitual, goal-directed) a thinking territorial and Wilson (detached, idealistic, ascetic) a thinking aethereal.

If we first determine which of the four basic functions best explains someone, we then have to decide which of the two possible spatial settings is most applicable, given the personality traits observed. Say we decide someone is a feeling type. We then need to know if he is a feeling volcanic or a feeling oceanic. Does he tend to rely on assertive action, or does he tend to be very open and subjective? If the first, he's probably volcanic, like Norman Mailer; if the second, he's probably oceanic, like van Gogh. Suppose, however, we are first able to determine a spatial area rather than the function. Then we might look next for a temporal clue. Does an oceanic appear to be continuous with regard to time (therefore, a *feeling* oceanic), or does he seem discontinuous (therefore, an *intuitive* oceanic)? Or, to take another example, since territoriality contributes both to thinking and sensation, we know, as soon as we perceive someone to have a territorial priority, that he is either a thinking or a sensation type, not an intuitive or a feeling type. In the thinking type we will find territoriality expressed through the theoretical principles and future orientation of *aethereality*, along with the plan making and logical consistency of *continuity*. Conversely, a sensation type's territoriality will be revealed in the physical, present orientation of the *volcanic* world and in the spontaneous immediacy of *discontinuity*. These factors combine to produce very different individuals, for instance, Humphrey Bogart—a sensation territorial—and Lauren Bacall —a thinking territorial. Yet, because of their shared primary areas such people would find that they held in common many attitudes about life.

Each of our psychetypes shares something with people of all other types. Take, for instance, an intuitive oceanic like Marilyn Monroe. She would have shared discontinuity with sensation territorial Humphrey Bogart but neither his volcanicness nor his territoriality. With thinking territorial Lauren Bacall,

Monroe would have had some access to aethereality but none of the latter's continuity or territorial attitude toward space. Oceanic structure would be common to Monroe and to feeling oceanic Elizabeth Taylor, who, however, would also be continuous and volcanic. Still closer to Monroe's own typology would be the intuitive aethereal personality—Orson Welles, for one—and of course, closest of all, another intuitive oceanic, someone with the exact same psychetype. Interestingly, Rudolph Valentino, perhaps closest also to being her male counterpart in the pantheon of Hollywood sex stars, seems to have been an intuitive oceanic, too.

Naturally, the types who would have the *least* in common would be those who shared the fewest primary areas—who had, therefore, no common function. These people are alike only in their subsidiary areas, and that similarity is a very distant one indeed. Leaving aside differences in extraversion and introversion, which would obviously further the breach, the most dissimilar types are: sensation territorials (like Stalin) and feeling oceanics (like Winston Churchill); feeling volcanics (like Eisenhower) and intuitive aethereals (like Patton); thinking aethereals (like Franklin Delano Roosevelt) and sensation volcanics (like Mussolini); thinking territorials (like De Gaulle) and intuitive oceanics (like Hitler).

Friendships or marriages between two such different people would have to exercise the most vigorous efforts of good will and understanding to surmount vastly separate attitudes and perceptions about almost everything. Such bridges can be built. But far more likely, even with the best will in the world, are the sorts of clashes that wrenched the friendship of Freud (a thinking territorial) and Jung (an intuitive oceanic) or the storm of incompatibility between the painters Gauguin (a sensation territorial) and van Gogh (a feeling oceanic).

A NOTE ON METHOD

What happens to these functions, areas, and traits, all of which we have been discussing in the abstract, when they are filtered through the catalyst of individual human beings? The best way to answer is by example, and so we will describe the traits either through specific hypothetical situations or through the actions and words of particular individuals, people with whom the reader is probably already familiar: statesmen, artists, and popular historical figures. These are for the most part people whom we could call megatypes, for they have developed the potential of their typologies to extraordinary degrees. In a sense, Eleanor Roosevelt is a thinking type's thinking type, Beethoven is an intuitive's intuitive, Charles Lindbergh the paradigm of sensation types, and Robert E. Lee a quintessential feeling type. Their psychetypes have been assigned, hypothetically, on the basis of biographies and personal writings.

To simplify discussion, we use standard abbreviations for all the terms that compose the eight basic psychetypes. This shorthand makes for a more manageable working vocabulary. These abbreviations are:

T = thinking
F = feeling
S = sensation
I = intuition
C = continuity
D = discontinuity
R = territorial   (We use "R" for territorial to avoid confusion with *T*hinking.)
V = volcanic
O = oceanic
A = aethereal

Thus, we will refer to Marilyn Monroe, an intuitive oceanic, as an IO; Orson Welles, an intuitive aethereal, would be an IA; Lindbergh, a sensation territorial, would be an SR, while a thinking territorial would be a TR, and so on.*

*If we were to give a *complete* psychetype description of an individual, we would include other factors. Walt Disney, for example, would be called an extraverted discontinuous intuitive aethereal oceanic with a secondary thinking function. However, it is unnecessary to include all this information. *All* intuitive aethereals are discontinuous and have a secondary oceanic area, and a secondary thinking function. We need, therefore, only say that Walt Disney is an IA.

While every effort has been made to avoid bias or mistyping, there may be occasional disagreement about the assignment of particular psychetypes. Anecdotes and quotations are used because they exemplify specific traits of a given type. No one trait will define a person. Nor will his psychetype encompass his entire personality. Each of us, as Walt Whitman said, contains multitudes; each of us contradicts himself. And none of us, neither everyman nor Leonardo da Vinci, is completely containable in any one category of any theory. Freud ended his study of Dostoevski with the admission that "before the problem of the creative artist, analysis must lay down its arms." This is ultimately true before the mystery of any human being.

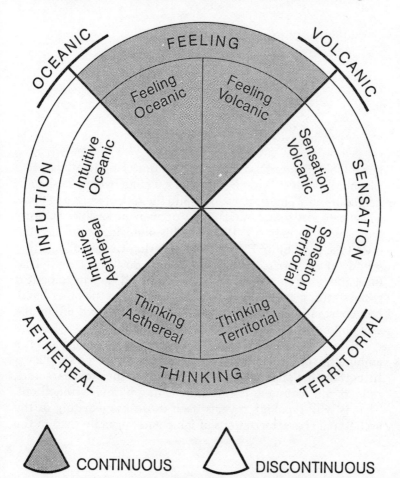

CONTINUOUS   DISCONTINUOUS

2.

A Practical
Approach to Psychetyping

If we look at the marvelous complexities of human lives, like Eleanor Roosevelt's, or Beethoven's, or our wives, husbands, neighbors, and children, we may find the task of assigning them a neat category somehow arbitrary or even impossible. Take my boss, someone may say. Which of his obnoxious traits are the ones that type him? He's always ordering people about; that sounds like a territorial, but he doesn't do it very well. That must mean he's an oceanic. Then again, all he cares about is social status, so maybe he's a sensation type. On the other hand, he's constantly asking for sympathy about the hard life he led as a child, so I guess he must be a feeling type.

The simpler something is, the easier it is to classify, and the ambiguities of life do not permit us the luxury of such simplicity. In certain fiction, however, we *do* meet lifelike characters, refined and flattened, their complicating wrinkles ironed out. That is why typology reveals itself more immediately in the archetypal characterizations of fable and fairy tale than in the

16

complexities of fuller personalities. And so it may be helpful to use such figures as preliminary handles for approaching experiential typology.

Take, for example, the cartoon children in Charles Schultz's *Peanuts*. Charlie Brown, sweet, passive, easily hurt, always involved, is a *feeling oceanic*. Lucy, the bossy, verbal organizer and sapiential authority, is a *thinking territorial*. Schroeder, the imaginative, Beethoven-obsessed pianist, is an *intuitive aethereal*. And Snoopy, the role-playing, pleasure-loving, mechanically ingenious dog, is a (very discontinuous) *sensation volcanic*. Like adult FOs, Charlie tends to be swayed by others, to anticipate negatively (he expects to lose the baseball game; he is sure the little red-haired girl will ignore him); and he is loyal, trusting, and very open to relationships. Like adult IAs, Schroeder is absolutely absorbed in his vision (playing the piano), so committed to it that he needs little from the outside world, including the flirtatious attention of an aggressive territorial like Lucy. The interactions among these cartoon figures caricature our own attitudes and our own responses to people of different typologies. We know them to be true, and that is why we laugh.

In *The Wizard of Oz,* the four functions are set forth even more directly. Each of the characters in Baum's fable is *literally* in quest of his primary function. The thinking-type Scarecrow wants a brain. The feeling-type Tinman wants a heart. The sensation-type Lion wants courage. Dorothy, who meets the Scarecrow first in this psychic quest, is herself a thinking type. The visionary Wizard whom they seek is an intuitive. Those familiar with the *Winnie the Pooh* stories will recall similarly basic psychetypes: the emotional donkey, Eeyore, an FO; the bouncy Tigger, an SV; the brainy Rabbit, a TR; and the irrepressible Pooh himself, an IO.

Fictional worlds are often permeated by one particular experiential world—often, but not inevitably, that of the author. *Alice in Wonderland,* the magical creation of TA mathematician Lewis Carroll, is largely a thinking-type world filled with aethereal characters who delight in zany gymnastics with language. It is quite a different country from the sensation-filled adventures of SV Robert Lewis Stevenson's sea stories, *Treasure*

Island and *Kidnapped,* in which volcanic personalities predominate. Then there are works like *Black Beauty, Heidi,* and many of the fairy tales of Hans Christian Anderson that are generally expressive of the feeling function, while the fantasy realms of Mary Poppins or Dr. Seuss are intuitive in atmosphere.

Popular adult fiction, because of its simple (or simplistic) characterizations, is another source of "pure" types. Take the detective novel. British versions tend to employ thinking-type and, in particular, thinking-aethereal crime solvers for whom detecting is primarily a cerebral process. Sherlock Holmes (a TA) is, of course, the master prototype of later thinking-aethereal sleuths like Agatha Christie's Monsieur Poirot. In American works, however, sensation-type heroes dominate and *sense* their way to solutions by slugging, shooting, and sleeping around with suspects. Spillane's Mike Hammer (an SR) and Chandler's Philip Marlowe (also an SR) are typical. But there are feeling-type private eyes as well; Ross McDonald's Lew Archer is a feeling volcanic who always involves himself emotionally in entangled generations of family traumas as he attempts to figure out who murdered whom. And there are the eccentric intuitives—Colombo (an IO) or Dorothy Sayers' whimsical Lord Peter Whimsey (an IA). And certainly not least, we have the enormously fat, megalomaniac, misogynous genius, Nero Wolfe, who solves crimes by sheer intuition, without ever leaving his study chair, for author Rex Stout has provided his master sleuth with a pair of sensation-type legs in the person of Archie Goodwin, Wolfe's supercompetent assistant.

"Pure" types are equally evident in the broad, formulaic characterizations of television. With the exceptions of the intuitive Colombo and the feeling-volcanic Baretta, most adventure series center around sensation or thinking territorials: Kojak, Mannix, McCoy, McCloud, McMillan. In television comedies, we see the stereotypic conflicts that result from typological differences. Both Rhoda and Maude are thinking-territorial wives with sensation-territorial husbands (Joe and Walter). Mary Tyler Moore is also a TR who argues with an SR, her boss, Lou Grant. In "All in the Family," the typological gap is widened: Archie Bunker is a particularly ignorant and belligerent sensation territorial married to a particularly "dingy" intuitive oceanic, Edith, and in constant conflict with the social and political principles of his thinking-type son-in-law.

But when we turn from the simplistic patterns of children's fables and television programs to the classics of literature, we find ourselves among characters who seem as full and intricate as living human beings. Mr. Toad, the mad motorcar enthusiast in *The Wind in the Willows,* is pure intuition. Now, Hamlet is also an intuitive; but to type so miraculously deep and so humanly complex a figure is not to define him in the same way. Such creations bring typology to life with all the subtlety of art; sometimes, indeed, they seem "larger than life." In general, however, we *can* say that different types of literature best lend themselves to one or another of the four experiential sets. Tragedy, for example, is basically *volcanic* in nature. Macbeth, King Lear, and Othello are all feeling volcanics. So is Sophocles' Antigone. Shakespeare's Antony and Cleopatra are, like the classical Medea, also volcanics. In the same way, the tragically fated people in Thomas Hardy's novels live in a volcanic world. Epics (like the *Iliad* and *Paradise Lost*) tend to be aethereal. Comedy and adventure are territorial. Romance is oceanic; fittingly, one of the best-known romances, *The Faerie Queene,* was written by a feeling oceanic, Edmund Spenser.

Or if we speak in terms of the functions, we might say that adventure and melodrama, from *Robinson Crusoe* to *Gone With the Wind,* derive from the sensation world, while tragedy and "psychological novels" (like *Jane Eyre* or *The Brothers Karamazov*) come out of the feeling function. Epic and romance (which include works like *The Lord of the Rings*) are based in intuition. Comedy of manners (*Pride and Prejudice,* for example), satire from Swift to Nabokov, and "novels of ideas" like those of Zola and Huxley are characteristic of the thinking function.

These broad suggestions should help the reader form at least a sketchy sense of what each of the four experiential worlds is "like" before beginning more detailed study of the traits that belong to them.

We will turn next to those perceptual and behavioral traits, examining them first through the temporal and spatial areas, then through thinking, feeling, sensation, and intuition. Finally, there are six points that are important to remember when learning the psychetypes, especially before applying them to innocent friends and relatives.

1. *Never evaluate an experiential type on the basis of one personality.* As we have mentioned, no individual displays all the traits of a type: Ingrid Bergman, van Gogh, and Mao Tse-tung, for instance, reveal very disparate aspects of the feeling-oceanic type. Nor do the traits completely explain any individual. Environmental, cultural, and psychological factors invariably modify our typological presets. Hitler, for example, was an intuitive oceanic. So was Marilyn Monroe. This certainly does not mean that intuitive oceanicness leads one to become a tyrannical psychotic or a suicidal neurotic; to explain psychosis and neurosis is the business of psychology, not typology. But it *is* true that the particular avenues their problems took were those to which their psychetype made them potentially vulnerable. Likewise, the vicious cruelty of Stalin does not come out of sensation territoriality per se but out of his particular background, character, and morality, funneled through sensation territoriality.

2. In an effort to be as precise as possible, *experiential typology uses different terms when describing comparable aspects of behavior for each of the areas or functions.* For example, in talking about the impact people have on others, we say intuitives are *charismatic,* sensation types are *magnetic,* thinking types *dynamic,* and feeling types *enchanting.* Actually, in common parlance these words are used almost interchangeably, but we have found that each suggests a particular atmosphere that should be distinguished. Intuitives seem to throw the self out at others like a dazzling display of fireworks. In the personality of an effective intuitive this projection can be extraordinarily inspiring; we need mention only the impact of Alexander the Great and Napoleon. Sensation types, on the other hand, seem to pull others toward them, as the term *magnetic* suggests; Robert F. Kennedy (an SV) had this ability to a remarkable degree. Thinking types awe others with their will, the power of their personality, the *dynamic* energy they command. In this way, Elizabeth I gained the enduring respect and

admiration of her British subjects. With feeling types, we respond to a unique warmth, a personal appeal, an emotional reaching out; Washington and Churchill were *loved* and honored by the people they governed.

Similarly, when we list "manipulativeness" as a sensation-type trait, we do not imply that people of other types never manipulate others. They do: feeling types by pulling on others' emotions, intuitives by refusing to make decisions, and thinking types by argument. All modes of behavior are open to each type, and our terms simply reflect differences in the "feel" that lies beneath the behavior.

3. *A type is not the same as a role.* Just as intelligence, body type, and physical and mental health are variables that affect personality, so we all learn to play roles in society that militate against our predispositions. For although some roles will be easier because more natural, all of us perform in even atypological ways, as our society dictates, as parent, wife, husband, student, professional, church member, socialite, whatever.

In the very broadest terms, Western civilization has been for the past five hundred years predominantly a "thinking territorial" culture, while the Far East has always espoused more *oceanic* attitudes. In other words, from the Roman Empire to European nationalism and imperialism to modern-day America, we have pre-eminently valued the qualities of *continuity* and *territoriality*, supported by *aethereality* and sensation (with its technical, physical competence; its emphasis on action and control). That is to say, we have valued order, consistency, decisiveness, seriousness, objectivity, structure, quantification, self-discipline, principles, and plans. We have esteemed those personality traits as prerequisites for "success." Independent, individualistic, impersonal, competitive, assertive, and purposeful—these are the people, we say, who get ahead, who go to the top, who "make it." They understand status; they know how to organize things, how to defend their territory, how to make plans and stick to them, how to control their feelings. They know how to *think;* they don't let present pleasures interfere with future goals. America's founding fathers were, in fact, predominantly thinking territorials (Jefferson, Adams, and Madison, among others), and we continue to equate our cultural values with this typology. We are, after all, a goal-directed, achievement-oriented society.

In the 1960s, a "typological revolution" began denigrating this thinking-territorial view of the world. The call of the "youth movement" (the "hippies" and "flower children") was to reawaken *discontinuity* with its existential spontaneity and playfulness. Such people wished also to reassert *oceanic* values in a territorial world. Let us, they said, be personal, receptive, reverential, nonjudgmental, open, unstructured, uninterested in status, achievements, in roles or goals. Let us go with the flow and let others be. In the battles of the generations fought during the 1960s, war was waged on essentially *typological* grounds, and it is significant that the youth movement interested itself in Far Eastern religions as well as the oceanic message of Christianity. The impact of this oceanic (feeling/intuitive) movement was to reach into the status quo territorial world; many there felt threatened. They weren't, in their own words, loose enough, free enough, weren't in touch with their feelings, were up-tight about their sexuality. Psychiatric approaches stepped in to assuage guilts and release tensions; in other words, to tap a little oceanic hole in territorial walls. Personal growth centers, Gestalt therapy, primal scream therapy, sex therapy, transcendental meditation, and many other programs—all provided outlets for the nonthinking-territorial impulses and needs everyone feels. All avenues to put us in touch with (a) our feelings, (b) our sensations, (c) our intuitions.

Cultural roles and social expectations, then, may disguise or even thwart our individual typologies. In a sense, all of us are "taught" to "act like" thinking territorials. This is particularly true in the business world and in academic situations, by their very nature thinking-type environments. Many a young feeling type, intuitive, or sensation type has had to *learn* the skills that come more naturally to young thinking types in order to succeed in structured, educational formats; this is so not because of a different *quality* of intelligence but a different *mode.* Say, for example, a very bright feeling type determines to go on to graduate school in which logic and abstract intellectuality are "the rules of the game." Her innate values, her emphasis on the personal, her variant conceptual mode, may make her feel misunderstood, unappreciated, or even less intelligent than she actually is. The danger is that this person may just quit in resentful reaction without making a conscious choice as to what she wants, based on a real knowledge of who she is. To help people to understand and by understanding to validate their own typological experience is the primary purpose of experiential typology.

One's psychetype need not determine one's profession; any career is accessible to any type. However, different professions do seem to attract certain types more than others: An intuitive, with his relative indifference to the practical, physical world and his distaste for bodily processes, is less likely to choose nursing as a career than someone with a *volcanic* acceptance of the body and a nurturing attitude toward other people. Sensation types are often drawn into courtroom law, politics, and surgical medicine. Thinking types tend to predominate in teaching, research, and administrative positions. Human services, like social fields, public relations, and practical medicine, attract feeling types, while work that allows free play of the imagination appeals to intuitives.

Sex and typology are not equatable, either. Sex *roles,* on the other hand, *are* affected by cultural training. In this culture, both men and women are asked to conform to typological expectations. Moreover, in a patriarchal civilization the most powerful (and most valued) roles are classified as masculine. Men, then, are supposed to be thinking types or sensation types. Women are supposed to be feeling types or intuitives. In the language of the areas, territoriality and aethereality are thought to be masculine traits, while volcanic and oceanic attitudes are called feminine. As a result, a feeling type or intuitive boy is going to have more trouble conforming comfortably to societal role demands than his thinking- or sensation-type peers. For he is *not supposed* to be emotional, tender, personal, and relatively uninterested in "theories," status, or technology; he is not supposed to be irrepressibly imaginative and impractical. To be so is to be thought "feminine"—a sissy.

Likewise, thinking- and sensation-type girls are likely to be told they are too intellectual, too athletic, too aggressive, too competitive, too interested in power—in other words, too "masculine." One of the stereotypic plots of sex comedies in the 1930s and 1940s was to show a successful TR career woman (usually Rosalind Russell, Katharine Hepburn, or Barbara Stanwyck) brought to her oceanic knees by the love of a good (TR or SR) man, who by the ninth reel had kicked her feet off the executive desk on which they were so inappropriately crossed. One of the goals of the Women's Liberation Movement has been to free women to express their thinking and sensation functions and at the same time free men to express the feeling and intuitive aspects of their personalities.

Many of the women whom the world has rewarded as successful have been those whose natural typology conformed to the *valued* typology, and who fought to be allowed to put that natural personality to use. Madame Curie, Susan B. Anthony, Florence Nightingale, Edith Wharton, and Eleanor Roosevelt were all thinking territorials. Simply contrast the achievement of Elizabeth I (a TR) with the tragic failure of her fellow monarch, Mary Queen of Scots (an IO). Women of typologies other than TR or SR are in a much more difficult situation, for they have to fight not only the stringent restrictions imposed by sex roles but the cultural devaluation of their natural typology as well. Even so, many manage to overcome these enormous obstacles: George Eliot was a feeling type, as were Emily Dickinson, Elizabeth Barrett Browning, and Clara Schumann; Queen Victoria, Mary Baker Eddy, and Emily Brontë were intuitives.

Margaret Mead (herself a TR) has devoted many years not only to the study of sex and temperment but also to the correlation between culture and personality in general. In her anthropological studies of primitive tribes she observed that specific cultures, such as the Samoan or New Guinean, tended to value one particular "temperament" above others, rewarding those who displayed it and denigrating those who did not. She suggested, too, that these temperaments might be equated with the four Jungian functions.

It was her hypothesis that such "temperamental types" had identifiable clusters of inborn personality traits. We will not deal here with the question of etiology—how do people *become* one type or another—except to say that we have observed in *very* young children definable, consistent typologies, and that this typology does not appear to alter, once established. A nine-month-old intuitive will be an intuitive at nine years and at ninety. There is some evidence of familial patterns (in which both father and mother and three of the four children, for instance, are all territorials), but as to whether this similarity is innate or learned has not been conclusively studied; in any case, we have also come across families of four in which each member was a different type.

4. *Each of the experiential worlds is just as valid as any of the others.* Experiential typology does not make the sort of normative judgments about personality types that too often limit human potential when imposed—whether by one's family or one's entire civilization. Each type has as much potential for use (or for abuse) as any other. One does not discover his own psychetype in order to imprison himself in it but in order to free himself by helping him learn which avenue of approach is probably going to lead to the most satisfaction. Finding out you are an intuitive should not lead you to throw up your hands at your plumbing problem and look for a sensation type to fix your pipes. Finding out you are a thinking type needn't mean you should forget trying to write love poetry. You are, of course, *you* first and a thinking, feeling, sensation, or intuitive type second.

5. *Each function is available to every person.* Whatever our primary perceptual set, all of us have a degree of access to the three other basic functions. Everyone in love is drawing on his feeling function. Everyone has inspirations and intuitive flashes. Everyone thinks, argues, keeps track of time, makes plans. Everyone occasionally gets fully absorbed in sensual experiences.

Why then bother to type people? If everyone has experiences that draw on all four functions, if no type is presumed more valid than any other, what is gained by discovering and acting on one's primary function? The answer is that the primary function is generative; it is there that our strongest potentials will be discovered. Like the dynamo that keeps the engine running, we most fully develop by creatively utilizing the special qualities of our primary function. It is the most productive and the most personally satisfying way to learn and grow. Some, in the name of a balanced personality, have suggested that the most productive path of growth would be to move around the rim of the circle, developing first one, then another of the typological possibilities. Experiential typology believes, however, that we learn better by starting with our natural typological base and from there moving inward, where the richest possible development of the self resides. To deny one's natural typology is to turn one's back on our most generative source of energy and substance. If we lived long enough to develop each of the four functions fully, perhaps the effort would be worthwhile. But we do not. Moreover, it is doubtful if we could ever succeed, using typological paths that are unnatural to our genuine perceptions. Self-actualization lies in the center, not in a tour of the rim. It *is* important that we become enlightened with regard to typologies other than our own, that we learn to value other worlds. We will best do this by first becoming enlightened about ourselves.

Each typology contains qualities that come to us as free gifts, talents and capacities born of our function and areas. People spend much of their lives in a search for identity, for their special gifts and talents. Experiential typology can help us recognize those already within us. Once discovered, we can then take them into the world, develop them, enlarge them, and offer them to others.

Within the perimeters of this theory, a person is productively functioning when he possesses (and puts to use) more of the strengths of *his* or *her* own type than its inherent weaknesses, those traits that lead to existential difficulties. It is never beneficial to attempt to change type (your own or someone else's—your child's, for instance); on the contrary, it will undoubtedly do damage. If being neurotic means deviating from "the normal," it is crucial for people to discover what is normal *for them.* Simply knowing the span of possibilities should assist us in actualizing our normal development as thinking, feeling, sensation, or intuitive types.

6. Finally, and most importantly, remember that *it is our experience of reality and not our behavior* that has primacy, for this is a theory of *experiential* typology. The way we perceive the world, the way we experience life, determines (generates) the way we will behave. If we recognize this, we are less likely to judge others negatively and often incorrectly. If we can see

that someone's action comes out of a valid, if personal, sense of a given situation, we are more apt to perceive that behavior as legitimate or at least as well-intentioned. We will pause to examine motivations and attitudes. Experiential typology offers a tool for empathy and tolerance. We may not always sympathize, we may not condone, but perhaps by learning to empathize we will less often condemn.

A final word of warning. Try not to apply the psychetypes *mechanistically*. Because this theory is so detailed and so thorough in its clarification of attitudes and its classification of behavior, it is easy to fall into the habit of automatically extending it to cover all elements of behavior. Typology is only one factor in a personality; it is where we begin, not where we end. Avoid using it to accuse or to excuse—yourself or other people.

Selected psychetype traits for each of the six areas and the four functions are listed at the back of the book in the order in which they are discussed. The reader may wish to glance through them before reading the chapters or may prefer to refer to the lists afterward. The quickest way to make an initial determination of someone's psychetype is to have him or her go down these lists, responding, "Yes, this is true of me," or, "No, I'm not like that," to each statement. Do continuity and discontinuity first, then the functions, then the areas. Suppose your friend says, "Well, I think I'm continuous." Give him, next, the thinking and feeling lists. If he affirms more of the thinking-type traits (no one will find all of them true to personal experience), ask him to choose between aethereal and territorial. Say he chooses aethereal; his psychetype is "thinking aethereal." If people say, "No, I won't do it. It's unfair to categorize human beings like this," chances are they're feeling types. A sensation type might tell you, "None of these words apply to me," and an intuitive might enthusiastically claim all ten of the lists. In general, however, we have always found that people of all the types are interested to discover how immediate one particular set of terms speaks to their experience.

3.

Determining
Our Perception of Time

While our perception of time is not as absolute as the set of our spatial areas, we are nevertheless basically either *continuous* or *discontinuous*. Continuous thinking and feeling types are time-bound; discontinuous intuitives and sensation types are situation-bound. These are indeed two different worlds; at their core, irreconcilable, and in our interactions with others, failure to recognize the gulf can lead to real difficulties. It is, for example, very disturbing for continuous people to be told that the past is irrelevant. Saying so is tantamount to denying the validity of the present.

" 'Tiggers never go on being sad,' explained Rabbit" in a Winnie-the-Pooh story. " 'They get over it with Astonishing Rapidity. I asked Owl, just to be sure, and he said that's what they get over it with.' " Continuous people find this "Astonishing Rapidity" with which discontinuous types change their moods and their minds, this insouciance about the past, perpetually confusing and frequently annoying. What does anything *mean* if it can be so easily forgotten, so cavalierly dismissed? But to a discontinuous person constant insistence on the importance of the past seems an intrusion, even a threat. Neither feels very comfortable in the other's experiential world, though, interestingly enough, perhaps because opposites attract, many people chose marriage partners across these temporal-typological barriers.

Let us take a hypothetical example of a continuous-feeling type and a discontinuous-sensation type who are married. One morning over breakfast they have a quarrel that is not resolved when they go off to their separate jobs. Eight hours later they return home, and the continuous member of the couple immediately reopens the argument. The discontinuous partner is incredulous and becomes chagrined. Why bring it up again? It's over, in the past, forgotten; why drag it out? But the feeling type hasn't gotten *closure* and so hasn't been able to put his hurt, anger, or confusion out of his mind during the day. The argument is still alive to him, and he feels a need to go on until it is resolved, or until he has worked through his own emotions about it. His mate simply does not feel the same needs.

The conflicts evoked by temporal disparity between romantic couples is one of the staples of fiction and film: Anna Karenina (an FV) and her lover Vronsky (an SR); Tom Jones (an SV) and his Sophia (a TR); Dr. Zhivago (an FV) and Lara (an SV) —down to the Captain Bogart (an SR) and the Lady Hepburn (a TR) in *The African Queen.* In *Gone With the Wind,* the discontinuous SV, Scarlet O'Hara, persists in preferring the continuous TA, Ashley Wilkes, to the man far closer to her own typological attitudes, Rhett Butler, an SR. Yet she fails to understand either Ashley's traditional values or his fidelity to the planned pattern of his life. She finds his yearning for the good, old ante-bellum past at the least, silly; and at the worst, infuriating. Nor does she see why he loves his wife, Melanie, who, as an FO, shares with him all the continuous attitudes that Scarlet does not. He, at the same time, is both horrified and fascinated by Scarlet's ability to adapt immediately to whatever the present brings and to simply disregard any long-term commitments or prior situations (like her sister's engagement to the man Scarlet decides she herself needs to marry) that might get in her way.

So, while continuous types may be attracted to the spontaneity and adaptability of their opposites, and discontinuous types may like the stable dependability that continuous partners can bring to their lives, nonetheless, each has to overcome the tendency either to dismiss or to attack the other's values and attitudes. Too often we are quick to see negatively what is really a positive quality in someone else. We can say, for instance, that a particular continuous person is constant, methodical, purposeful, and deferential. Or we can say he is inflexible, mechanistic, stubborn, and obsequious. A discontinuous person can be seen as versatile or fickle, open or unorganized, ardent or immoderate, adaptable or capricious. Naturally, our response depends on which of these interpretations we choose to make.

In general, the charges brought by continuous types against discontinuous types are that the latter are too changeable, too impulsive, too quixotic, too volatile; that they are inconsistent, unreliable, impatient, and moody. They don't stick to things, they get bored too easily, they require too much stimulation, they don't value traditions and established forms. They aren't "serious."

The countercharges made by discontinuous people are that continuous types are too static, too stiff, too stodgy. They're platitudinous, pedantic, plodding. They're insufficiently spontaneous, inventive, or enthusiastic. They weigh things too carefully and too long. They hang on to their feelings too long, they think too much, they plan too much. They aren't "free."

The following chart demonstrates how these personality attributes may appear first to those who have them and second, to those who don't—and don't like them.

CONTINUITY	DISCONTINUITY
CONSISTENT	CHANGEABLE
constant/inflexible	versatile/fickle
steady/static	adaptable/capricious
solid/rigid	supple/irresolute
dependable/monotonous	mobile/erratic
methodical/mechanistic	resilient/opportunistic
systematic/compartmentalizing	flexible/unstable

CONTINUITY	DISCONTINUITY
DELIBERATIVE	SPONTANEOUS
purposeful/stubborn	free/wayward
resolute/obstinate	unconstrained/impulsive
stalwart/headstrong	imaginative/thoughtless
serious/dull	playful/improvident
philosophical/platitudinous	uncontrived/negligent
unwavering/tedious	open/unorganized
studious/pedantic	easygoing/careless
TRADITIONAL	INNOVATIVE
ceremonial/sententious	inventive/quixotic
formal/stiff	creative/whimsical
decorous/prim	original/bizarre
"tried and true"/square	ingenious/perverse
conventional/stereotypic	outspoken/ill-mannered
established/"old-fashioned"	casual/unseemly
loyal/diehard	up-to-date/newfangled
TEMPERATE	ENTHUSIASTIC
reserved/inhibited	exuberant/volatile
deferential/obsequious	ardent/immoderate
patient/plodding	fervent/rabid
habitual/"in a rut"	ebullient/manic
imperturbable/cold-blooded	wholehearted/intemperate
stoical/impassive	intense/extravagant
staid/stodgy	zealous/impatient
objective/disinterested	mercurial/temperamental
"steers a middle course"/"straddles the issue"	impassioned/moody

CONTINUITY

To the continuous person, time is vitally important. With feeling types, the past itself is a rich source of comfort and delight. They cherish it for its own sake, as well as its ability to inseminate and thereby enrich the present. For thinking types time is linear: past to present to future. Of the four typological sets it is thinking types who care the most about the passage of time—in their own lives and in the abstract. It is as if they constantly felt time like a pulse, or a claw, at the back of their necks. They talk more, write more, and study more about their sense of time than other people. Thinking types are interested not only in the proper timing of personal progress but in the historical progress of the human race, the earth, the universe. It is thinking types who write *The Rise and Fall of the Roman Empire* and *The Story of Civilization*. Through such vast telescopes they view the recurrent and patterned events that join together each moment of time into one meaningful design.

All continuous people sense these patterns; because life repeats itself, nothing stands in isolation, and the past never loses its significance: "My life closed twice before its close," wrote FV poet Emily Dickinson. "It yet remains to see / If Immortality unveil / A third event to me." As they desire to connect the present to their pasts, such people take pleasure in planning or even simply musing about their futures. They enjoy following the process of their lives. During her youth, Virginia Woolf (a TA) wrote in her diary that she wondered what the "old Virginia" would think of the way she was acting now: "She will be a woman who can see, Old V., everything—more than I can, I think." People like this take great pleasure in imagining events as future memories.

That is why we find continuous children so much more curious about what they will be like as adults, so much more impatient, often, to "grow up" than young intuitives and sensation types appear to be. What will I look like. Where will I go to college? What sort of person will I marry? What will I do? How old will I be when I die?

In the world of continuity, time moves along an evolutional path, with each person working, as TR Madame Curie said, "toward his own highest development, accepting at the same time his share of responsibility in the general life of humanity." It is out of this attitude that George Bernard Shaw (also a TR) said he wrote his plays for "the progress of society."

Because people of this type are guided in their present involvements by their sense of the past and future connections that exist, they have a strong desire for familiarity. They like to go back to what is known, familiar, and therefore loved—as Washington (an FV) always returned to Mount Vernon, or as Jefferson (a TR) felt: "All my wishes end where I hope my days will end, at Monticello." Many continuous people are content to live in the same town, even, like Immaneul Kant (a TA) or Emily Dickinson, in the same house throughout their entire lives. Familiar surroundings are reassuring. Thomas Wolfe devoted an entire (mammoth) novel to the agony he felt when his home town Ashville ostracized him for writing about it in his first novel. He called the book *You Can't Go Home Again.* Familiar surroundings include not only places and objects (like an old armchair still in the den or a treasured family Bible), they include people, too.

Continuous types place a high value on relationships that have a history. They like to be around old friends, people who knew them in the past, and who therefore know more fully who they are. This is less important to the discontinuous person, who delights in making new acquaintances, moving to new places, having new experiences, and who, in fact, may be baffled or even displeased by old (but to him now unfamiliar) faces showing up in his life again. He is likely to be baffled, too, by the continuous person's memory of names and faces from elementary school classes, by his references to long-past relationships, by his interest in college yearbooks and reunions, by his desire to trace the family line or find out whatever happened to "old so-and-so."

We observe in the biographies of many continuous personalities instances of uninterrupted, lifelong friendships (like those between Swift and Pope or Thomas More and Erasmus), of extremely close ties with relations (like van Gogh's with his brother Theo), and of stable marriage partnerships—for example, those of Pierre and Marie Curie or Will and Ariel Durant (all thinking types). This is, of course, not invariably the case, nor do we never find lifelong relationships among discontinuous types; they are, however, less frequent. Moreover, continuous people seem to recover more slowly from the loss of relationships than do their typological opposites. John Dewey (an FV) remained a widower for twenty years before remarrying. Brahms (a TR) loved Clara Schumann for decades, and though she did not return his romantic affection, he never married anyone else. She, meanwhile, an FO, lived out those decades mourning the death of her husband, Robert Schumann, devoting her life to popularizing his music. FV George Eliot spent many, many years (and one book, *The Mill on the Floss*) trying to adjust to her brother's rejection of her when she began living with George Lewes. In general, thinking and feeling types do not give up easily on relationships.

Just as they love familiar places and faces, continuous people are fond of recurrent celebrations, of the traditional forms that men have through generations established and held on to. Christmas, Thanksgiving, Easter, marriages, christenings, graduations. These are made the more moving because they carry with them the accumulated treasures of the past, all the collected thoughts and feelings of past generations.

Since they tend so much to become accustomed to things, continuous types may dislike innovations or at least have difficulty dealing with them. Many are fairly conservative or traditional in their views, preferring the "tried and true" to the "new fangled." In their view, "To innovate is not to reform." Such people therefore like to familiarize themselves with what might happen so that the event will not seem too strange or surprising when or if it does occur. If he is driving his car to an important confrontation with his girl friend, a continuous person will probably spend the trip fantasying the conversation that is likely to transpire: "I'll say this, then she'll say that; but if she says this instead, then I'll say that." If he is going to be interviewed for a job, he will find out everything he can about the situation he's getting into. If he's never been to Bermuda before, he will study Bermuda before he goes there.

Continuous types do not like things "sprung on" them. A continuous wife who had planned to go to Bermuda would be very upset with a discontinuous husband who at the airport decided suddenly they'd have more fun skiing in Aspen, and exchanged their plane tickets. In fact, they so dislike it that they are sometimes at a disadvantage when dealing with the new. Shakespeare puts this typological trait to dramatic use in *Othello*. Iago, a discontinuous sensation type, "springs" something on the continuous FV Othello. He tells him his new wife,

Desdemona, is sleeping with someone else. Othello has known Iago a lot longer than he has known Desdemona; his tendency is to trust that longer-lasting relationship. He believes Iago. Meanwhile, Desdemona, also a continuous feeling type, cannot quickly enough adjust to this new, inexplicable behavior on Othello's part—behavior that is, as far as she can see, completely underived from their past experiences together. Iago, taking every advantage of their confusion, masterfully and diabolically brings about their tragic deaths.

All the qualities of temperament we have been discussing lead continuous types toward consistency and moderation. They are not, for the most part, erratic, improvident, or impulsive people. Instead, they manage their lives, like their budgets, thoughtfully and carefully. Few of them would, like the discontinuous IA Frank Lloyd Wright, simply keep writing checks until the bank returned them marked "insufficient funds." Nor like the intuitive Napoleon would they tear their clothes off and rip them to shreds if they seemed to be a little too tight. They will keep records of their expenses, get their income tax in on time, call ahead for reservations, shelve their books in chronological or alphabetical order, put the records back in their jackets, and if they tell you they will be there Thursday at nine, they probably will. In general, they will be pretty much the same way Wednesday as they were on Tuesday, and you can be fairly confident that a year from Wednesday they will still be that way.

For the most part, continuous types prefer not to take too many risks. A comparison between the military tactics of continuous generals like Wellington, Eisenhower, or Montgomery and those of discontinuous strategists like Napoleon, Patton, or Rommel is symptomatic of this difference. Rommel (an SR) would draw a few arrows on a scrap of paper a few minutes before he went into battle; Napoleon (an IA) didn't even bother with the arrows. On the other hand, Wellington (an FU) and Montgomery (a TA) fought by the rule book and were appalled at the chances their opponents were willing to take. Similarly, Schubert (an FO) and Brahms (a TR) were far more conservative in their music, took fewer "leaps" than, say, Beethoven (an IA) and Wagner (another IA). In fact, Schubert always remained

troubled by Beethoven's "eccentricities," and Brahms considered Wagner "excessive."

Because they are not always seeking new arenas of activity,
continuous people are far less easily bored than discontinuous
ones. On the contrary, they tend to be very self-sustaining—
which can prove frustrating for a discontinuous partner who is
relying on them for constant and varied stimulation. This capacity to fill the self from within is even more true of introverted
continuous people. Karl Marx, an introverted TR, revolution-
ized the world not by climbing barricades or by making
speeches throughout Europe. He spent nearly all his adult life
quietly sitting at a table in London's British Museum, reading
or writing. Each evening he walked home to his family living
in a small apartment nearby. The next morning he walked back
to the museum. *Das Kapital* was the result.

Along with consistency and moderation, people of this type
have tremendous patience. They neither rush into things, nor
—once in—do they easily give up. "Our patience," said Burke,
"will achieve more than our force." The remark was addressed
to the British Parliament in a speech warning them in the 1760s
that intemperate measures might push the American colonies
into revolution. One hundred and fifty years later, Churchill, by
holding patiently, tenaciously and continuously to his resolu-
tion, was to keep the embattled British from defeat days, weeks,
months longer than many had believed it possible for the island
to withstand German attack: "We shall fight them on the
beaches. We shall fight on the landing grounds. We shall fight
in the fields and in the streets. We shall fight in the hills. We
shall never surrender." Meanwhile, Hitler's discontinuous impatience hurried him into an invasion of Russia before England
had capitulated.

Churchill's continuity found political expression in a generally conservative philosophy that, he said, he had inherited
from his father. He wished to turn back to the stable, enduring
traditions since threatened in a world of mad dictators and Iron
Curtains. Throughout his life he devoted himself to learning the
lessons of the past; like most people of this type, from Cicero to
John F. Kennedy, he venerated the glories of former epochs.
And so he wrote histories—his own, his family's, his nation's.

Such people, with their strong memories of the past, consider their childhood extremely important, as we see in the works of writers like Thomas Wolfe or Dostoevski or in biographies like Churchill's *My Early Life* or Eisenhower's *At Ease: Stories I Tell My Friends.* Compare these books with the "biography" of an SR like Richard Nixon; *Six Crises* has very few nonpolitical reminiscences in it and certainly does not dwell on childhood memories. Discontinuous people lack that desire to relive moments in one's personal past, to recapture that "remembrance of things past" so typical of thinking and feeling types—at least, they do not have the impulse to the same degree.

Few things, then, are more distressing to continuous people than to have the past invalidated, to find out that the way they remember things is not the way others remember them, to go back home and find their old neighborhood replaced by a shopping center, to discover that a friend is not what they thought him, to have a theory, years later, proved wrong. This kind of person is relying on those past perceptions and experiences to explain the present; whatever he has learned, he is continuously applying in the present. It is naturally, then, most painful to find out one had misperceived, misinterpreted, (and therefore misapplied) the past. When Othello finally realizes he has done so, he kills himself. So does Tolstoy's Anna Karenina, another feeling volcanic.

So that they will *not* make such disastrous mistakes, continuous people tend to be careful and thoughtful. Even young children are likely to seem more "serious" about life than their discontinuous peers. Sometimes this seriousness (and studiousness) subjects them to schoolmates' mockery: TA Einstein was called "Old Father Bore" as a boy; TA Milton earned the title "The Lady of Christ's Church" when a child in school.

A natural corollary of their thoughtfulness is the importance continuous people attach to making plans, whether on the scale of Eisenhower's and Montgomery's D-day invasion or a housewife's schedule of family meals for the week. Such people take their decisions very seriously, carefully considering situations before acting and making sure they have availed themselves of every possible option. French novelist Flaubert (a TR) would spend two days on a single line of *Madame Bovary*. For ten full years TR Susan B. Anthony trudged from town to town, legislature to legislature, talking, arguing, reading papers, collecting supporters, in order to force the New York State senate to pass a bill granting equal economic rights to women. Such care and persistence requires the tremendous patience that continuous people are able to bring to their experience. "The only proper attitude is patience," said Einstein, who worked more than thirty-five years on his unified field theory and died still unsatisfied with his results.

For all these reasons continuous types are very wary of the possibility of negative outcomes. They are so aware of all the conceivable outcomes that they tend to be worriers. No matter how carefully they consider the options, no matter how thoroughly they plan, no matter how temperately they decide, still, something could go wrong. A person of this type may spend six months studying all the consumer guides on automobiles; he then checks out a dozen car dealers and talks to a dozen previous owners; finally, he chooses a car. But somewhere in the back of his head there is still likely to be the nagging thought: This car may be a lemon. "The only thing I should ever claim for any view of mine," wrote Bertrand Russell, "would be that it is in a direction along which one can reach truth—never that it *is* truth. The skeptical intellect, when I have most wished it silent, has whispered doubts to me." He was in his nineties at the time. Similarly, in his eighties, Freud wrote that the only thing he was really certain of, the only real contribution he had made to psychology, was the concept of the ego, superego, and id. Everything else, he said, was either unessential or would have soon been supplied by other theorists.

Many continuous types seem to come into their own in their later years. The consistent, moderate, purposeful progress of their lives seems to evolve and expand very much like their perception of time itself. On the other hand, it is almost as if discontinuous people flare up and then burn out. These are, of course, not absolutes; Pablo Picasso (an SR) and Frank Lloyd Wright (an IA) were both creatively vital in their nineties, while Lawrence of Arabia (a TA) and Thomas Wolfe (an FO) both died quite young. Nevertheless, there is a certain pattern among illustrious thinking and feeling types to develop at gradual and steady paces, many reaching their peaks in late middle age or even afterward. Shaw produced a number of his best-remembered plays in his sixties and seventies; he wrote still more plays in his eighties and nineties. John Dewey's most active decade was that of his sixties; he kept working until his death at ninety-three. Thomas Hardy began publishing his poems in his sixties. Freud wrote *Civilization and Its Discontents* at seventy-four. Churchill was eighty-five when he finished the sixth volume of his history of World War II. Similiar patterns are revealed in the lives of Bertrand Russell, De Gaulle, Florence Nightingale, Madame Curie, Albert Schweitzer, Mao Tse-tung, and others.

Contrast this picture with a fairly random sample of discontinuous types: Alexander the Great, king at twenty, dead at thirty-eight. Custer, general at twenty-three, dead at thirty-eight. Gershwin wrote his major works, including more than thirty musical comedies, by thirty, dead at thirty-eight. Byron died fighting for Greece at thirty-six; Shelley drowned at thirty; Keats dead at twenty-six. Mozart at thirty-five. Robert Burns at thirty-seven. Sir Philip Sidney at thirty-four. Valentino and Jean Harlow in their twenties. Marilyn Monroe at thirty-six. The point of this rather morbid thanatopsis is not to advise all those who have typed themselves as discontinuous to be sure they buy some life insurance but to suggest the comparative youth at which many sensation types and, even more so, intuitives make their contribution to the world.

Continuous people have so much fuller a sense of time's continuum that they feel psychologically free to develop slowly, to wait, to postpone; they don't feel they have to do everything, see everything, write everything, be everywhere at once. Brahms allowed himself twenty years' preparation before he wrote his First Symphony. At twenty-two, Schweitzer resolved: "I would consider myself justified in living for art and science until I was thirty in order to devote myself from that time on to the direct service of humanity."

What a difference in attitude from Alexander the Great, who feared his father's military successes would leave him no worlds to conquer. Or Keats, who at twenty-one, only six months after deciding to be a poet, undertook to write a major work of four thousand lines in four months—and then spent fewer weeks revising *Endymion* than he had months writing it. Bertrand Russell was listening to another kind of clock: "I have devoted the first eighty years of my life to philosophy. I propose to devote the next eighty years to another branch of fiction."

DISCONTINUITY

"It's the doing that interests me. Once it's finished, I'm no longer interested. It's ejaculated, gone forever. The past for me is absolutely disgusting." Captain Jacques Cousteau, the oceanographer, is an SR, and as this remark makes abundantly clear, he is discontinuous. We could hardly find a more concise statement of the discontinuous tendency to perceive pastness as insignificant. For such people, each moment exists in its own discrete particularity. Its existential significance is self-contained. It is from day to day that discontinuous people live, and each day (each event, each moment in each day) is unique. They see life go past them like faces glimpsed from a train window; they do not really expect to see those faces again. As a result, people of this type may be quite distraught at partings, even those involving very temporary separations, for somewhere in them (though they may know the fear is irrational) is the suspicion that life will never bring the other person back around again. Of course, the continuous person who seems so much less upset may then board his plane and spend the entire flight thinking about the leave-taking, while his discontinuous friend, having promptly recovered, goes off without further worry, merrily on his way to the next experience.

Viewed simplistically, in the parable of the ant and the grasshopper or the fable of the tortoise and the hare, ant and tortoise are continuous, grasshopper and hare are discontinuous. The clichés of their temporal world find expression in phrases like "There is no tomorrow." Or "Take no thought for tomorrow." Or the cry of lovesick poets: "Gather ye rosebuds while ye may." *Carpe diem*— seize the day.

This "existential" approach to time can be erected into a principle, a philosophy of what life is *really* like (as Sartre, a continuous thinking type, did), or espoused as a creed for what life *should* be like (as did even typologically continuous members of the 1960s hippie movement, for example, thinking territorial Janis Joplin). But for intuitives and sensation types this attitude is so deeply natural that they may not even be conscious that such is their perception of time. There are discrepancies between these two psychetypes, however, for in general intuitives (being aethereal) tend to disregard the past in favor of an imagined future, whereas sensation types (with their volcanic physicality and immediacy) are likely to disregard the future as well as the past, while focusing almost exclusively on the present situation. Compare, for example, the attitudes of Charles Lindbergh (an SR), who loved to fly because in the air he could "live only for the moment," and Napoleon Bonaparte (an IA), who lived for what men would say of him "ten centuries hence." It is fairly atypological for someone with a leading sensation function to even conceive of or much concern himself with such theoretical possibilities. Lindbergh, the first man to fly solo across the Atlantic, said it never occurred to him to consider what would happen *after* he made it to Paris. In *The Spirit of St. Louis* he recalled that while actually circling the airfield, he had been asking himself, "What *will* I do after I land at Le Bourget?" He decided, Well, I'll find someplace to put my plane, cable home, then look for a place to spend the night; maybe I'll be in trouble. After all, I'm a tourist in a foreign country without a visa. And so on. The wildly cheering thousands who stormed his small silver plane when it touched ground on that Paris airstrip completely surprised Lindbergh. He had never thought that people would be waiting to welcome him if he made it.

Napoleon, however, would have anticipated crowds in Paris even before he left New York—just as, once he took Italy, he imagined himself conqueror of Spain; once he ruled Europe, he saw himself dictator of the world.

But all discontinuous people share the attitude that each moment of time is disconnected from all the rest of time, and so their involvements (either with present happenings or future visions) are sensed as cut off from whatever might have led up to them. If that past has been a painful one, this capacity can serve to make such people quite resilent, even unstumpable, in

the face of former adversities. And, in fact, we find discontinuous people on the whole more optimistic, more easily cheered
or comforted than feeling and thinking types. The ability to
"bounce back" is commonplace in fictional characterizations of
discontinuity, all the way from the irrepressible Mr. Toad to the
equally irrepressible Don Quixote—both intuitives. SV Tom
Jones is despondently carving his unattainable Sophy Western's
initials in a tree; the wench, Molly, comes lecherously around
the side of the trunk, and Tom hurriedly changes the "S" for
Sophy to an "M" for Molly. SV Scarlet O'Hara loses father,
mother, child, husband (s), home, love, but each time she clen-
ches her fist, straightens her back, and reminds herself that
"after all, tomorrow *is* another day." Dickens's immortal intuitive Mr. Micawber constantly tells David Copperfield that he
has "fallen back only for a spring," that inevitably "something
will turn up." For discontinuous people tomorrow always is
another day, and something undoubtedly will turn up—if not
better, well, at least different. If their electricity is shut off
because they neglected to pay the bill, maybe candles are pret-
tier, anyhow. If they sell their business in Ohio to drive a cov-
ered wagon to California to look for gold, and the wagon breaks
down in the Dakotas, maybe it's a beautiful place to live, anyhow. Or if they make it to California and don't find any gold,
there's bound to be a lot of money in raising oranges. Or. Or.
Or.

There is, however, a less positive side to this attitude: the
tendency to devalue or simply dismiss the accomplishments
and commitments, the *meaning* of the past, a tendency that can
make discontinuous people seem to others either incredibly
forgetful or ungratefully indifferent, even unscrupulous. (The
360-degree about-faces on foreign and domestic policies announced by Presidents Johnson (an SV) and Nixon (an SR)
shocked and/or outraged journalists and reporters, many of
whom, as might be suspected, are continuous thinking types.)
But the past is past to such people. According to Plutarch,
Alexander (an IA) told the exhausted troops who had been
fighting ten years for him that if they chose to return to their
families in Macedonia rather than cross the Ganges and conquer India with him, then "he owed them no thanks for any-

thing they had hitherto done, and that to retreat now was to confess himself utterly vanquished." Similarly, it is her own typological door that Rhett Butler (like her, a sensation type) shuts in Scarlet O'Hara's face. "But you used to love me, and I love you now," she tells him. "That is your misfortune. Frankly, my dear, I don't give a damn" is his reply. When it's over, it's over.

This sense of the irrelevance of pastness makes many discontinuous people far less traditional and conservative than their typological opposites. For they are willing, like Caesar (an SR), to take risks: to cross the Rubicon or to preach a funeral oration for his wife when Roman convention did not allow women to be so honored. Such people are willing, as Mary Queen of Scots prophetically announced when she embarked for Scotland, "to hazard all I have." Such willingness can lead to success, to inventiveness, to radical breaks with orthodoxy in science, religion, or in the arts: innovations typified by creators like Beethoven (an IA), Picasso (an SR), Frank Lloyd Wright (an IA), or Dylan Thomas (an IO).

Of course, taking risks can also lead to disastrous follies such as IA General Custer's last charge. IO Mary of Scotland hazarded all she had and was executed by TR Elizabeth of England. SV Mark Anthony's excesses cost him (at the hands of the methodical thinking ethereal, Augustus) not only the Roman Empire but his life. For the same quality that allows discontinuous people to respond so quickly and so fully to situations, that same reliance on immediate perceptions which makes them so versatile and ebullient, can as easily make them dangerously immoderate when they fail to compare the importance of the present to the past; in other words, when they fail to evaluate the relative significance of events. One might prefer to go to the movies the night before an exam, but in the long run that movie will matter far less. One might believe he is destined to conquer Russia; realistically, however, a good plan might be to defeat England first. Lindbergh almost crashed into the Atlantic because he was nearly incapacitated from lack of sleep during his solo flight. The reason he was so exhausted was because he had decided, on the spur of the moment, to take off at a time when he'd already been awake for more than twenty hours; he then had to be in the air thirty-three more. In the same way, the horrendous financial debts and difficulties that tormented discontinuous artists like Robert Burns, Wagner, Beethoven, and F. Scott Fitzgerald were no doubt exacerbated by their lack of continuity and the methodical habits of temperateness and organization that go along with it. Wagner owed money all over Europe. Fitzgerald was always asking editors for advances on stories he had not yet begun. Beethoven told his impatient publisher that the Ninth Symphony had been "completed by the copyists during the last few days" when actually he hadn't even finished, much less copied, it.

But discontinuous people get too easily involved in whatever is presented at the time, regardless of long-term situations, to maintain the sort of steady, even keel we have seen in thinking and feeling types. Able to throw themselves into current activities without reservation, they are apt to be rather impulsive and changeable. Some are more conscious of this characteristic than others. SV John Keats wrote to a friend:

> *Tonight I am all in a mist; I scarcely know what's what. But you, knowing my unsteady and vagarish disposition, will guess that all this turmoil will be settled by tomorrow morning. . . . I am now reading Voltaire and Gibbon, although I wrote to Reynolds the other day to prove that reading was no use.*

This flexible quality can be a strength or a weakness. While acknowledging the dangers of such simplifications, we could generalize that when discontinuous people succeed, they can succeed rapidly and spectacularly; conversely, when they fail, they can fail catastrophically. Especially is this so for intuitives, as the careers of Alexander, Napoleon, Hitler, Custer, Kaiser Wilhelm, Sir Walter Raleigh, Marie Antoinette, Charles I of England, and Mary Queen of Scotland (the last four of whom had their heads chopped off) indicate.

The mood of a discontinuous person cannot be relied on to last longer than the availability of something new. This does not necessarily suggest inconstancy of emotion; sensation types and intuitives can, of course, be in love for life, or depressed for ten years, or in mourning, like Queen Victoria, for half a century.

But such people are in general temperamentally changeable. At eighteen, when the just widowed Queen Mary decided, against much advice, to leave France, she was in an agony of grief because she *was* leaving. As long as a speck of coastline could be glimpsed, she stood waving and sobbing at her ship's stern. "Adieu, France! Adieu, ma chere France!" "Good-by, my dear France. I think I shall never see you again." She said she was inconsolable. Five days later Mary landed exuberantly in Scotland, happily eager to begin life as its queen. She quickly ran into trouble, disregarded wise counsel, acting precipitously, and ran into more trouble. Escaping from captivity once, she raced nearly a hundred miles on horseback despite ill health. Captured again, she attempted to escape disguised as a washer-woman carrying a bundle of dirty clothes. The Scottish lairds returned her to imprisonment on the island fortress of Loch-leven. From there, she wrote an anguished letter to Queen Elizabeth, beseeching her to "have pity on your good sister and cousin, for you alone can save me." The same day she wrote to her former mother-in-law, Catherine de Medici, to beg her to send French troops to the rescue. Yet within twenty-four *hours* of writing these impassioned, helpless pleas, Mary, dressed as a country woman, walked boldly right past the courthouse guards, through the gate, and hid beneath the seat of a rowboat while a young, enamored courtier rowed her to freedom.

Such rapid recoveries typify the moods of another intui-tive-oceanic queen, Victoria, each time a new prime minister was elected. When Lord Melbourne was deposed, she wrote in her diary, "All ALL my happiness gone! That happy peaceful life destroyed, that dearest kind Lord Melbourne no more my Minister!" His successor, Robert Peel, was to her a detestable man with a smile "like the silver fittings of a coffin." Yet when it was Peel's turn to be replaced, *he* was revered, the "greatest" of her prime ministers, and his replacement a "dreadful" man. It is easy to see why Cervantes gives his intuitive hero, Don Quixote, a discontinuous partner in adventure: the sensation volcanic, Sancho Panza. No continuous person would have been willing to endure all the disasters the two encountered on their adventures, all the buffetings, deprivations, and mockery, with the easy going, undefeatable enthusiasm and the readiness to forget the past and hope for the best that typify Sancho's attitude.

People who are continuous find such mercurial shifts and swings inexplicable and untrustworthy. TR Shaw wrote of the irreconcilable statements in IA Richard Wagner's autobiography: "They explain nothing but the mood in which he happened to be on the day he wrote them." The discontinuous refusal to be bound by past statements and the concomitant belief that words may change their meaning in different situations (traits much in evidence during the presidency of SR Richard Nixon) represent another area of misunderstanding and mistrust between people of this type and those who are continuous. But as intuitive William Randolph Hearst (founder of the newspaper chain that enthusiastically championed a vast number of utterly irreconcilable political positions) said, "It is not that important to be consistent." Nor was sensation-type Henry Ford as dismayed as his supporters when he espoused and dropped causes as rapidly as his assembly line manufactured automobiles, abruptly terminating his fervent and expensive presidential campaign with the laconic remark that he was not a politician and canceling his vicious anti-Semitic attacks with a brief statement that he had been "mistaken."

With their weak sense of the past such people reject even yesterday as long ago and no longer relevant. As a result, they can be relatively unperturbed by former mistakes or failures. SV Tolstoy said that throughout his life he kept making resolute vows to overcome his three sins, "gambling, sex, and vanity," and time after time he kept breaking them, just as he was able to win the Medal of St. George for military bravery, then be sent to the guardhouse the next morning for oversleeping and missing the presentation ceremony.

One of the reasons discontinuous people are so forgetful is that they really *dislike* the past impinging on the present. In other words, they are uncomfortable with continuity. "Do not think too much about things which have already been accomplished," warned SR scientist Louis Pasteur. Even worse is others' insisting that you do so; the publicity that for years followed Lindbergh wherever he went was intolerable to him. "The New York–Paris flight is past. I wish that people would just remember it as something that happened in 1927 and then forget about me."

Not, of course, that discontinuous types have no memory of, or no interest in, their own pasts. But they are likely to remember that past as a spotty and disconnected series of peak experiences rather than as an unbroken continuum. Needing, naturally, some sense of continuity, of "roots," they often derive it from maintaining strong ties with their families, ties that thinking and feeling types may not need to insist on in the same way, moment to moment, for typologically they carry *within* them the knowledge that such connections will always exist, even if not constantly acted upon. They don't worry that their families will forget them if they fail to write or call; the discontinuous person, himself likely to forget about things not presently experienced, *will* worry. Another way such people connect to the past is by creating what we might call mythic Gestalts of their childhoods, which may or may not be literally accurate. These may be myths of misery (as with Hitler or Marilyn Monroe) or myths of ecstasy. SR Mark Twain, in a way, made a literary career out of his myth of his childhood: "I can call it back and make it as real as it ever was, and as blessed." He called it back, of course, in the persons of Tom Sawyer and Huckleberry Finn.

In the discontinuous world every moment needs to be intensified because the moment, present or future, is all there is. Thus, when the young Caesar left to run for a disputed office in the priesthood, he did not say, "Mother, wish me luck. But if I lose, I'll consider what steps to take next." He said, "Mother, today you will see me either high priest or an exile." When Alexander received a letter accusing his favorite physican of trying to poison him, he did not call in the accuser or the accused for questioning. Instead, he accepted a goblet of medication from the physican, handing the man the letter to read with one hand, drinking the potion with the other.

Intensify the moment. Charge the windmills. Cross the Rubicon. Hazard all you have. People like this see life as a drama, whether they be SR John Donne preaching his own funeral sermon at St. Paul's or IA John Barrymore caricaturing his own dissolution in Hollywood. They seek out experiences, believing that something new is not only desirable but doubt-lessly available. Before he became a writer, Mark Twain was a printer, a soldier, a prospector in the wild West, a Mississippi river-boat pilot, and a foreign correspondent. Many of these psychetypes, from Sir Francis Drake to Walt Whitman, are in-veterate wanderers, for all discontinuous people are afraid of "missing something." Whatever they're doing they fear is keep-ing them from doing something else. Rather than methodically walking from one room of a museum to another, they want to be in all the rooms at once and will probably drive a continuous companion mad by racing erratically in and out of the galleries. It is likely to be the same with their exploration of cities or countries. People like this may seem too "playful" to more serious thinking and feeling types. A friend of Mozart's, dis-tressed about the composer's dire financial straits, was shocked to find Mozart and his wife merrily dancing about their small living room—dancing, Mozart told him, to keep warm, for they had run out of firewood. But sensation types and intuitives *like* to see their lives as play, game; "seriousness" sounds like dull-ness to them.

Because they are rather easily bored, discontinuous types require continuous stimulation from the present. (Edison once worked simultaneously on forty-five different inventions.) Not only do they dislike things that go on too long; they also hate having to repeat tasks or processes and are intolerant of routine. For this reason they may have negative attitudes toward "thoughtfulness" and learning. Someone of this nature has a propensity to assume that things can be learned only as they are needed and may be unwilling, therefore, to learn traditional things—those things he thinks others believe he "ought" to learn. "If I had read as much as other men," wrote sensation-type philosopher Thomas Hobbes, "I should have known no more than other men." The same attitude was shared by intui-tive composers like Beethoven, Wagner, and Gershwin. Gersh-win, commented Oscar Levant, "could never accustom himself to such restraints as sonatas, rondos, or any of the classical molds."

One result of this impatience with the orderly process of sequential learning is that discontinuous types tend to be less successful in terms of their formal schooling than thinking and feeling types; many simply quit. It is not that they can't do the work, rather that they feel constricted within the routine of educational systems. This is true even of those whose work is in a sense "intellectual." Benjamin Franklin and Mark Twain never went through high school. Hemingway refused to go to college. Tolstoy, Fitzgerald, Faulkner, and Frost never graduated from college; Shelley was expelled from his university. Frank Lloyd Wright told a gathering of young architecture students that if they applied themselves and studied, they could graduate and become "nice mediocrities." "A schoolboy may be defined as one who can tell you what he knows in the order in which he learned it," said Frost, who quit Dartmouth after three months, claiming he could not learn things out of books. After wandering about trying various occupations, he gave Harvard a try, but after two years there, decided it wasn't worth it and quit.

Lindbergh had to force himself back after two or three false starts to get through college: "Why should one spend the hours of life on formulae, semicolons, and our crazy English spelling? I don't believe God made men to fiddle with pencil marks on paper. . . . For so long, I can sit and concentrate on work, and then, willy-nilly, my body stands up and walks away." Such people can even be contemptuous of the "intellect," as Hemingway's vituperative outbursts against "eggheads" demonstrate. Many prefer not to have their own intellectualism taken seriously. "I'm just a farmer who happens to write stories now and then," William Faulkner somewhat disingenuously told critics. But, of course, as the achievements of many of these people make splendidly clear, they can indeed take themselves most seriously.

For all four types, continuity and discontinuity exist on a sliding scale. Remember that, unlike the spatial areas, temporal perceptions are not absolute. For example, though both Charles Darwin and Dylan Thomas were intuitives, Darwin was a far more continuous intuitive than Thomas. Similarly, Lawrence of Arabia was a more discontinuous thinking type than Karl Marx. We have been discussing these traits in their most diametrically opposed positions, but, of course, in individual human lives one would rarely meet a completely discontinuous or an invariably continuous person. Moreover, the scale can shift somewhat in different periods of a single life. SR Thomas Edison at eighty was more habitual, more orderly, less impulsive, more continuous, than he was at twenty; so, for the most part we all gain in continuity as we age. Nevertheless, Edison at eighty would be more discontinuous than TR Sigmund Freud at eighty, or probably at twenty.

Though sensation types, because of their intense involvement with the present, may seem theoretically more discontinuous than intuitives (who are likely to hold to a particular future-oriented vision), this difference is moderated by the difference in the two types' social attitudes. Sensation types, worried about their own fiercely independent aggression, tend to be tremendous believers in external social controls. They have great respect for traditional codes and status hierarchies. As they age, this incipient conservatism can grow more and more resistant to change. Since people of this type generally respect (or at least notice) the rules of law and social order, they are likely, especially in their later years, to *appear* more continuous than the less socially sensitive (or conformable) intuitive. Robert Frost (an SV) at sixty was the poet of the Establishment. Ezra Pound (an IA) at sixty was no more moderate than Ezra Pound at twenty, and the aging Beethoven (an IA) cared no more for the rules than the youth had.

For different reasons, feeling types will perhaps seem more continuous than thinking types if we define continuity in terms of "past-maintaining." Conversely, thinking types are more continuously structured with regard to their future plans and with regard to the connection of those plans to what preceded them. Being volcanic and oceanic, the feeling type will be less orderly and purposeful about his overall "life direction."

And, of course, whether we are extraverted or introverted affects our temporal perceptions. Highly introverted discontinuous types like IO poetess Christina Rossetti or SR Alexander Fleming, discoverer of penicillin, will display fewer of the more volatile and extravagant qualities of discontinuity than extroverts of the same types. They will, for instance, require less (and less varied) stimulation from the external world. In the same way, extremely extraverted thinking types (like De Gaulle) or feeling types (like Judy Garland) will share with discontinuous people a greater need for varied stimulation and new experiences.

Differences in primary area's also have some effect on continuity-discontinuity. SRs will seem less discontinuous than SVs, for the former can draw on the goal-oriented, structuring habits of territoriality to control their volcanic impulsiveness. (SR Stalin was, for one thing, better *organized* than SV Mussolini.) Likewise, an IA will seem more continuous than his receptive, anarchical IO counterpart, who is able to draw less upon aethereal detachment and future-oriented theoretical capacity. (Here we see one of the crucial typological differences in Napoleon (an IA) and Hitler (an IO).

Having learned that the bell does not toll the same time for thee and me, we can turn now to the spatial dimensions, where we find that we don't even see the same bell nor look for it in the same places. Some of us look at it, some of us look through it, some look east-south-north-west, and some look all around.

4.

Our Perceptions of Spatial Substance: Aethereals and Volcanics

The aethereal-volcanic split describes two opposing ways of viewing the *substance* of space; in other words, differing perceptions of what makes up reality. We could call aethereals "Platonic" and volcanics "Aristotelian," for the former are theorists and the latter, empiricists. Philosopher William James considered these antipodal positions the fundamental contrast between types of minds, though he used different words to describe them. What we are calling "aethereal," he labeled "monist," "absolutist," and "rationalist." Our term "volcanic" is synonymous with his "pluralist," "pragmatist," and "meliorist." The two world views are diametrically opposed. As James quipped, "What is mind? No matter. What is matter? Never mind." Thus, being an intuitive aethereal, the poet Shelley's psychetype would be made up of discontinuity, aethereality, and the oceanic. He would not share in the volcanic world at all.

Each of us has a primary and a secondary area. If our primary area is concerned with spatial substance, our secondary area will indicate our sense of spatial structure, and vice versa. Shelley's primary area is aethereal (substance); his secondary area is, therefore, oceanic (structure). Each of the four functions has two areas available to it, and each of the four areas consequently participates in two of the functions. (See chart, p. 00.)

In other words, only thinking types and intuitives can be aethereals; only sensation types and feeling types can be volcanic. Territorials are either thinking types or sensation types; oceanics are either intuitives or feeling types.

AETHEREAL

When we imagine an "aethereal personality," we probably think of somebody like the perennial "absent-minded professor," his head in the clouds, as, musing over philosophical conundrums, he walks past his wife without recognizing her. However, although a great many aethereals do enter the theoretical branches of science and academia, others are politicians (like John F. Kennedy and Franklin D. Roosevelt); still others, adventurers (from Sir Walter Raleigh to Lawrence of Arabia); still others, like Isadora Duncan, dancers. As always, typology does not limit behavior. Secondly, if we think of aethereals as very tall and very thin, we need only recall that while this stereotype often holds, Napoleon was little more than five feet four inches tall, and Orson Welles could hardly be called willowy. Nor are aethereals "flighty" or unusually "angelic."

Aethereals are people who are interested in the possible and the theoretical as opposed to the actual and the immediate. They care less for the way things are than the way things *could* be or *ought* to be. In fact, they tend to object to things "as they are." Life should be "optical, not practical," said IA Ralph Waldo Emerson, fittingly enough, popularizer of the philosophical system "Transcendentalism." For all aethereals want to *transcend,* transcend the body for the mind, the real for the ideal, the present for the future.

Such people live not only *for* but actually *in* the future. "My heart is full of futurity," wrote the Romantic poet William Blake. It is the emergent (what's over the horizon, the far-off vista) that attracts them, for they are interested much more in what "will be" than what "is" or "was." This is, of course, far more in evidence in discontinuous intuitive aethereals like Blake than we find it in continuous thinking aethereals whose continuity links them with the whole progression of time, including the past.

But even for thinking aethereals it is the possible future that evokes their deepest engagement. "That man is right," said TA Henrik Ibsen, "who has allied himself most closely with the future." It was out of the same belief that FDR, when unveiling the Jefferson Memorial, offered as his highest praise to the author of the Declaration of Independence that "he was an exponent of planning for the future."

To such persons the future may actually seem more *real* than the present. At twenty-four, Cecil Rhodes wrote a will in which he left his entire fortune (a fortune that at the time he did not possess) for the furtherance of a future dream: a society whose object should be to extend British rule throughout the world, capturing for the Empire, Africa, the Middle East, South America, coastal China and Japan, and the "ultimate recovery of the United States of America." He took a friend into his study and, solemnly laying his hand across the map of Africa on his wall, said, "That is my dream, that—all British." And ultimately he *did* get them Rhodesia, and he did make his fortune. It supports the Rhodes scholarships, which he endowed to provide to American and German youths an opportunity to come in contact with British moral values.

Out of this view of life Wagner entitled his treatise on music "The Art Work of the Future," and Walt Disney, who built "Tomorrowlands" in his theme parks, was planning to create "The City of the Future" on land adjoining Disneyworld in Florida—a vast metropolis, still to be constructed, enclosed under a temperature-controlled dome and capable of accommodating 300,000 residents. "Disneyworld," he said, "will never be finished."

The idea of things going on and on is very appealing to aethereals, particularly intuitive ones. They are fascinated with possibilities and reluctant to have them closed off. As a result, they proliferate goals. At his death, Frank Lloyd Wright was designing a 510-story building on the Chicago lake front. Throughout his career he kept extending the perimeters of the possible—to the horror of more conservative architects. His Imperial Hotel in Tokyo, they said, was impossible. It would never last through a Japanese earthquake. In a way an appropriate symbol of aethereality, the hotel was not locked in foundations but designed to freely rest on them, to float over the earth beneath. The earthquake came, and every building around it crumbled; the Imperial Hotel shuddered, adjusted itself, and stood. Thereafter, until it was destroyed by bombing, Wright's impossible structure was the place everyone ran to whenever earthquakes were announced.

Goal proliferating can produce remarkable achievements in amazingly short periods, as the first years of FDR's Presidency attest. It can also provide avenues for diverse and innovative productions; Gershwin, for example, was always trying out new musical forms and fresh orchestral possibilities. On the negative side, the aethereal runs the risk of spreading himself too thinly, starting something new before he finishes the old. In 1845, Darwin wrote an associate, "I hope this summer to finish my South American Geology, then to get out a little Zoology, and hurrah for my species work!" The little zoology turned out to be a book on barnacles that took him eight years to write. And the *Origin of the Species* was not published until fifteen years later. The problem was that each new insight sidetracked Darwin into writing a book about it.

Aethereals, then, tend to experience themselves as being pulled by multiple possibilities, none of which they wish simply to shut out. They are, therefore, likely to be distrustful of "skepticism." Every possibility must be considered before something may be legitimately dismissed as unviable. In their view, other people are too quick to reject ideas simply because there is insufficient evidence to support them; one should not worry so much about "being right." Darwin, who considered skepticism "a frame of mind injurious to the progress of science," wrote of his fellow botanist Robert Brown, "Much died with him, owing to his excessive fear of making a mistake." Darwin himself was quite willing to make mistakes and made a great many of them by taking at face value information about plants or animals that later proved totally inaccurate; it was not his practice to check on the qualifications of his informants. Contrast this attitude with the "seeing is believing" propensity of the sensation-territorial scientist Louis Pasteur, who refused to trust in the accuracy of any data he had not *personally* observed, and who, when asked to find the disease-infecting silkworms in Alais, France, spent four years living in the orchards there to learn the answer.

Aethereals deeply resent having their ideas (or anyone else's ideas) dismissed at first hearing as impractical, untenable, or—as frequently happens—"crazy." "Why not?" they ask. "I'm ahead of you. Catch up!" "Why should we not occupy Malta?" asked the youthful French officer Bonaparte (an IA). "We shall be masters of the whole Mediterranean." To his startled, skeptical followers he promised a glorious future. "Today these may seem like the vague anticipations of a visionary enthusiast, but a cold, pertinacious man will make them a reality." However, the desire to mount, as Napoleon put it, "higher and higher" makes aethereals seem to others more visionary enthusiasts than pertinacious realists. Both in their thoughts and their lives they are always off to the next, the newest, the biggest possibility. For their emphasis is usually on the scope rather than the depth of an idea, and their delight is to generalize, moving always to the next level of abstraction, the ultimate idea, the Big Theory. Perhaps nowhere has this impulse found more awesome application than in Albert Einstein's thirty-five-year search for a single, unifying principle that would explain all forms of universal creation and prove that the entire universe is nondualistic, not uncertain but governed by one continuous immutable law. Einstein was never able to *prove* this unified field theory, but his tireless effort to do so is typical of the tendency toward generalization displayed, on all levels, by aethereals.

Underlying such impulses is a deep belief in the power of ideas, a commitment to one's theories or visions that may override all other considerations. In this regard, thinking-aethereal Woodrow Wilson's absolute fidelity to his League of Nations resembles intuitive-aethereal Isadora Duncan's unwavering faith in her revolutionary theory of dance, though the *objects* of their commitments could not be more different.

Similarly, aethereals are likely to be more theoretical than people of the other three primary settings, more so, say, than even thinking territorials, for the latter tend to be more involved with practice than theory per se, that is, with the organization and implementation of ideas. Not only aethereal intellectuals but those of all professions and interests share this theorizing impetus. We find it in composers like TA Stravinsky, and in IA Gershwin's fascination with the application of mathematical concepts to music. We see it in Napoleon's love of conversing with the thinkers and scientists of his French Academy, in Alexander the Great's delight in Indian mystics and Greek sophists, in his statement that were he not Alexander, he would choose to be Diogenes the philosopher.

Another prevailing aethereal mode is *idealism.* Such people believe in acting according to principles: "Principle," said IA Frank Lloyd Wright, "is the only safe precedent." These are principles not about acceptance of the norm but adherence to ideals. Aethereals always "aim high"; they insist on things as they *ought* to be and often find it difficult to compromise: "I know not what course others may take, but as for me, give me liberty or give me death!" said Patrick Henry, an IA. The erroneous assumption that their idealism is shared by others can lead to painful disenchantment. Woodrow Wilson began by making this sort of assumption: "Sometimes people call me an idealist. Well, that's the way I know I'm an American. America is the only idealistic nation in the world." He died bitterly disabused of that notion after his Congress and his nation proved unwilling to accept his peace-conference proposals for a world "as it ought to be." The problem was, as thinking *territorial* Eleanor Roosevelt analyzed, that Wilson was "the idealist, with no knowledge of practical politics, and therefore without the ability to translate his dreams into facts," whereas what was needed was "a practical knowledge of how to achieve political results." Wilson, she thought, failed to understand people as individuals and was occasionally blinded by his own self-righteousness.

Because of their own commitment to ideals and principles, all aethereals can become righteously indignant with those who fail to "live up." According to her biographer, Joseph Lash, Eleanor Roosevelt tried hard to guard her aethereal husband Franklin against this tendency. "Isn't it just a bit patronizing?" she would write the youthful FDR about his contemptuous criticism of an older colleague. "If I were he, I would rise up and smite you for an impertinent youth." Of such "chastenings" Lash wrote, "If [FDR's] audacity did not more often lapse into presumption, he probably had Eleanor to thank for it." However, aethereals actually take pleasure in their indignation; it may feel to them completely justified. Indignation seems, for example, to have been TA Cicero's almost perennial attitude toward life, and much of his biting sarcasm against the rest of the Roman populace comes out of it.

The unwillingness of some aethereals simply to *accept* the weaknesses and failings of fellow humans can lead to problems in relations with others, who may find them "self-congratulatory," "cold," "contemptuous," "prissy," or, as we shall see, "arrogant." Remarks like "You are fools!" or "Who can live with such spoiled children?!" (which IA Beethoven used to address to his concert audiences) are not likely to endear one. Aethereals run the risk of alienating people by a kind of moral absolutism that too readily dismisses the value of other individuals.

All these high aims go hand in hand with a love of glory. TA John F. Kennedy's favorite speech in Shakespeare was one spoken by another TA, Henry V, before the battle of Agincourt, and it is a stirring address on the subject of glory given to his troops on St. Crispin's Day; "If it be a sin to covet honor," he tells them, "I am the most offending soul alive." "Death is nothing," wrote Napoleon in the same vein, "but to live defeated and inglorious is to die daily." He believed himself another Alexander, another Caesar, and kept near him trophies of the military glories of former heroes: busts of Scipio and Hannibal, the sword of Frederick the Great. His study was the tent of an ancient warrior; his crown, a small circlet of golden laurel leaves like that of Augustus; his Arc de Triomphe, a Roman one. And as Napoleon worshiped Alexander, Alexander (another IA) worshiped Achilles and slept with the *Iliad* beneath his pillow, announcing at his hero's Trojan grave site, "Happy is he who has so famous a poet to proclaim his actions." To ensure his glory, Alexander would not surprise attack at night: "I will not steal a victory." He wanted to inherit from his father not a prosperous kingdom but a troubled one that would give him more opportunities to achieve a glorious name. General Custer lost his life in the pursuit of glory. In World War II the daringly unorthodox tactics of General Patton outraged colleagues. And Benedict Arnold, petulantly infuriated by what he considered George Washington's slighting of his military achievements, betrayed his country. All these men were intuitive aethereals.

Glory appeals to aethereals because it stirs the imagination, and such people believe so strongly in the power of the imagination that they may feel at the core that the only truly exciting life is the life of the imagination, the internal life of visions and plans. We certainly find this the case with the many aethereal artists (people like Blake and Wagner) who have appeared to others to be living only for, and only in, their creative work. No one but an aethereal would write, as Shelley did, that "life like a dome of many-colored glass, stains the white radiance of eternity." Life may offer the beauty of its variously colored multiplicity, but it lacks that pure, abstract perfection that the imagination can provide. For life is messy and cluttered with concrete details. Aethereals have very little patience with those details, with the random grocery items, the passing sidewalk scene, the data of a trivial game. An aethereal shaving before a mirror is much less likely to be absorbed in the texture of his beard or a crack in the plaster than in some idea or imagining going on in his head. Someone of this type can, in fact, become so abstracted that he seems to others to have left the ground, to have lost touch with the "real world." The poet Blake's wife had to remind him that they were out of money by putting an empty plate in front of him at supper, and she told waiting guests to excuse her absent husband by explaining that he was upstairs "talking with God." But when critics complained that Blake's drawings looked like nothing in nature, he replied that he did not see with their eyes: "To me this World is all One continued Vision of Fancy and Imagination."

In communicating these intricate internal goings-on, aethereals may use imagery or analogies so complex or idiosyn-

cratic that they cannot be understood easily. The impulse behind such highly symbolic language is the effort to capture and
express those truths that best reveal the underlying essence of
things, what thinking-aethereal T. S. Eliot called "the objective
correlative." Unlike volcanics, who tend to be more involved
with the process of living per se, aethereals are highly engaged
in the intellectual process. That to them *is* life, or at least life
at its best. The aethereal is therefore concerned with intellectual achievement, is eager to acquire knowledge and careful to
gather relevant information to support cherished ideas or inspirations.* At times, thinking may become an end in itself, so
much so that such people find it difficult to turn off the mental
activity currently absorbing them, whether to eat dinner, mow
the lawn, turn the corner left at the correct intersection, allow
the conversation to move to another topic, or remember to pick
up the dry cleaning—or any of the other, to them, tiresome
details of day to day routine.

Given their cerebral bent, aethereals are apt to rely pervasively on language in order to deal with the world. But doesn't
everyone? No, not to the same extent that thinking and intuitive aethereals do. Feeling types (oceanics and volcanics) depend heavily on often unspoken emotional perceptions and
interactions, while sensation types (volcanics and territorials)
prefer action to talk and may actually distrust words: "You
either do it and you don't talk about it. Or you talk about it and
you don't do it," said Humphrey Bogart, an SR.

But aethereals love to talk, and they have a strong appetite
for conversation. Appreciative of verbal elegance themselves,
their own verbal skills are usually considerable. It is through
these that they prefer to relate to others. As would be expected,
many of the famous "wits" were aethereals: Cicero, Voltaire,
Pope, Jane Austen, and in our time, William Buckley and Gore

---

*Most aethereals, of course, do not have visions of conquering the world,
thoughts about Unified Field Theories, or imaginations like William Blake's.
The point is, rather, that *whatever* the focus of their thoughts or visions—
whether it be an engineering problem or a new lawsuit at the office, a beginning
love affair, aspirations to be an actor or an inventor, political campaigning or
religious meditation—the aethereal is likely to be deeply absorbed in thinking
about it.

Vidal, whose love of language is as similar as their politics are different. Puns and word play have an irresistible appeal to personalities of this type, from the verbal magic of Lewis Carroll and James Joyce to the five-year-old aethereal's tireless fascination with the nonsense rhymes of Dr. Seuss.

Aethereals may also use language as a way of distancing themselves. Volcanics have tremendous difficulty staying uninvolved, but aethereal types display a great capacity for detachment, a potential to be indifferent to all things (including other people) that do not happen to form a part of the mental or imaginative world currently engaging their thoughts and energies. This capacity to detach gives aethereals a valuable intellectual toughness; they can analyze their own mistakes as dispassionately as they may their friend's. However, it also leaves them open to charges of coldness and insensitivity. Wagner's wife endured many years of her husband's insolvencies, infidelities, and indifference, only to be told by the composer, "Your suffering will be rewarded by my fame." He was faithful only to his music. While Wagner's personality was, in most regards, an extreme one, many aethereals find that their way of relating strikes people of other types as aloof or even arrogant. And it is true that some may simply not value people or things for themselves but, as Beethoven put it, "as instruments upon which I can play as I please." In an even more sweeping statement, Napoleon is reputed to have dismissed his disastrous Moscow retreat with the remark, "Do you think I give a snap of the finger for the lives of a million men?"

In most aethereals, of course, this attitude is simply the need to keep interactions at a low emotional level. Nor does it derive from a dislike, or a disdain, of other people; once an aethereal bridges what can be to him a difficult gap between himself and intimacy with another, he may take consummate pleasure in the intensity of the contact. Rather, his detachment comes out of his feeling that the real world is an abstract and private one, a mental world, and that, in most situations, strong emotions are best kept out of it. The aethereal's world is also an idealistic one, and so people are valued not as individuals but as manifestations of those ideals. Thus, when Alexander the Great destroyed Thebes, he spared the house of Pindar's descendants—not because he felt sorry for their personal plight but because Pindar represented to him an ideal of the poet. Nor do aethereals usually take offense when they themselves are treated in a detached manner. In fact, they tend to prefer this impersonality, for they wish to be valued for their achievements, for their "doing" rather than simply their "being."

Related to their mistrust of the personal, aethereals are likely to mistrust the corporate existence as a whole. Volcanics find it very important to be accepted by the society in which they live, to be a part of the mainstream. But one of the favorite words aethereals have for the mainstream is "the herd," and the herd is not a group they are terribly eager to join. In general, they prefer to stand alone (and ahead) of the crowd of their fellow men, or as Milton—a TA—called them, "the owls and cuckoos, asses, apes, and dogs." "I lack the gift of orthodoxy," said the playwright Ibsen with some relish; "I must of necessity say, 'the Minority is always right . . . that minority which leads the van, and pushes on to the point which the majority has not yet reached."

Aethereals are highly individualistic people, and they pride themselves on having the courage of their difference. "The people and the herd are angry with me," Nietzsche has his prophet Zarathustra announce. "They are herdsmen, but they call themselves the good and just. Whom do they hate most? The one who breaks up their old table of values, the idol-breaker, the law-breaker. He, however, is the creator." This iconoclasm is more prevalent among intuitive aethereals than their thinking-type counterparts, and the former may carry their individualism to the point of deliberate eccentricity in personal styles, as the dancer, Isadora Duncan, or the painter, James Whistler, delighted to do. We see the trait, too, in the directorial styles of IA film makers Orson Welles, Federico Fellini, and Alfred Hitchcock. Some proclaim their uniqueness through a distinctive manner of dress, like the flowing golden locks and fringed buckskins of General Custer or General Patton's pearl-handled revolvers.

An aethereal is not necessarily a "loner." He may incorporate into his vanguard a few other like-minded individuals. Henry V's fellow soldiers at Agincourt were "We few, we happy

few." The blind Milton, writing *Paradise Lost* "in darkness, and
with dangers compassed round, and solitude," hoped he would
"find fit audience, though few." But to aethereals the fact that
they are *few*, as well as happy or fit, is not a negative consideration.

Aethereals are willing to stand alone, and almost nothing
is allowed to oppose their individual principles. Nothing else is
sacrosanct; every common idea, every ordinary value, is held up
to scrutiny. "I will not serve that in which I no longer believe,
whether it calls itself my home, my fatherland, or my church,"
wrote James Joyce, who left his native land of Ireland for self-
imposed exile in Paris. Taken to its absolute, this stance
becomes the sort of cynicism typified by Napoleon's admission:
"I became a good Catholic when I wanted to end the war in
Italy; in the East I was a Turk. If I reigned over the Jews, I would
build Solomon's temple again." But for the most part, there is
a core truth espoused against which the aethereal judges the
rest of the world. If you try to get him to compromise his
position, modify his behavior, or simply bend from a fixed
stance in some everyday situation, you may find him rather
unwilling to adapt—as fellow liberals found when they attempted to persuade the philosopher Bertrand Russell to disa-
vow his pacificism during World War I. "Intellectual integrity,"
he said, "made it quite impossible for me to accept the war
myths of any of the belligerent nations. Indeed those intellectuals who accepted them were abdicating their functions for the
joy of finding themselves at one with the herd."

However, while aethereals can be troublesomely inflexible,
their "nothing-sacred" attitude can also make them refresh-
ingly free from pomposity and jingoism. They are often willing
to see themselves as no more sacred than anything else. It was
Napoleon who said there is only one step from the sublime to
the ridiculous, and who, in the midst of his coronation as Emperor, was capable of prodding his brother in the ribs with his
scepter and whispering, "If only father could see us now!" The
same willingness to be good-humored about himself was part of
the charm of John F. Kennedy's press conferences.

This is not to say that aethereals are inordinately modest
about their just desserts. On the contrary, they have a strong

propensity toward arrogance. It was the same Napoleon, able to laugh at his own shortcomings, who could seriously say, "I closed the chasm of anarchy and put an end to chaos. . . . How can I help it if a great power drives me on to become dictator of the world?" It was the blind, forsaken Milton who said his poem would do things "unattempted yet in prose or rhyme," for it would "justify the ways of God to man."

Sometimes this arrogance is cheerfully confessed; sometimes it can be a life creed. "Early in life," explained Frank Lloyd Wright, "I had to choose between honest arrogance and hypocritical humility. I chose honest arrogance and have seen no reason to change."

As a whole, aethereals are relatively indifferent to the material world. Their world, as we have seen, is internal rather than external. "As for living," the poet Yeats liked to quote, "our servants will do it for us." Some people of this type strongly prefer the inanimate world of art or ideas to the animate one of nature. They may even find the sensual distasteful and natural processes something one should rise above. Author Rex Stout has his intuitive-aethereal sleuth, Nero Wolfe, actually refuse ever to leave his house unless driven out by a rare emergency. Next to the outdoors, his hatred is reserved for the notion of sexuality; he'd much rather read a book. Moreover, aethereals need little from their physical environment, for they are often rather aesthetic or spartan. Such were the personal life styles of both Alexander and Napoleon. Neither cared for luxurious food, clothing, or surroundings. They were lavish in bestowing extravagances on others but had little interest in such things themselves. According to Plutarch, Alexander said that sleep and sex "chiefly made him sensible that he was mortal" because "weariness and pleasure proceed from the same frailty and imbecility of human nature." Napoleon, who could completely refresh himself with twenty minutes of sleep, would have agreed.

George Gershwin said he needed nothing in life but his piano. "My piano is my wife and mistress." Asked where his laboratory was, Einstein held up a pencil. People like this may, as a result, be quite unobservant of their surroundings; they simply don't notice things and so may act in socially insensitive or awkward ways. The lack of attention to details can also lead aethereals to be careless or absent-minded. Lawrence of Arabia left his only copy of his autobiography in a railway carriage. When Beethoven's clothes became too ragged, his friends would simply take them away in the morning and put a new wardrobe out for him. He never seemed to notice the difference. In *Don Quixote,* Cervantes takes this aethereal trait to its absurd extremity. The intuitive Man of La Mancha is so totally absorbed in his dream of knight errantry that he is completely unobservant of his real surroundings. He does not notice that giants are windmills, armies are sheep, Dulcinea is an ugly peasant girl. And he is sublimely indifferent to the fact that he and Sancho are constantly beaten, starved, and mocked. Sancho is very aware of it all. Sancho is a volcanic.

In a more serious vein an aethereal's world can be severely damaged when a sudden, hitherto unnoticed event in reality contradicts an essential element in the person's theory or vision, when a tiny fact destroys a beautiful hypothesis or a splendid dream. In December of 1913 Woodrow Wilson told Congress, "Many happy manifestations multiply around us of a growing cordiality and sense of unity among the nations, foreshadowing an era of settled peace and good will." Eight months later, Western Europe was at war, and his programs of domestic reform had to be disrupted. A few years afterwards, an even more cherished ideal was to be shattered when the American people rejected his plan for a League of Nations. Wilson could not compromise or barter with his opponents. Lyndon Johnson would have. Johnson was a volcanic.

VOLCANIC

For the aethereal Blake, poetry—founded in the imagination—was mystical and revelatory: "I assert for My Self that I do not behold the outward Creation and that to me it is hindrance and not Action; it is as the dirt upon my feet." For Walt Whitman, the volcanic, poetry was grounded in that dirt and trees and leaves of grass: "I will make my poems of materials for I think they are to be the most spiritual poems. And I will make the poems of my body and of mortality. For I think I shall then

supply myself with the poems of my soul and of immortality."
Each of these poets seeks to discover reality, but aethereals and
volcanics search in different places and in different ways.

Volcanics live in the here and now. They are people deeply
engaged with life, often with strong vital energy to give to
living it. As such, volcanic types are far more interested in the
actual and the immediate than in the aethereals' hypothetical
future. In the volcanic view, the present is where the focus
should be. The American educator, John Dewey (an FV), constantly warned theorizers: "Cease conceiving of education as
mere preparation for later life, and make of it the full meaning
of the present life." It is the same emphasis that led the SV
Tolstoy to devise a new religion, the gospel of the brotherhood
of man as a "practical religion not promising bliss in the future
but giving happiness on earth." That is the happiness to which
the twentieth-century Pope John, a feeling volcanic, gave
predominance in the title of his 1963 encyclical, *Pacem in Ter-
ris,* peace on earth.

The term "volcanic," then, refers not so much to the explo-
sive, eruptive aspects of this personality but to the in-rootedness
of the type. In other words, volcanics seem to live not only on
the earth and in it but to gain energy and sustenance from deep
within its sources. An aethereal can ignore his current surroundings; a volcanic cannot. People of this type greatly dislike
having to act out of accord with actual situations. They feel
uncomfortable with the notion of infinite possibilities infinitely
unfolding. In fact, they may have trouble assessing things that
they are not presently experiencing; this is, of course, the opposite problem of the aethereal's difficulty in dealing with immediate situations. Take two fictional characters for examples. The
volcanic Othello has no trouble at all coping when confronted
with a sudden military crisis; what he cannot do is cope with the
possibility that Desdemona may be betraying him, a hypothesis
that he must accept at secondhand from Iago. That is why he
demands of Iago "give me ocular proof," "give me a living
reason she's disloyal"; and that is why he can be duped by the
trick of a planted handkerchief. Conversely, the aethereal Sherlock Holmes has no trouble at all mentally reconstructing a
crime committed in another country; he may, however, fail to

remember that Dr. Watson is sitting across from him while he does it.

Volcanics like "to be there." As an aethereal, Darwin said that if a fact interfered with a theory, his tendency might be to throw out the fact. A volcanic would throw out the theory. He is the sort of person who says, "I felt it. I saw it. That's how I know it's true." The eighteenth-century philosopher, Bishop Berkeley, an aethereal, believed that the physical world was nothing but an idea in God's mind. Dr. Samuel Johnson, a volcanic, kicked a stone, hurt his foot, and cried, "Thus I refute Bishop Berkeley."

As a result of this concentration on present happenings, volcanics may fail adequately to anticipate potential eventualities, though this is more true of discontinuous sensation volcanics than of feeling volcanics who develop a sense of the recurrent patterns of experience from their perception of temporal continuity. But both have far less natural impulse than do aethereals to anticipate the future; they may actually consider such hypothesizing if not somehow "wrong" then at least a futile exercise.

Volcanics rely on action. They are likely to be pragmatic people and, as such, feel uneasy away from facts. Aethereals distrust the personal; volcanics distrust the impersonal. To them, all those theories and abstractions that make up the aethereal's ideational world are false to life, even dangerous. In an episode describing a military rout in *A Farewell to Arms,* Hemingway wrote, "Abstract words such as glory, honor, courage were obscene beside the concrete names of villages, the number of roads." Not all abstractions are obscene, but they are not, to the volcanic perceptual world, as innately meaningful as any particular actuality. "I have no rules and no method," said the painter Renoir. "Nothing can be taken for granted; nothing is stereotyped." Everything must be taken individually, in its concrete, specific, relative is-ness. The real *is* the ideal: "And a mouse is miracle enough to stagger sextillions of infidels," Walt Whitman insisted.

The volcanic believes that each human being should be seen as unique and special, that each detail of this "multiverse" is relevant and must be attended to. He does not consider the multiplicity and mutability of the material world a cluttering barrier between him and some ideal; it does not give him the nervous fear that permanence and unity cannot be found on earth and must be sought in ideas. On the contrary, he delights in the fact that "beauty derives its charm from diversity," as Renoir believed. In the profusion of natural images common in the works of volcanic poets like Frost, Whitman, Keats, Robert Burns, all the way back to Chaucer, we can enjoy this sensitivity to the charm of physical diversity, as we see it, too, in the multitudes of individual characters created by volcanic novelists like Dickens and Tolstoy.

"Damn the Absolute!" William James exclaimed. "Why is 'One' more excellent than 'forty-three' or than 'two million and ten'?" Volcanics do not think that the truth can be found in abstract theories or individual people be helped all that much by philosophical generalities. "No sort of scientific teaching," Dostoevski wrote, "will ever teach men to share property and privilege with equal consideration for all." This assumption does not mean that volcanics never operate from a broad perspective intellectually or work in a generalized way for the benefit of mankind. They do. But as Lewis Fischer wrote of Gandhi's nationalist movement, "His was not a loyalty to abstractions; it was a loyalty to living human beings."

During his early period of political agitation in South Africa, Gandhi at times shocked his devoted followers by his willingness to compromise with the detested authorities in order to gain a particular advantage he thought important. As we have seen, an aethereal might have more difficulty bending his ideals to meet a contradictory force halfway. But volcanics are far more adaptable. For one thing, they are generally able to accept life simply, as it is given. "We love the things we love for what they are," Frost said. An aethereal would probably say instead, "We love the things we love for what they *could* be."

This kind of acceptance, joined to their perceptivity about their surroundings, makes volcanics very socially and emotionally aware people. Thus, they are usually able to fit easily into the mores of the age and culture in which they live. It is fortunate that they have this capacity because not fitting in is much more traumatic for them than being excluded from the mainstream would be for an aethereal, who might simply not notice he was being excluded. The volcanic, with his sensitive social antenna, would be quicker to pick up other people's negativity or shock and, lacking the aethereal's protective ability to detach himself, could be quite wounded. This is especially true of younger volcanics; in adolescence everyone's tender psychic skin is more easily lacerated; as we grow older, our hides thicken, and while we may still feel the barb prick us, it doesn't seem to hurt as much or as long. But when some variety of "unacceptable" behavior does bring down on a volcanic the wrath and censure of society, as happened to nineteenth-century novelist George Eliot when she began living with a married man, the person may suffer tremendous psychological pain because of the imposed isolation.

More often than not, however, volcanics can easily integrate themselves into the corporate existence, even an adopted and initially quite foreign one. Observers were struck, for instance, with how totally at home and how completely accepted by the native population both Dr. Livingstone and, years later, Albert Schweitzer were when living in African villages. Volcanics can be, in fact, so secure in their base as members of the corporate whole that their idiosyncrasies may not strike others as being quite as odd as, say, similar eccentricities in an aethereal would. Because volcanics naturally pick up social customs, they know how to respond to them whether they genuinely share the values or not. So people sense that the volcanic is really "one of them." Robert Frost was the people's poet, however much fun he might poke at the people, while his contemporary, the aethereal Ezra Pound, was considered completely insane and retaliated by dismissing the entire United States as one huge insane asylum.

Volcanics also tend to make friends easily. One reason why is that they strike others as "natural." They are good-natured people. The immense popularity of the late Pope John derived in part from the feeling everyone had that he was "just himself," unpretentious and natural despite all the protocol and ritual that surrounds the papal office. He forbade people to kneel to him, invited the Vatican gardeners in for lunch, laughed and joked with his visitors. He was not being strategic in behaving this way; it was just his very personal style. As he told his parishioners to whom he opened his palace day and night when he was Cardinal of Venice, "I am only a parish priest, and wish to remain so." One of his favorite expressions was "May God have patience with us fat men." Nor did the papacy change his unassuming manner; he said that if he did suspect himself of becoming pompous, he would have John the Pope tell John the man, "Don't make yourself so important, please."

Such easygoingness also means that volcanics are generally not very goal-oriented but can be content puttering around, wandering about on trips, tinkering with projects without feeling pressured—as a territorial would—to "get the thing done" and move on to the next task, the next sightseeing stop in the agenda, the next step in the plan. In fact, they resist the imposition of such rigid structures. Tolstoy wanted to found a school in which there would be no compulsory lessons, no orders, no rewards or punishments; the children could work, play, come, go, pay attention or not, as they chose. Years later, this "progressive" system of education was popularized in America by another volcanic, John Dewey.

But more than simply easygoing, the volcanic temperament is, in a deep sense, an acceptant one. Whatever life presents can be endured with dignity, for everything in life ought to be considered real and meaningful, a part of the human condition. Death as well as birth, sorrow as much as joy. This capacity is one of the explanations why so many volcanics do well in the medical and nursing professions, social services, and other work in which there is intimate contact with human suffering.

To say that is not to conclude that volcanics accept everything with enthusiasm. Of course, they do not. Being such highly involved people, they are also highly responsive to anything that touches their emotions, and that naturally includes negative as well as positive emotions. A volcanic is likely to have little success in detaching himself from his own experience—in standing back, as an aethereal can, to analyze it. As a consequence, he is at times capable of uncontrollable explosions of strong emotions. He erupts. The tempestuousness of fictional works like *Romeo and Juliet* or *Wuthering Heights* is based in the volcanic personalities of both sets of lovers: Romeo and Heathcliff are feeling volcanics; Juliet and Catherine Earnshaw are sensation volcanics. Works written by volcanics, like D. H. Lawrence's *Sons and Lovers* or Dostoevski's *The Brothers Karamazov*, are likely as well to reveal this sort of passionate engagement with the emotions. Similarly, a volcanic's theory of the function of art is apt to be founded not in intellectual but in emotional criteria. A poem, said Robert Frost, "is never a put-up job, so to speak. It begins as a lump in the throat, a sense of wrong, a homesickness, a lovesickness. It is never a thought to begin with." Emily Dickinson, an FV, wrote that she knew something was poetry if she felt "physically as if the top of [her] head were being taken off."

The emotionality of volcanics is expressed both in affirmative and in critical ways. Take, for example, their great tenacity, which may be in one case an unshakable loyalty and in another, unforgiving vengefulness. On the one hand, they are very protective of other people; at the same time, they have a tendency to find fault and scold them. In relation to the volcanic personality, these attitudes are not all contradictory but are, instead, psychologically connected. If someone feels a great deal of responsibility for another person's well-being, feels himself involved in it, he finds it hard not to nag at the recipient of his concern, while a more detached individual wouldn't worry so much and therefore wouldn't find so much to worry about. Again, volcanics are able to be very tough about negative feelings (those they have about themselves or other people as well as those that other people have about them); meanwhile, they may be quite willing to manipulate the feelings of those around them, and they expect others to be as emotionally tough as they are. In *Gone With the Wind,* the volcanic Scarlet O'Hara endures an unmitigated series of disasters with admirable courage; in addition, she faces her own moral pragmatism—by which I mean her readiness to "lie, steal, cheat, and kill" to protect Tara—with some honesty. But she certainly expects everyone else to be as strong as she is. So, having manipulated her sister Suellen's fiancé into marrying her instead, she has no patience with Suellen's outraged reaction. Nor can she tolerate

Ashley Wilkes's aethereal idealism when the real "facts" contradict it: He *is* sexually attracted to her, and the genteel Old South *is* dead.

In whatever ways they develop their moral codes or philosophies, volcanics have a profound sense of personal integrity and are horrified if they feel they have been unfaithful to their true selves or their "best" selves. We can see this attitude in distilled form in tragedy, in which most of the heroes are feeling volcanics whose death follows their realization of and repudiation of such interpsychic betrayals: Othello and Mark Antony are so filled with self-contempt for having been unfaithful to their own integrity that they commit suicide.

All people of this type have a deep sense of honor and are capable of great moral indigation, which is different from the righteous indignation felt by aethereals against those who fail to live up to idealistic and ideational standards. Volcanics are outraged by those who fail to live up to ethical and humanistic standards. It is perhaps more often the feeling volcanic whose moral quality impresses us as particularly inviolate. Discontinuous-sensation volcanics tend to believe, as we shall see, in a more flexible "situational" morality than the cumulative, traditional systems of ethics espoused by their continuous feeling-type counterparts.

When eminent public figures are of the feeling-volcanic psychetype, as George Washington and Dwight Eisenhower were, they are likely to inspire in people great affection and loyalty. We admire them not necessarily because they are brilliant thinkers or charismatic innovators, nor because they are politically astute. We admire them primarily because they seem to exemplify within their own persons unassailable honor and human virtue. They are great because they are good. Sensation volcanics can evoke a similar sort of personal devotion, as the careers of Robert F. Kennedy and Gandhi suggest. We are responding to what we believe to be the heart of another human being, not the head.

Volcanics themselves are more concerned with personal development than theoretical speculation, more interested in the depth than the scope of things. Not just the individual self, though. We are all together, man and nature, involved in a communal growth. "One generation playing its part and passing on. Another generation playing its part and passing on in turn." Walt Whitman, like all volcanics, felt a deep attraction to those enduring aspects of life's processes: the inevitability of death and winter, the perennial coming of birth and spring, an ancient tree that has outlasted centuries of storm and frost, the awakening of love in the young, the turning of the seasons, the old face that traces the experiences of years in its lines, the old river that just keeps rolling along. Hemingway's *Old Man and the Sea* is, in this sense, a paradigm of the volcanic experience.

People like this feel a very close relationship to their physical environment. "The land was ours before we were the land's," said Frost, and we are best off when we learn how to become the land's again, to be at one with nature. Volcanics, like Frost, usually show a tremendous respect for nature and the animal world; they have that love of all living, growing things, which FV Albert Schweitzer called "reverence for life." Many volcanics are devoted pet owners; they can be passionately attached to horses or dogs. They feel comfortable around animals and enjoy raising them, like to be outdoors, are fervent gardeners, boaters, hikers, and campers. For unlike many aethereals who are rather indifferent to their physical environment, or even feel uneasy in it, volcanics have a natural aptitude and a high sense of competence about working with their bodies, with animals, and with the land. They are physically oriented people.

As such, they can accept all the natural processes that go along with being human. Lyndon B. Johnson, to take a perhaps less usual instance of this trait, had no compunction about matter-of-factly pulling up his shirt to show White House visitors his gall-bladder scar nor (if rumors are to be believed) about holding conferences from his toilet seat. Somehow, one doesn't think of Woodrow Wilson doing such things.

Their physicality also makes them much more concerned about the state of their bodies than aethereals usually are. Volcanics worry about illness, about aging, and about losing their looks. "How," wrote Tolstoy, "can a man with so broad a nose, such thick lips and little grey eyes like mine, ever find happiness on earth?" It is hard to imagine Albert Einstein seriously asking himself that question. But volcanics are extremely sensitive about their appearance; they dress to please others, and themselves, in the most fashionable and appropriate way possible. Despite his little gray eyes, the young Tolstoy was considered quite a fop. This is true even of those volcanics whom we might expect to be "above" such considerations. When he was a student in London, Gandhi dressed everyday in a banker's formal morning coat, a silk top hat, gloves, and cane. And one of the reasons his neighbors were so surprised at the subsequent calling of St. Francis of Assisi was that, as a youth, he had been the leader of a group of dilettantish dandies who strolled about the town wearing the most lavish of outfits. However, as we have seen, all volcanics are highly aware of their social surroundings; they want to belong. They are very attuned to the physical world; they want to be an attractive part of it.

To sum up the two different perceptions of spatial substance: Volcanics see the composition of reality as concrete, substantial, specified, actual, and realistic, while to aethereals reality is abstract, imaginative, absolute, theoretical, and symbolic. The volcanic mode of relating to this world is involved, personal, active and experiential, pragmatic, humanistic, acceptant, communal, and physical. Conversely, the aethereal's mode is detached, impersonal, verbal and intellectual, rational, idealistic, speculative, individualistic, and aescetic. No individual will relate completely and exclusively in his typological mode, but his basic manner of perceiving and responding to his experience will fall into one or the other of these areas.

AETHEREALS

Cicero, TA	Alexander the Great, IA
Henry V of England, TA	Patrick Henry, IA
John Milton, TA	Benedict Arnold, IA
Voltaire, TA	Napoleon Bonaparte, IA
Jane Austen, TA	William Blake, IA
Bishop Berkeley, TA	Percy Shelley, IA
Friedrich Nietzsche, TA	Ralph Waldo Emerson, IA
Lewis Carroll, TA	Ludwig van Beethoven, IA
Woodrow Wilson, TA	Richard Wagner, IA
Henrik Ibsen, TA	Charles Darwin, IA
Lawrence of Arabia, TA	General George A. Custer, IA
Bertrand Russell, TA	Isadora Duncan, IA
T. S. Eliot, TA	Cecil Rhodes, IA
Franklin D. Roosevelt, TA	William Butler Yeats, IA
Igor Stravinsky, TA	Frank Lloyd Wright, IA
Albert Einstein, TA	James Joyce, IA
John F. Kennedy, TA	George Gershwin, IA
Gore Vidal, TA	Walt Disney, IA
William F. Buckley, Jr., TA	Alfred Hitchcock, IA
	Orson Welles, IA
	Federico Fellini, IA
	General George Patton, IA

VOLCANICS

St. Francis of Assisi, FV
George Washington, FV
Dr. Samuel Johnson, FV
Emily Dickinson, FV
George Eliot, FV
Dr. David Livingstone, FV
Feodor Dostoevski, FV
William James, FV
John Dewey, FV
D. H. Lawrence, FV
Dr. Albert Schweitzer, FV
Dwight D. Eisenhower, FV
Pope John XXVIII, FV

Geoffrey Chaucer, SV
Robert Burns, SV
John Keats, SV
Leo Tolstoy, SV
Walt Whitman, SV
Auguste Renoir, SV
Mohandas Gandhi, SV
Robert Frost, SV
Ernest Hemingway, SV
Lyndon B. Johnson, SV
Robert F. Kennedy, SV

5.

Understanding Spatial Structure: Territorials and Oceanics

TERRITORIAL

In some personalities a perception of the *structure* of reality takes precedence over an awareness of its *substance;* in other words, their attitudes derive more from their sense of the external make-up of reality, than its internal composition. When this is so in a thinking type or a sensation type, they are territorials rather than, respectively, aethereals and volcanics. When it is so for intuitives and feeling types, they are oceanics, as opposed to, again respectively, aethereals and volcanics. In its most simplistic formulation territorials see the world as structured, and oceanics see it as unstructured.

"Structure" is, in fact, the most important word in the experiential vocabulary of territorials. They are the people for whom some kind of organizing structure in their lives, thoughts, social relations, spatial surroundings, and own psyches is an absolute prerequisite of well-being. First of all, they need to define the "self," to experience their specific positions, functions, and relationships not as a merging part of the corporate whole but as distinctive from others. Next, they want to be able, with some clarity of purpose, to make that self-definition effective in the world.

Humphrey Bogart was an SR who became notorious in Hollywood for his nonconformist attitudes and his insistence— in a town in which group pressure had the power to ruin a career—on maintaining his personal freedom. But as he said, "I don't see why I should conform to Mrs. Emily Post, not because I'm an actor and believe that being an actor gives me special dispensation, but because I'm a human being with a pattern of my own and the right to work out my own pattern in my own way." As Rick in *Casablanca,* Philip Marlowe in *The Big Sleep,* or Sam Spade in *The Maltese Falcon,* Bogart brought this same individuality to his film characterizations, in which he always played a strong man who, as Richard Schickel summarized, "unflinchingly followed his own code of ethics," a man who could "get interested in a fight for justice or principle only when his own, direct stake in the outcome was made painfully clear to him." He was his own man, who kept his own counsel, lived by his own creed, and made you respect it.

Being by nature independent people, territorials prefer to make their own structures. Sensation types with high territoriality are especially sensitive to being "fenced in." For example, the novelist William Faulkner could apparently so little tolerate the enclosure and regimen of a classroom that he was never able to stay in one long enough to graduate from high school. During World War I, despite his eagerness to be a pilot, he would not enlist in the air force because he could not tolerate the idea of being bossed around by "Yankees." Back home in Oxford, Mississippi, after the war, he took a job in the local post office. According to biographer Louis Untermeyer, he was reputed to have been the worst postmaster in the small town's history.

> *He was never on time; he was whimsical about sorting mail, keeping accounts, filing records; he opened and closed the office without regard to the convenience of the customers. When com-*

plaints reached the authorities, he resigned. He said he was glad he would no longer "have to be at the beck and call of anyone who happens to have two cents."

Superficially, it might appear that we are talking about an attitude indistinguishable from the individualistic stance earlier categorized as an aethereal quality. There is, however, a very real difference. In general, territorials do not see themselves as apart from, ahead of, at variance with, or uninvolved in the rest of society; rather, they insist that their rights within its organization and their position in its hierarchy be carefully demarcated and respected. Obviously, Faulkner did not consider the post-mastership of Oxford, Mississippi, his rightful station. Once again we see how typological differences lie not so much in *behavior* as in our underlying experiential attitudes and motivations.

In order to maintain their individual boundaries, territorials try hard to be as impersonal and objective as possible. Such control helps to ensure their freedom. To reach a state of economic, psychological, intellectual, and sentimental freedom is, according to SR oceanographer Jacques Cousteau, the best way to live one's life. By "sentimental freedom" he means not being dependent on human relationships; by "intellectual freedom" he means not being "imprisoned by the ideas and intellectual patterns" with which society conditions us. Economic freedom enables a territorial to avoid being in another's debt. People of this type greatly dislike owing anything to others, as they feel it interferes with their independence. To keep himself from financial obligations to his studio, Bogart put his earnings in an account he called the "Fuck You" Fund. The money meant he could feel free to say just that to Warner Brothers if he ever felt like leaving Hollywood. George Bernard Shaw refused to marry his wealthy fiancée until his income matched hers.

But "debt" can mean things other than money. A territorial is likely to feel uneasy until he has repaid a favor, given a gift in return, "evened the score." He may even be unwilling to ask street directions from a passer-by or request a neighbor's assistance in putting up a fence. Charles Lindbergh flew across the

Atlantic alone not because he had to but because he wanted to: "Besides costing more, a big plane isn't as efficient, and it would need a crew. I'd rather go alone. . . . What advantages there are in flying alone! I know now what my father meant when he warned me, years ago, of depending too heavily on others." "Above all," he added, "I've gained in freedom." The "We" of his first autobiography would be just he and *The Spirit of St. Louis.*

Closely related to this attitude is the territorial's love of privacy and his need to keep that privacy from being invaded. For most individuals there's no necessary incompatibility between hospitable openness and privacy, but with public figures there is a direct conflict, for their lives are, literally, publicized. The problem becomes more acute when the territorial is introverted, especially in the case of a sensation territorial whose need for control and secrecy is more intense than that of thinking types. Richard Nixon, an introverted sensation territorial, carried secrecy to a neurotic, not to mention criminal, degree. More understandably, Lindbergh was so maddened by the invasions of his privacy during the famous kidnapping trial that he left America to live in England, where he hoped people would have the courtesy to leave him alone.

Thomas Jefferson was always fighting an internal battle between his need to be involved in political affairs and his need to be a private person. As a result, he becomes a member of the Virginia legislature but spends only sixteen days of an eight-week term in residence. He comes to Philadelphia, writes the Declaration of Independence, but retreats to Monticello in September of 1776 and does not re-enter national politics until six years later, ignoring the pleas of the many political friends, like Edmund Pentleton, who urged him to return to the service of his country: "I hope you'll get cured of your wish to retire so early in life from the memory of man." He begins an autobiography but quits after 120 pages with the remark, "I'm already tired of talking about myself." Moreover, he gives us very little personal information in what he does write. As Fawn Brodie, his recent biographer, points out, we know an incredible amount about Jefferson, but we still do not feel that we know the *man* behind all those collected and preserved records; not in the way, for example, we feel that we know volcanics like Andrew Jackson or Teddy Roosevelt.

Even highly extraverted territorials are annoyed by intrusions into what they consider their private affairs. Elizabeth I sharply reprimanded Parliament, which published her replies to their queries regarding her marriage plans: "I know no reason why my private answers to the realm should serve for a prologue to a subsidies-book. Neither yet do I understand why such audacity should be used to make without my license an act of my words."

Because Elizabeth wished to protect both her privacy and her objectivity, she, like all territorials, strove all her life for absolute emotional control. In her lifetime and position, of course, to lose it might be to lose her head, as she had learned from the fate of her volatile, intuitive-oceanic mother, Anne Boleyn—and from the similar fates of countless other high-ranking men and women who had gone to the scaffold at the command of her father, Henry VIII, or her sister, "Bloody Mary." Self-discipline and self-preservation thus became, in a sense, synonymous to Elizabeth, and an asset to that discipline was her territorial ability to resist emotional arousal, to treat her own feelings objectively, and at the same time to treat others' feelings impersonally, as irrelevant to the political situation at hand. Had her feeling-volcanic sister, Queen Mary, been able to be that dispassionate, she might have had the more popular Elizabeth (in the Tower at that time as a threat to her throne) executed. Years later, when Elizabeth's beloved Earl of Essex threatened *her* throne, she did have him executed. Despite his impassioned letters (of a sort not unlike those she had once written to Mary), she condemned him as one who had proved himself "a senseless ingrate" and a political hazard. Elizabeth was not a vindictive person; she was, in fact, far more temperate and humane than most of her contemporary monarchs. She would have preferred that others control themselves as well as she did and not force her into the position of having to protect herself and her throne against them. But if they persisted, as her very uncontrolled intuitive-oceanic cousin Mary Queen of Scots did for almost twenty years before Elizabeth finally had her beheaded, then the kingdom came before the kinship.

Elizabeth's objectivity often made her seem to others "too clever and sly," "more than a man, but rather less than a woman." Likewise, Jefferson—who, according to his daughter Martha's personal knowledge, only lost his temper twice in his life—was considered by some acquaintances to be as "cold as a frog." We find similar remarks made about most territorials, including those equally noted for their human compassion, like John Adams, Florence Nightingale, or Eleanor Roosevelt. But control makes possible that structured equilibrium so integral to territorial values. "Peace is my passion," said Jefferson. It was Elizabeth's and Eleanor Roosevelt's as well.

Naturally, no one can always resist emotional arousal, at least not without paying a high price to do so. For instance, Jefferson made only a matter-of-fact entry in his journal: "My mother died about eight o'clock this morning in the fifty-seventh year of her age." Period. That was it. But he promptly got an excruciating migraine headache that kept him in bed for weeks. One way territorials have of protecting themselves from strong emotions is by simply staying away from situations in which they are likely to occur. So Lincoln, a TR, who apparently had a rather problematic relationship with his father, refused to go visit him when he was dying, writing instead to his step-brother, "Say to him that if we could meet now, it is doubtful whether it would not be more painful than pleasant."

Or, territorials may choose to maintain control in distressing situations through a wry sort of humor. Refusing to go out socially after he learned he had terminal cancer, the Russian writer Chekhov told friends, "It would be awkward to fall down and die in the presence of strangers." In the same circumstances, Humphrey Bogart responded to journalists' vulturelike curiosity with sardonic news bulletins: "You can say that I'm down to my last martini, but I'm fighting to hold my head above the press." Territorials dislike sentimentality—in themselves as well as in others—and consequently may be curt with those whom they think are trying to offer them unwanted sympathy, unwanted because it may break through their control. Adlai E. Stevenson wrote of the last weeks before Bogart died of cancer that "he made a most gallant effort to keep gay. He had an impatience for weakness, an impatience with illness." According to his TR wife, Lauren Bacall, he had "always hated sentiment and sincerely resented a public display of affection. . . . Although he was sentimental, when he gave me a present, it was usually with a crack to take the sentiment from it." Territorials are more embarrassed by emotional displays than aethereals because they are less detached; on the other hand, they don't feel as comfortable with their feelings as volcanics do, so they are likely to cover them up by making a wisecrack or changing the subject.

One emotion that territorials may have particular trouble suppressing is their defensiveness, an outgrowth of their strong self-protective impulses. This defensive response to supposed insults or injuries or criticism can lead them to overreact, to defend themselves needlessly when perhaps the best thing to do would be to let the matter drop and be forgotten. Instead, they may put themselves in the position they most want to avoid, for their attitude exposes them emotionally and costs them their private impersonality. But territorials are so aware of the demands a social structure puts upon their function within it that they must justify to themselves, if not to others, their failure to meet those demands. As Jefferson said, "I am always mortified when anything is expected of me which I cannot fulfill." But he only made matters worse when he insisted on defending himself in a public hearing against a rather *pro forma* censure by the Virginia legislature for his actions as governor. He learned his lesson, and when he ran for the Presidency, he wisely simply ignored all the insinuations about his sexual immorality with a slave mistress. In a far more extreme example, Richard Nixon's obsessive and defensive efforts to justify his conduct about the Watergate situation pushed him in a deeper and deeper entrenchment and finally helped cost him the office he was willing to do so much to protect.

Ironically, because territorials struggle so continually (and usually so successfully) to maintain an emotionally neutral objectivity, when their feelings *do* get the best of them, they may momentarily go more out of control than people of other spatial settings; or at least, because such behavior is infrequent, they *seem* more out of control. For one thing, territorials simply haven't the familiarity with their own emotional barometers that, say, volcanics have developed. Thus, they can lapse from cool control to mawkish self-pity, as happened in Nixon's televised farewell to his White House staff, to the ungoverned fits of rage that terrorized Queen Elizabeth's courtiers, or to the bouts of melancholia that disrupted Lincoln's nights.

Just as a structured psyche is vital to a territorial, so is a structured intellect and a structured life. They tend, consequently, to be very orderly people, believing, as Edmund Burke wrote, that "good order is the foundation of all good things." We can contrast the orderly routine of family life in the homes of territorials like Freud or Marx with the rather chaotic turmoil in the homes of even introverted volcanics like Eugene O'Neill or Teddy Roosevelt, or oceanics like Dylan Thomas. Territorial order derives from a habitual, self-disciplined frame of mind. Of course, the continuous thinking territorial with his secondary aethereality is likely to be somewhat more consistent in his habits and structured in his life style than his sensation-type counterpart, whose discontinuous, volcanic orientation toward the present can distract him from overall goals, but a sensation territorial will seem highly organized if compared with a "just take it as it comes" sensation volcanic. Both SRs and TRs are people who need closure on things, need to see problems resolved, answers given, and everything put in its place. Jefferson kept journals, farm records, and account books in which every expenditure of his adult life was duly noted. He also methodically preserved twenty-five thousand letters written to him as well as copies of his own correspondence. For eight years he recorded statistics of the earliest and latest appearance of every single vegetable that arrived at the Washington, D.C., marketplace. His many practical inventions (including a huge compass on his ceiling) were designed to improve the functional orderliness of Monticello.

These habits also illuminate a related territorial trait: the enjoyment derived from quantification, from lists, charts, statistics, maps, records, and so on. Such individuals love to read maps, are excellent at finding their way around places, at giving directions, at figuring out diagrams. On a vacation trip a territorial will happily study maps and navigate, plan agendas, read all the literature handed out at spots of interest, and will be glad to tell you how many years it took how many craftsmen to carve how many statues on Notre Dame cathedral.

Disciplined habits and quantifying skills lead many territorials into successful careers as scientists, technologists, and engineers; among them, Benjamin Franklin, Madame Curie, Louis Pasteur, Thomas Edison, and Henry Ford. A territorial is the type who likes to solve problems; if an aethereal delights most in creating theories, a territorial delights in putting theories to work. Jefferson did not only design a theory of education, he designed the University of Virginia and built it. Edison was interested in the idea of electricity insofar as that idea helped him figure out how to put electricity to use—in lightbulbs.

A structured world is an organized one, so territorials take tremendous pleasure in organization; they are very good at it, too. Among his many other achievements, Benjamin Franklin managed to organize for his home town of Philadelphia a fire department, a post office, a police department, the Pennsylvania Hospital, the University of Pennsylvania, the American Philosophical Society, and a subscription library, as well as getting the city streets paved. Meanwhile, he served on many committees to help organize not just a city but a new nation. So did Jefferson, on thirty-four of them, in fact, between 1776 and 1777. As they not only enjoy organizing events and understand how to do it but also appreciate organizations per se, territorials work well on committees; they like the way people can work together within formal structures to accomplish common goals. Florence Nightingale, Susan B. Anthony, and Eleanor Roosevelt are laudable instances of thinking territorials, like Jefferson, whose organizational skills, joined to tireless patience with committee work, enabled them to bring to fruition significant advances in human rights and welfare. Their accomplishments grew in good measure out of those considerable administrative abilities that we typically find in territorials. The careful organization and management of government, including the establishment and efficient use of bureaucratic structures, distinguished the reigns, or leaderships, of a long line of territorials: Caesar, Cleopatra of Egypt, Vespasian, Charlemagne, Eleanor of Aquitaine, Cromwell, Jefferson, Lincoln, Bismarck, Stalin, and De Gaulle had very different ideas about the purpose and power of government, but all of them shared the territorial's capacity to administer effectively. Against great odds Elizabeth I did so for forty-four years (far longer than the eight monarchs before her managed to stay on their thrones) and became the first British ruler to leave her name to an age.

Believing as they do in the importance of social structures, territorials tend to be very concerned with status. They want status for themselves, and they notice it in other people. Almost automatically, a territorial recognizes the subtle differences in rank that are awarded people in social hierarchies on the basis of their nobility, their land, their money, their power, their family. While TRs and SRs are willing to acknowledge the status of others and to be deferential to their superiors, they are equally insistent that their own status be appreciated by those "beneath" them. "A strange thing it is," snapped Elizabeth when her Parliament kept urging her to marry, "that the foot should direct the head in so weighty a cause."

Territorials also pay close attention to all the totems that symbolize status: the kind of car, the brand of Scotch, the suit label, the size of an office and how many windows it has, who sits where at a conference, who has his name on the door and a Bigelow on the floor, who's on his way up or his way down. They may choose to ignore this knowledge; the point is not that territorials are necessarily power-hungry opportunists, but simply that they naturally "pick up" the layout of power structures. Mozart, who was at one time palace musician to Archbishop Hieronymus, wrote home that he had to eat with the servants and that even then "the two valets sit at the head of the table. I have at all events, the honor to be placed above the cooks." An oceanic in a similar situation would probably never notice that his prestige was being coordinated with his place at the table, or if he did, it would not matter as much to him as it obviously did to Mozart, an SR. But territorials, who appreciate the significance of role differences—those public roles we assume or are given in social life—have a propensity to define people by their *function*. That is, they are apt to see cook, valet, clerk, wife, policeman, Congresswoman, or army officer rather than individual men and women. And in ordinary situations they are likewise apt to relate to people in terms of those functions: A soldier is a soldier, a patient is a patient, a secretary is a secretary, a captain is "higher" than a lieutenant, a composer ought to be "higher" than a cook. Even in personal circumstances, role and function may supersede relationship at appropriate times. In a real sense, when they worked on political matters, FDR was to Eleanor Roosevelt "the President," not her husband. Because of this attitude, a territorial needs to have information about people that tells him how to relate to them properly. "Who is so-and-so?" may therefore mean: "What does he do, what's his background, what's his position, to whom is he married, who are his friends?" Conversely, when an oceanic asks, "Who are you?" he or she more likely wants to know: "What are you like as a person?"

One of the ways territorials learn the "rules"—the principles, codes, values, skills by which they live in the world—is by choosing role models to follow. These mentors can be decisive and lasting influences; in the biographies of young TRs and SRs we find continual mention of gratefully remembered superiors (often teachers) who performed this function, for instance, Eleanor Roosevelt's French schoolmistress or Jefferson's tutor ("my antient master, my earliest and best friend"). The intuitive-aethereal Beethoven said he had learned nothing innovative from his teachers, but Mozart deferentially acknowledged Haydn as his musical role-model, revealing here another difference in aethereal and territorial "individualism." Role models need not always be people personally known; a young territorial scientist might choose Madame Curie or Albert Einstein to model her aspirations after.

Their concern about their own respectibility is another reason why territorials are so respectful of the rules or codes of honor adhered to by groups and organizations to which they belong. In all public relations people of this type are very attentive to their duties as well as cognizant of their rights. Until a higher principle (fidelity to his spritual truth) led Martin Luther to break with the Catholic Church, he was an exemplary member of his monastic order, just as Sir Thomas More faithfully served his king, Henry VIII, as Chancellor until a higher duty (his allegiance to the Catholic Church) brought about his fall.

Perceptivity about social relations and events also helps

territorials to appraise accurately the viable limits of a given situation so that they do not unknowingly transgress them by violating protocol, behaving in a tactless way, misreading or ignoring social cues. All the above factors contribute to the ceremoniousness of this psychetype. As would be expected, they prefer structured forms in which to express their (very genuine) feelings, and so ceremonial displays (church services, graduations, military parades, inaugurations or coronations, all varieties of rituals) can move them deeply. Outside the form that makes the feeling appropriate, such displays might embarrass them.

As with all other parts of life, *spatial* structure matters a great deal to territorials; they need to have, literally, their own territory. That territory, as Jefferson said of Monticello, is a true expression of one's self. Jefferson was surveyor, designer, draftsman, and engineer of his beloved Virginia estate. Not many territorials have the opportunity to so completely create their dwelling place, but most would like to. They are very sensitive to spatial needs and quite creative about the use of space— architecture and engineering are often among their career choices. On a private level, they enjoy working on their houses. Show a territorial a room and a bunch of furniture, and he or she will immediately begin to arrange it (or rearrange it) at least in their heads. In fact, sometimes they cannot resist suggesting to others that they "move that chair to the right side of the fireplace" or "don't you think you ought to put the study here instead of there." Thinking territorials, in particular, are willing to spend hours mentally creating and furnishing spatial structures.

Moreover, that special place with which the territorial has identified exerts a strong pull on his psyche, and if away from it, he may experience periodic seizures of homesickness. This yearning to return to old, special places may be intermittent, but it is quite intense. Driving back home after years' absence, such people will become increasingly excited and nostalgic as the *physical* landscape grows more and more familiar. Mark Twain lived in Connecticut, but his books took him back, time after time, to the Hannibal, Missouri, of his boyhood.

Because territory matters so much, territorials are very

sensitive to its being invaded. "Good fences make good neighbors." "Territoriality" is, in fact, the term used to define the protective instincts animals have about their "space." Human territorials feel a similar sort of protectiveness toward theirs. Most, for example, do not at all appreciate having people enter their homes without first knocking and waiting to be *invited* in. It might simply not occur to an oceanic to wait for that official welcome, but if not, he probably would not mind if others strolled into his home unasked. However, a territorial would never do that until he was assured that such informality was the custom there, for they never cross "No Trespassing" signs, including symbolic ones like closed doors. They try not to crowd people, physically or emotionally, and they dislike being crowded, physically or emotionally.

Territory does not simply mean one's home; it can be a captain's feeling about his ship, a citizen's about his town or his nation; it can be a profession or an area of intellectual expertise. "Territory" also includes the people who "belong" to it: family, neighbors, colleagues, countrymen. A territorial will defend and protect people even if he does not personally know them, or does not like them, when they are members of what he calls his "space." Elizabeth I felt territorially protective of every British subject in her kingdom. People with this area primary in their psychetype are thus likely to find themselves taking care of others. Chekhov, who was caretaker to quite a gathering of impoverished relatives, called them his "benignant tumor," but he never threw them out. Jefferson took in his sister and her family for six years when her husband's insolvency made it impossible for him to provide for them. It is constitutionally very difficult for a territorial not to respond to the needs of someone for whom he feels responsible, and that includes those he has allowed into his "space," from offering a guest "something to eat or drink," to giving a poor cousin a loan, to protecting a member of "his team" from whatever threatens them or defending his country against invaders.

All the traits we have been discussing go to make up a personality that is competitive and assertive, that likes to control things. Territorials want power. Most are willing to admit it. "I had rather," said Julius Caesar, "be the first man in a village, than second in Rome." But unlike many aethereals, territorials are willing to work within the system, to manipulate existing structures, in order to acquire power—however ruthlessly autocratic some (like Cromwell or Stalin) may be in wielding it, once obtained. Thus, Bismarck refused to accept the Prime Ministry of Prussia under Kaiser Wilhelm I unless he were given clear rights to direct foreign policy. Once he had that legal power, he was so dictatorial that Wilhelm quipped, "It is not easy to be the Emperor under such a Chancellor." However, since their typological deference and desire for respectability make them reluctant to override completely the structures in which they live, their political careers tend to be less meteoric than those, say, of intuitive aethereals. But if their rise is slower, their staying power is greater. Meteors fall as fast as they climb, while leaders like Charles De Gaulle have seemed durable as granite.

The struggle for power is not onerous to territorials; as a matter of fact, they are often at their best when opposed; opposition spurs them on by challenging their competitive instincts, whether the arena be a love affair, a college exam, a political campaign, a technical problem, a deadline to meet. In a way, they almost prefer to perceive the world as a dangerous opponent to be overcome. Science, wrote TR James Watt, inventor of the steam engine, must "find out the weak side of Nature and vanquish her." The implicit attitude here is a distinctly territorial one, the need to face dangers and overcome them. It led Stanley into the African wilderness to find Livingstone; it took Lindbergh across the Atlantic Ocean alone; it drove Caesar to be the first Roman over the Rhine and into pagan Britain; it sent Florence Nightingale to the disease-infested military hospitals of Turkey.

George Bernard Shaw wrote five novels, none of which he could sell to publishers. Far from ending his literary career, these rejections aroused his will to succeed: "Fifty or sixty refusals forced me into a fierce self-sufficiency." Territorials do not resign easily. "If they will have my office," retorted Benjamin Franklin, "they shall take it from me!" These are people with very strong wills. "Will. Work. Wait" was, in fact, Louis Pasteur's credo. "To will is a great thing for Action and Work follow

Will." That is why those who expected to find a manipulable ruler in Elizabeth I because she was a woman were quickly disappointed. "She seems to me," the Spanish ambassador wrote in alarm, "incomparably more feared than her sister, and gives her orders, and has her way as absolutely as her father did." (Her father, Henry VIII, was, incidentally, also territorial —an SR.) So she promptly let her subjects know that while she did not intend to act in a manner unsuitable to her station, still "if she ever had the will or had found pleasure in such a dishonorable life, she did not know of anyone who could forbid her." And she assured her Parliament that she was quite capable of taking care of herself and them, too.

> *And though I be a woman, yet I have as good a courage, answerable to my place, as ever my father had. I am your anointed Queen. I will never be by violence constrained to do anything. I thank God I am endued with such qualities that if I were turned out of the realm in my petticoat I were able to live in any place in Christendom.*

Elizabeth rather enjoyed her battles with Parliament, for territorials like having worthy adversaries with whom to match wits. Arguments and power plays give them an opportunity to exercise that sort of social gamesmanship that makes relations with others, including sexual ones, more interesting and exhilarating to them. Elizabeth used her mastery of sexual gamesmanship to play one royal suitor off against another for forty years without permanently alienating any of them, thereby raising flirtation into a diplomatic skill. Not many territorials are in positions to use their sexuality to implement foreign policy, but all are sexually aggressive people who enjoy the intricate moves of the mating dance. They are capable of distinguishing purely sexual energy, in themselves and in others, and of responding on that level alone. Even if personally uninterested, territorials will automatically pick up and sort out the sexual vibrations in a roomful of people. They can do so because sex is important to them. The need to acknowledge its vital significance to human psychology is therefore fittingly stressed in the theories of a territorial, Sigmund Freud: "In a normal sex life, no neurosis is possible." This premise was one that Freud's student and colleague, Carl Jung, rejected. Jung was an oceanic.

OCEANIC

The oceanic world is the antithesis of territoriality, as the terms suggest. Territoriality implies boundaries, limits, organized and defined space, whereas our impression of the ocean is one of undifferentiated, uncontained, undefined, boundless expanses. And that, at the core, is how oceanics regard the world, which is one reason why the oceanic attitude has been traditionally more highly valued in the Orient than in the Occident. In the philosophy of Zen Buddhism, in Chinese civilization, in the spiritual messages of Eastern mystics, we are more likely to find analogies of oceanic traits than in our culture, for the latter has, at least since the Roman Empire, placed a premium on territorial qualities like objectivity, control, order, habitual self-discipline, deference to status, goal-directedness, determination, and a strong sense of competitiveness. That is why territorials, and especially extraverted ones, have enjoyed an extremely high success rate in our society; they are predisposed to value what their culture values. Not having to force their personalities to behave in ways that are typologically uncongenial makes it easier for them to achieve positions of power and status.

In the experiential world of the oceanic, the terms "power" and "position of status" have much less meaning, even perhaps negative meaning. But our civilization has placed very little emphasis on oceanic values, for they are not the attitudes that make for conquest, for industrialization and upper mobility, for imperialism. They are not the values by which you get to the moon first or the head of the corporation fastest. As a consequence, there are fewer oceanics in our political history books than individuals with other primary areas, Winston Churchill and Robert E. Lee being two of the pre-eminent exceptions.

When many young people turned against the Establishment in the 1960s, they held up an essentially oceanic vision of the self and society; in effect, they offered a secularized statement of the message of the Gospels of Christ. Love. Peace.

Good will. Brotherhood. In the songs of the "hippie movement," even when the spokesmen are thinking types like John Lennon or Janis Joplin, the lyrics talk in oceanic language. That language is subjective and emotional; its attitude is reverential, receptive, flexible, and passive. "Do your own thing." "Go with the flow." "Let it be."

Let all things merge and unite in one connected process. "Let a hundred flowers bloom, let diverse schools of thought contend." With this announcement, Mao Tse-tung inaugurated his thought-reform campaign under the oceanic assumption— later retracted—that in an open arena conflicting points of view could naturally resolve themselves into harmony.

What matters to oceanics is that their individual personhood be given the freedom to be its "self." Not as distinctive and separate from others; oceanics are relatively uninterested in self-definitions that are, in their view, restrictive: doctor, clerk, Republican, American, middle class, uneducated, Catholic, wife. The self floats outside such formulations; it may contain them, but it is not synonymous with them. "Who are you?" "I'm me." "What do you do?" "I am."

It is not in the nature of oceanics to spend that much time introspectively "assessing" the structure of their personalities or evaluating other people's. They may learn to do so, especially if in the past they have gotten "in over their heads" into situations that they subsequently discover they were ill-equipped to deal with, given their particular characters and abilities, or if they find themselves getting burned because they have failed to make an accurate appraisal of someone else's character or abilities or motivation. This is what happened to Mary Queen of Scots when she came from the refined civilities of France to rule a native kingdom she was temperamentally unsuited to govern successfully. She had not prepared herself to cope with the rather barbaric codes and customs of her Scottish lairds, nor did she grasp the significance of the highland rivalries among them that were eventually to depose her. Oceanics are unsuspicious, trusting people, and, true to type, Mary consistently put her faith in those who would later betray her.

Moreover, unlike territorials, oceanics tend to be nonjudgmental; they are willing, instead, to accept others as they find them. Robert E. Lee, for example, was always reluctant to criticize either the military efforts or the private behavior of his officers and disparaged attacks on them by others. "I know how prone we are to censure," he wrote Jefferson Davis, "and how ready to blame others for the non-fulfillment of our expectations. This is unbecoming in a generous people, and I grieve to see its expression." Oceanics are far more likely to blame themselves for failures; if they consider themselves to be in the wrong, they will readily admit it. In intuitive oceanics like Mary, self-reproach may be a way of ensuring that one's charismatic appeal to others is not diminished. In feeling oceanics like Lee, the impulse often comes out of a sense of guilt that one has caused another's unhappiness or misfortune.

In a letter to Davis, written after his defeat at Gettysburg, in which Lee offered his resignation as commander of the Confederate forces, he said, "I have no complaints to make of anyone but myself. I have received nothing but kindness from those above me, and the most considerate attention from my comrades and companions at arms."

Such willingness to assume blame combined with such charity toward others often makes oceanics vulnerable to the ridicule or reproaches, or even the self-interested manipulations of those less trusting than they. For people of Lee's spatial setting usually lack guile; they tend to be frank and open, with little aptitude for secretiveness; nor are they instinctively self-protective. When someone with these characteristics becomes involved, as Mary Queen of Scots did, in political intrigues and surreptitious plots that require the utmost circumspection and cunning, the results can only be disastrous—as Mary's fate was. At Machiavellian maneuvering, her contemporaries, Elizabeth and Catherine de Medici, both territorials, far surpassed her; just as Lincoln, also a territorial, far surpassed Lee. Historian Fletcher Pratt points out:

> Lee's one defect as a leader was that he really was the kind of plaster saint Lincoln is in danger of being made by admiring schoolboys. There was something unearthly about the man's best moments. He was foreordained to failure by a devotion to duty so inhuman that it would not let him step a hairsbreadth beyond

*the legal bounds of his office, even to save the Confederacy. He
had no humor and none of that talent for intrigue without which
real statesmanship is unattainable. Lincoln, on the other hand,
would have delighted Machiavelli.*

In ordinary situations this inability to protect oneself
reduces some oceanics to a sort of defenseless standing about
while others take advantage of them. The composer Schubert
apparently just accepted whatever sums publishers chose to
give him for his compositions even when the money was clearly
less than their value, and even after he achieved some degree
of fame. He relinquished copyrights, gave away symphonies,
and lent out songs, all without recompense. A friend subsequently collected over a hundred Schubert songs that the composer had forgotten to get back.

But because oceanics so greatly dislike conflict, they may
choose not to press a point or raise a controversial issue rather
than have to pit themselves against another. This is one reason
why General Lee found it almost impossible to fire subordi-
nates; he could not bear to hurt their feelings or, by so doing,
place himself in a conflictual situation. Violent quarrels made
Mary Queen of Scots physically ill. Oceanic discomfort with
controversy reflects a broader habit of mind, one in which process is more intellectually important than progress or goal. The
territorial mind is analytic and synthetic. It differentiates by
taking things apart and putting things together in the right
divisions. But the oceanic mind sees things as Gestalts, undefined, a-temporal and a-spatial. This mode of perception
gives them that mental flexibility, a certain rippling, flowing
quality of mind, whose rhythms we hear in the poetic voices of
Gerard Manley Hopkins or Dylan Thomas.

The same impetus to join mentally what appears to be
separate lies behind the purposefully loose, freely associative
structure of novels like Lawrence Sterne's *Tristram Shandy,* in
which the narrator takes four whole volumes to get his hero
born and named, and five more to reach childhood. This habit
of mind can become problematic if it makes any organizing
principle difficult to sustain. Thomas Wolfe's manuscripts just
went on and on, the words rolling out in, as he put it, a "torren-

tial and ungovernable flood," literally filling packing cases with pages. Told by his editor Maxwell Perkins to cut a book to a reasonable length, Wolfe would make a conscientious effort to do so but often ended up adding twice as much as he deleted. An introductory chapter grew to one hundred thousand words; a heavily edited manuscript was still twice as long as *War and Peace*. Wolfe could not bear to leave out anything that might contribute to "the full flood and fabric of a scene in life itself." Fortunately for him and his readers, Maxwell Perkins was a superb editor who managed to condense and organize Wolfe's "life" into the structure of a novel, once going so far as to send the text off to the printer's while Wolfe was out of town to keep the author from adding even more material to *Of Time and the River*.

Wolfe's reliance on his editor's judgment is indicative of another oceanic tendency that derives from their subjective approach; they often feel unable to evaluate their own ideas objectively. Lee sent daily, sometimes hourly, reports to Jefferson Davis, with whom—as his President—he thought he should check out all his military decisions, preferring not to act until he had received official approval even when such procedure made for dangerous delays in action. Most oceanics want to "check things out" with others: a piece of furniture they are planning to buy, a letter they've written, an opinion they've formed. The intellectual diffidence of many oceanics is related to their before-mentioned discomfort in realms other than the personal. Marilyn Monroe, at the time an eminently successful film star, attended acting classes at Lee Strasberg's studio, where she sat shyly in the back of the class, hesitant to contribute to discussions about performing. Hollywood jokes over her attempts to educate herself had deeply pained her but had also enhanced the intellectual insecurity that made her reluctant to verbalize her ideas on art, or literature, or even on acting. As a friend said, "The trouble with Maryilyn was she didn't trust her own judgment. So she always had someone around to depend on." She was probably the only beginning studio starlet to bring her own acting coach on the set, to help her with what was almost a walk-on role in *The Asphalt Jungle*.

Preferring as they do to relate on a personal level, oceanics need to arouse emotions in themselves and in others. In contrast to territorials, who have almost a horror of intrusive emotionality and will endeavor, if possible, to suppress it, oceanics like to be in emotional states. They seek and respond well to love, to loyalty, to passionate expressions of feelings in general. Winston Churchill raised to oratorical sublimity the ability to arouse people with words. His message to Britain during her war years concerned itself far less with theories and facts than evocative appeals to his countrymen's courage, honor, pride, defiance, and endurance. It is the oceanic way to thus personalize things. Churchill did not offer England his plans and projects, his experience and expertise; he offered his "blood and toil, tears and sweat." Mao did not say to the Chinese peasants, "Down with imperialism!" He said, "Down with the rich foreigners!"

Lack of ease with impersonality affects an oceanic's priorities about life styles. For example, in direct contrast with her predecessor Queen Elizabeth, Queen Victoria was willing to relinquish much of the abstract theorizing and organizational business of government to her counselors and her husband, "Dearest Dearest Albert." "Really," she confessed in her journal, "when one is so happy and blessed in one's home life, as I am, politics (provided my country is safe) must take only a second place."

Oceanics are, in fact, rather uninterested in social structures, like governmental hierarchies. They prefer a world of social openness—unstructured and unstratified. Developed into an ideology, this attitude tends to be one sympathetic to egalitarianism: America's great populist, William Jennings Bryan, was himself a feeling oceanic. And to the young Mao Tse-tung, the form of a government should grow from a grass-roots movement of the people. He saw the world as one-third capitalist, two-thirds proletarian; no nations, races, or castes were distinguished. His achievement would be the Chinese People's Republic. From a less politically sophisticated perspective, Marilyn Monroe, when asked why she seemed to be sympathetic to Communists, responded, "Why not? They're for the people, aren't they?"

Someone of this type is unlikely to define another, as a

territorial might, by his function or his status, for oceanics believe that everyone is entitled to the same rights and consideration. "It is a dreadful thing," the poet-priest Gerard Manley
Hopkins wrote of English laborers, "for the great and most
necessary part of a very rich nation to live a hard life without
dignity, knowledge, comforts, delights, or hopes, in the midst of
plenty—which plenty they make." The reflection is not original. Politicians make it all the time; the point is that oceanics
feel on a personal level that such inequality violates the personal freedom that is of paramount value in their experiential
world. Once in his early twenties, Mao wrote nine articles in the
thirteen days following the suicide of a young girl forced by her
parents to marry against her will. He passionately denounced
such restrictions on women's rights and called for "the great
wave of the freedom to love" to sweep the old hierarchies away.

For themselves, oceanics are apt to pay more attention to
someone's personal qualities than his or her station. Consequently, they are more likely than other types to disregard
status distinctions. To Lee, his staff officers and his troops were
his "brothers" and "companions in arms," nor did he see any
reason why his son, Robert, should not serve in the ordinary
ranks like any other young man. To Mary Queen of Scots, there
was nothing wrong with choosing counselors from among foreigners or the middle class, but to the Scottish lairds these
intruders into the social hierarchy were ignoble "vile, crafty
strangers." Worse, she did not think it unbecoming her station
to make her musician, David Riccio, her secretary and her
friend. She was imprudent enough to permit him to attend her
and her ladies in her private room, where a conspiracy of the
lairds trapped him and stabbed him sixty times with daggers
before her eyes. Rumor had it that she and the commoner
Rizzio must be lovers; why else would she be so personal with
him?

Oceanics often puzzle or even outrage others with their
apparent unconsciousness of "proper roles." Even his affectionate and patient brother Theo was horrified by van Gogh's announcement that he planned to marry a public prostitute because she had been good to him, was wretched and alone, and
needed someone to help her care for her child. Moreover, he

intended to live with her in The Hague where the van Gogh family were respectable citizens. All London was horrified when the middle-aged Queen Victoria became close friends with her coachman-groom John Brown, whom she allowed to scold her with the rather unregal appellation "Woman!" Ignoring the consternation of her family and court, the Queen brought Mr. Brown to all official functions and governmental meetings, while town gossip began referringto her as "Mrs. John Brown." She named him in her will, right beside kings and princesses, and she was only just dissuaded from publishing a loving memoir of their friendship.

This kind of disregard for propriety and custom results in oceanics' frequent failure to present themselves in the most socially advantageous manner; they may be careless about protocol, about their appearance, or, as we have seen, about their "proper role." Moreover, they simply don't like to handle situations involving complex structures, like very formal gatherings in which complicated nuances of protocol are involved. They don't see any sense in such rigid ritualization of life. For young oceanics, inflexible school structures may present a problem. Churchill, later to distinguish himself in many intellectual arenas, was one of the worst students (in his studies and his conduct) ever barely to scrape his way through a succession of British schools.

Spatial, as well as personal, freedom is vital to an oceanic's well-being. They need plenty of free space. Territorial boundaries strike them as oppressive, and they tend to ignore them. However, if they are insensitive about invading other people's territory, they are equally untroubled by intrusions on their own; in fact, they don't see the presence of others as necessarily intrusive at all. What a territorial might consider "crowded," an oceanic could consider "closeness." It was a territorial—Benjamin Franklin—who wrote, "Fish and guests stink in three days." On this typological discrepancy the friendship of van Gogh and Gauguin collapsed, for van Gogh, eager to share his home in Arles with someone, to make it a community of brotherly painters, invited the territorial Gauguin to live with him, happily fixed him up a room, cooked for him, gave him money —and infuriated Gauguin by persistently invading his "space" and his psychological privacy with solicitude and emotional demands.

The receptivity of oceanics—that "going with the flow" suggestibility—leads them, or rather does not *lead* them, allows them to drift rather aimlessly if not anchored by a purposeful vision or stable relationship. After only six months in the Hunan Revolutionary Army, Mao left it to register first at a police, next at a soap-making school. Then he was persuaded by one advertisement to become a lawyer, by another to go into commerce. A month's worth of commercial classes (most of which were in English, which he did not understand), and he transferred to the First Provincial Middle School in Changsha to study history; he quit there after six months and decided he might do best studying on his own at the library. The early years of Adolf Hitler reveal a similar sort of vocational drifting.

The same qualities sometimes make it difficult for oceanics to maintain a position firmly; they may appear "wishy-washy" like the cartoon oceanic Charlie Brown. In political spheres such indecisiveness can have dire consequences. It helped to cost Mary of Scotland, Charles I of England, Louis XVI, and Marie Antoinette of France their thrones—and their heads. Napoleon analyzed the many moments during the French Revolution when Louis, had he been sufficiently firm, could have controlled the situation; instead, he one day paraded in the revolutionists' bonnet; the next, opened fire on citizens.

On the positive side, many oceanics benefit from a mental flexibility that works with change rather than being swept away by it. Accused by critics of constantly switching his political allegiance in an inconsistent manner, Churchill replied, "To improve is to change. To be perfect is to have changed often." He defined a fanatic as "one who can't change his mind, and won't change the subject."

An oceanic, drifting through experiences he finds difficult to communicate, may feel almost as if he is not a part at all of this bustling, busy world. Life seems to be dreamily floating along. In the oceanic romantics, Samuel Taylor Coleridge and Thomas De Quincey, that dreamlike mist was enhanced by their use of opium, but even a stone-sober oceanic may strike others as somewhat whimsical, perhaps naive and innocent.

Another reason why oceanics may appear so innocent is that they tend to be less interested in sexuality than people of other types. The classic films of IO director D. W. Griffith, films like *Birth of a Nation* and *Orphans of the Storm,* take us into a world in which the female (usually Lillian Gish) is a vision of pure childlike, quivering vulnerability, always sexually threatened but never sexual. "The animal side of our nature is to me —too dreadful," confessed Queen Victoria, who gave her name to what are now considered repressed and restrictive sexual attitudes. This does not mean, of course, that oceanics don't like to make love but simply that "sexuality" in the abstract, so to speak, does not particularly intrigue them. In this way, her typology helps us to define the very particular sexual appeal of the intuitive oceanic Marilyn Monroe. While Hollywood packaged and publicized her as an erotic object, her psychetype gave to her sexuality a detached, innocent ambiance, a pure, almost unearthly quality, as though she were floating somewhere above her body, naively unaware of its provocative effect on others. She could say the most risqué line and convince you that she was absolutely unconscious of any implicit double-entendre. She could talk baby talk, as Jean Harlow did; but with Harlow, a sensation volcanic, you knew the technique was a put on. With Monroe you could never be sure. Her mouth slightly agape, her eyes widely open, she seemed to drift through her movies like a helpless child.

As they often feel defenseless, oceanics very much want to be protected and safe. One other person can fulfill this need: Prince Albert for Victoria, Georges Sand for Chopin, Robert Browning for Elizabeth Barrett Browning. The pliant Mary Queen of Scots was guided first by her strong-willed mother, then by her French uncles, then by a succession of men, including three husbands. Elizabeth Taylor has demonstrated the same oceanic tendency to require a strong, stable relationship to lean on—five, so far. Marilyn Monroe required the whole world: "I wanted to become famous so that everyone would like me and I'd be surrounded by love and affection." Moreover, oceanics are apt to be swayed by those with whom they are in relationship, even to adopting their values and life styles—Elizabeth Taylor converted to the Judaism of one husband, the Welsh poetry and Shakespearean drama of another.

Another way of looking at receptivity is to see it as passivity. The passive nature of many oceanics can be used as a method of controlling others, of dealing with problems by not dealing with them, thereby forcing others to do something, as Marilyn Monroe's "inability" to be anywhere on time, learn her lines, pay her parking tickets, or manage her life pushed her colleagues, friends, and husbands into a position of taking care of her. If territorials have the potential to try to dominate other people, oceanics have the potential to try to engulf them. They themselves may be engulfed by their problems, for just as they cope with emotional pain by absorbing it, allowing it to flow through them, so they allow a difficulty in one area of their lives to flow over until it affects all others. One thing goes wrong, and because it is hard for them to isolate and actively deal with it, their whole life can be, so to speak, contaminated. We can see this trait dramatized in the character of Shakespeare's Hamlet, an intuitive oceanic. Because of his mother's hasty remarriage, the entire world seems to him "weary, stale, flat, and unprofitable," "an unweeded garden." All oceanics can be swamped by this kind of pervasive negativity; moreover, in feeling types, because of their continuity, the spill-over can flow on and on, whereas discontinuous intuitives are more readily distracted.

When, on the other hand, an oceanic is not in the midst of a "funk," it is his or her nature to look for, and to find, the good in other people. They are, for the most part, extremely kind, goodhearted individuals, often willing to do for others things they cannot bring themselves to do for their own benefit. As we saw in Lee's resignation letter, they can have true generosity of spirit and will give praise and gratitude as quickly as the contents of their pocketbooks. The helplessness of others (of the poor, of children, of animals) touches them deeply. It is these aspects of the oceanic personality to which Arthur Miller paid tribute in his characterization of Rosalyn (his wife, Marilyn Monroe) in his film *The Misfits:* a guileless, loving woman, incapable of seeing evil anywhere except in those who would take away the right of all creation, animate and inanimate, to its own integrity.

The spiritual reverence of many oceanics shines through the devout faith of such different people as Queen Mary of Scotland, Robert E. Lee, and William Jennings Bryan. It illuminates the paintings of van Gogh and the poetry of Gerard Manley Hopkins. "Glory be to God for dappled things." Dylan Thomas said, "My poems were written for the love of man and in praise of God and I'd be a damned fool if they weren't." However they define "God," however they express love, most oceanics would agree that they'd be damned fools to place other values higher.

TERRITORIALS

Cleopatra of Egypt, TR	Julius Caesar, SR
Martin Luther, TR	Emperor Vespasian, SR
Sir Thomas More, TR	Charlemagne, SR
Elizabeth I of England, TR	Eleanor of Aquitaine, SR
John Adams, TR	Henry VIII of England, SR
Thomas Jefferson, TR	Benjamin Franklin, SR
Edmund Burke, TR	Oliver Cromwell, SR
James Watt, TR	Wolfgang Mozart, SR
Abraham Lincoln, TR	Louis Pasteur, SR
Florence Nightingale, TR	Thomas Edison, SR
Anton Chekhov, TR	Sir Henry Stanley, SR
Susan B. Anthony, TR	Mark Twain, SR
George Bernard Shaw, TR	Henry Ford, SR
Karl Marx, TR	Otto von Bismarck, SR
Madame Marie Curie, TR	Charles Lindbergh, SR
Eleanor Roosevelt, TR	Joseph Stalin, SR
Charles De Gaulle, TR	William Faulkner, SR
Sigmund Freud, TR	Richard Nixon, SR
Lauren Bacall, TR	Humphrey Bogart, SR

OCEANICS

Louis XVI of France, FO	Mary Queen of Scots, IO
Lawrence Sterne, FO	Charles I of England, IO
Thomas De Quincey, FO	Marie Antoinette of France,
Frédéric Chopin, FO	IO
Franz Schubert, FO	Samuel Taylor Coleridge, IO
Elizabeth Barrett Browning,	Queen Victoria, IO
FO	D. W. Griffith, IO
Vincent van Gogh, FO	Gerard Manley Hopkins, IO
Robert E. Lee, FO	Adolf Hitler, IO
William Jennings Bryan, FO	Dylan Thomas, IO
Thomas Wolfe, FO	Carl Jung, IO
Winston Churchill, FO	Marilyn Monroe, IO

The Thinking Type

"All I want is the truth, Jason."
   BILLIE JEAN KING TO A LINESMAN
   DURING A TENNIS MATCH

If it were possible to choose a word that would summarize what matters most to a thinking type, that word would be the "truth." When Janis Joplin paused in a rock concert to explain the meaning of a song—"You might even call it the truth"—then added, "No, I wouldn't heavy-up on anybody like that," she was speaking out of the same thinking-type reverence for truth that is carved around the rotunda of Thomas Jefferson's memorial: "I have sworn upon the Altar of God eternal hostility against every form of tyranny over the mind of man"—the same values that made Anton Chekhov vow that his plays would be written to tell "the absolute and honest truth," and that led the Roman lawyer Cicero to let a client know why he could not win a case for him: "I have more truth than eloquence." And so the eight-year-old thinking-type girl who tells her friend that his exaggerations are nothing but fibs lives in the same experiential world out of which Aristotle said, "Plato is dear to me, but dearer still is truth."

The thinking psychetype is made up of aethereality, continuity, and territoriality. Being continuous, they consider it important to incorporate the past into the present; being territorial, they structure time in a linear progression—the past relates to the present relates to the future. Act A led to act B, and act B should lead to act C. "Since I did well in the sciences in high school, I am prepared to take advanced courses in college; having mastered those, I should be accepted into a medical school," and so on. Time can, of course, flip open a trap door between acts B and C. Few things distress thinking types more than when such invalidations of past experiences and future expectations occur. Cleopatra (historically a TR, as far as we can judge, though in fiction usually depicted as an SV) assumed from her successful relationship with the Roman general Julius Caesar (an SR) and from his regard for Mark Antony (an SV), that the Roman general Antony could bring to fruition her plan for joining the western and eastern worlds into an Alexandrian empire. She was right about Antony's willingness but wrong about his capacity.

Thinking types have a great respect for the proper timing of things; they prefer not to rush precipitously into events but to await the logical moment to act. Lincoln, for instance, had his Emancipation Proclamation prepared long before he decided the most propitious moment had come to revitalize Northern spirit by issuing it. Similarly, TR John Adams was far more cautiously deliberative about aligning himself with American revolutionaries than his intuitive cousin, Sam Adams. While the radical Adams was out rousing colonists to rebellion, the future president was in court defending—on legal principle—those British soldiers who had fired on and killed protesters in the "Boston Massacre."

Although thinking types are inclined to believe that things will get better with the passage of time and are generally patient enough to wait for events to unfold in what Shaw called "the creative evolution" of time, those events do have to proceed at the proper pace. Both TAs and TRs are constantly evaluating the progress of their lives. Since they are careful to ensure that they are moving in the right direction (and, unlike sensation types and intuitives, do not change directions that easily), it distresses them to feel that their pace has been slowed down or, even worse, come to a halt. Suppose a thinking-type woman makes a break with her continuity and accepts a job in a new town. Should that job not prove to be the next best step forward in her "life plan" but instead a step sideways, she will probably be more frustrated by the "lost time" than persons of other psychetypes. For like Virginia Woolf, she will have "an internal, automatic scale of values which decides what I had better do with my time." That will hold true for daily schedules as well as life schedules. The thinking type always hears a clock ticking inside the head. Kept day to day in an erratic, purposeless structure, such a person becomes increasingly anxious. "I'm not getting anywhere!" "Everything's in chaos around here. Where's the time gone?"

In people of this type, concern with time broadens out to a general interest. Most share a deep love of history; in fact, many of our eminent historians have been thinking types. Moreover, nearly all thinking types like reading about past events and enjoy visiting historical sites. In their conversations and writings they are inclined to use a great many historical referents or analogies. Remarks like "The situation in France today is very reminiscent of difficulties Britain encountered when . . ." Or "Euripedes could never have written the play that opened tonight. Thank God." Or "She may think she's Dolly Madison, but . . ." Whatever the arena, thinking types take pleasure in following the overall process of things, for they believe, like Burke, that "people will not look forward to posterity, who never look back to their ancestors." TA Gore Vidal has been doing just that in recent books—*Burr* and *1876* among them. To understand how situations, beliefs, or movements have come into being through the process of time is therefore important. It is one of the traits that leads so many thinking types, including Barbara Walters and Walter Cronkite, into journalism, for the news is simply current history.

Because of their aethereal emphasis on the future, individuals of this psychetype (especially TAs) believe strongly that they have a significant place in history to fulfill. (A TR would, in all likelihood, call it a particular "function.") In John Kennedy's favorite speech, Shakespeare's Henry V promises his soldiers that the day of their battle "will ne'er go by, from this day to the ending of the world, But we in it shall be remembered." To be thus remembered may matter more than one's past reputation or one's present status. It is because their contribution to history matters to them, is actually a responsibility they must meet, that they care so much about being on the right path and about having their achievements properly recognized. It distressed Herman Melville that while his South Seas adventure books had been immensely popular, few people would read *Moby Dick* or other works he considered to be his real literary accomplishments. "Think of it!" he said. "To go down to posterity as the man who lived among the cannibals."

In the thinking type world, the focus is essentially ideational, rather than, say emotional or active. It is far easier for such people to live without much external stimulus than to live without a "chance to think." All TAs and TRs enjoy having ideas, and consider it crucial to do so. Of course, everybody "thinks," but these two psychetypes specifically *crave* ideas, almost for their own sake. "Had any new ideas lately?" "Let me tell you what I've decided about the Republican Party."

Thomas Jefferson was astonished that Alexander Hamilton should consider Julius Caesar the greatest man in history; *his* three heroes were Francis Bacon, Isaac Newton, and John Locke, all of whose contributions were in the realm of ideas, not deeds. Like these three men, thinking types are highly capable of logical thought, with a great proclivity for making theories out of everything. They take pleasure in any work that entails synthesizing the logical components of a task, from putting together a household budget to taking apart a space missile. For TAs—Einstein, Newton, and Nietzsche, to take rather lofty examples—it is generally the theory itself, with its speculative ramifications, that most appeals. For TRs like James Watt, Lenin, or Susan B. Anthony, it is more the practical application of ideas to actual situations in the external world.

These ideas are not usually, of course, so grand as the theory of relativity, the invention of the steam engine, and the emancipation of women. They may be theories about one's children's behavior, or a spouse's career, or why inflation has gotten so bad, or how to improve efficiency at the office. Children of these two psychetypes are always asking, "Why is this so?" "What does that word mean?" "What should I do if?" And they are always telling you, "I know! I know!" "Want to know why it snows? It's because . . ." Adult thinking types are just the same, simply more sophisticated (most of the time) in their questions and answers. As a result of this typological disposition, such people periodically require a random input of information; otherwise, the tendency of continuity to resist change, coupled with the internality of the thought process itself, may run them into a rut in which the same old thoughts are played over and over in a quagmired mind. At that point, some external stimulus, preferably of an emotionally neutral nature, is necessary to crank the mind up and set it back in motion. A newspaper in the morning, a magazine in the bathroom, a new book, a television documentary, an intellectual conversation with a stranger at a party, all are typical channels of input. A bored thinking type may cry, "I've got to have something to read!" the way a famished child calls for food. Some will read anything available: cereal boxes, subway posters, old catalogues, anything with information in it. In the same way, thinking types need time alone to think; that is how they figure out who they are, what they want, how to solve their problems. Those who are sufficiently introverted naturally take the time. When hectic circumstances make this impossible, they are apt to become jangled and tense.

Such internalizing moments are often spent in fantasizing conversations; it is not only a solace for loneliness, but a way of working things out, for solving personal or intellectual problems and deriving theoretical formulations. On occasions when the conflict involves someone else, the thinking type will take both parts in these interior dialogues, running through all the variables of a future real interchange. Unfortunately, once the TA or TR has worked out his script, he may expect the conversation to actually take place precisely as he has planned. So, if it doesn't he is prone to feel thwarted, even cheated.

Both thinking psychetypes try to let the head guide the

heart; in other words, they prefer to let ideas generate feelings, not the reverse. TAs, with their capacity for detachment, are frequently more successful. Herbert Spencer, the British philosopher, noted down in his diary all the pros and cons of married life; deciding that for him the negative aspects outweighed the advantages, he remained a bachelor. General Montgomery, of World War II fame, went through the same process but came to the opposite conclusion. He then promptly set out for a holiday resort where he theorized he would probably meet numerous eligible women. And though his friends were horrified by his unfeeling approach, Montgomery did find someone vacationing in Switzerland, married her, and lived happily with her until her death.

Realizing their tendency to intellualize their emotions, thinking types are very interested in the problem of how and when to *stop* thinking, of when it may be futile or damaging to try to reason out solutions of, for example, romantic ambivalences. Their conflict is perfectly emblemized in the four-thousand-word letter Thomas Jefferson once wrote to Maria Cosway entitled "Dialogue Between My Head and My Heart." In it, he presents her with a "divided empire": His head advises, "Advance with caution" because "the art of life is the art of avoiding pain," while his heart counsels that pleasures like love are worth the price we pay for them.

It was too high a price for Queen Elizabeth; torn between personal love for the Earl of Leicester and public responsibility to her throne, she chose the monarchy, not the man. Passionate imprudence had cost her mother's life, and so should it never hers. It had cost the life of her girlhood infatuation, Thomas Seymour, whose scheme to place the young Elizabeth on Mary's throne had led him, and almost her, too, up the steps of the scaffold. Elizabeth had loved Seymour but could still remark of his fate, "There died that day a man of much wit and very little judgement." To obey her judgment was a principle by which she lived and died, alone.

Principles. Like truth, a core word to this type. Every event, actual and possible, is governed by a strong sense of the appropriate principle involved. Encountering new situations, young TAs and TRs learn how to act by looking for the principles to be derived from them. Once learned, the same principle will be applied to all such situations. And having been embraced, these principles are generally inviolable. Rather than renounce a principle, Sir Thomas More died (and became St. Thomas More). It was an irrevocable principle that led Martin Luther to reply to his judges when they offered him a chance to recant his heresy, "Here I stand. I can do no other." In defense of principle, Martin Luther King, Jr., offered no resistance to the physical attacks of Southern state troopers. And it was for the principle "all men are created equal" that Abraham Lincoln paid his highest tribute to a fellow thinking territorial:

> *All honor to Jefferson—to the man who in the concrete pressure of a struggle for national independence by a single people, had the coolness, forecast, and capacity to introduce into a merely revolutionary document, an abstract truth, and so to embalm it there, that today, and in all coming days, it shall be a rebuke and a stumbling block to the very harbingers of re-appearing tyranny and oppression.*

Today we hear other political TRs, Barbara Jordan, Jimmy Carter, George McGovern, echo the same language out of the same inherent values. Surely, someone may object at this point, principles are not unique to thinking types. "Principles," as we use the term here, are abstract, intellectually derived absolutes, and experientially they are particular to the thinking-type world. For a feeling type, personal loyalty will often take precedence over such general precepts. Sensation types tend to live by situational, group-bonding codes, while intuitives are faithful to individual visions. But to a thinking type, one's principles comprise one's selfhood; to live without them would be to live without a soul. Hence, not even his beloved family's entreaties nor his own desire to live could bring Thomas More to take a vow in which he did not believe. To do so would already be death.

Of course, not all principles are so lofty as More's or Lincoln's or Barbara Jordan's. Maximilien Robespierre's principles about the French Revolution included mass guillotinings of the entire nobility during the period known as "The Reign of Terror." A thinking type may have a principle about the need to discipline children physically, or keep women in their place. Principles cover the private sector as well: Always answer letters within a month. Never have an affair with a married man. Never loan money to a friend.

It annoys thinking types when others fail to understand why they must act in certain ways. "Don't you see, it's the principle of the thing" is a common expostulation of theirs. When Mrs. Patrick Campbell wrote a distraught letter to George Bernard Shaw (who loved her devotedly), telling him that her son had been killed in battle, the pacifist Shaw wrote back: "I can't be sympathetic. These things simply make me furious. I want to swear. I *do* swear. Killed, just because people are blasted fools." It was the principle of the thing.

Even more distressing to these psychetypes is when two principles come into conflict. Jefferson, for instance, was never able to resolve the contradiction between his belief in equality and his ownership of slaves. One method thinking types commonly use to deal with this problem is to defer their decisions in the hope that an overriding principle will resolve any apparent contradictions. We may call this a "megaprinciple." Let's say a young TA or TR woman has a principle that she should never lie to her parents; say she also has a political commitment to civil disobedience, which she knows her parents cannot approve of. Her megaprinciple might be: "I will not tell my parents now that I plan to participate in a demonstration. It will only hurt them, and it is wrong to cause people pain. They do want me to be true to myself, and if they only understood, they would agree that I am right to follow my conscience. Someday they *will* understand. At that time I will tell them what I have done."

A willingness to compromise in order to evolve a principle acceptable to themselves and others as well is a quality perhaps more often found in TRs than in TAs—who can be, as we saw with Woodrow Wilson, rather absolutist. In the writing of our constitution, the capacity of TRs like John Adams and James Madison to work out effective compromises was of crucial importance. But to aethereals Alexander Hamilton and Aaron Burr the results were "a frail and worthless fabric," "a miserable paper machine."

A third basic commitment of thinking types is to justice.

Like their belief in truth and in principles, their love of justice is, in a sense, impersonal. In other words, they can usually divorce their theory of ethics from personal emotions. The TR or TA who says to his friend, "I saw you cheating on that exam. If you do not turn yourself in, I feel obliged to do so" is not, by his own lights, behaving in a vindictive or heartless manner. He is simply saying, "Justice transcends even friendship." To be dispassionate is often to be tolerant as well and their very impersonality allows many thinking types not only a compassion for humankind as a whole but a great capacity to let other people be. Having no desire, as she said, "to open windows into men's souls," Queen Elizabeth strove to put an end to the religious persecutions that had martyred so many devout Christians in her brother's and her sister's reigns. Her tolerance was considered by many more passionate dogmatists to be a "minglemangle" and mediocre moderation, but her compromise between Catholic and Protestant doctrines survives today as the Anglican/Episcopalian Church.

Loving justice in the abstract, thinking types are often willing to take up crusades in which they have no individual stake. "I disapprove of what you say," wrote Voltaire (a TA), "but I will defend to the death your right to say it." Jefferson agreed: "It is a singular anxiety some people have that we should all think alike." To vindicate the Jewish officer, Dreyfus, from false charges pressed by an anti-Semitic court, Emile Zola devoted years of his time and talent, beginning with his stirring article which opens each paragraph with the sentence "J'accuse!"—I accuse. Thinking types often do. That is what Ralph Nader keeps saying to industry, what Luther said to the Church, what Marx said to capitalism. Such people are inclined to be judgmental, and nothing outrages them more than when, in their view, others are not following the rules of justice.

One of the dangers people of these two psychetypes face is their propensity to get so swept up in their righteous indignation that they begin to enjoy it for its own sake, while the precipitating cause gets left behind, even forgotten. Someone steps in front of them in a line, cancels a plane reservation without letting them know, tells a lie, doesn't live up to responsibilities, whatever the case may be, and they (especially TAs) are off on what we might call an "indignation trip."

Love of justice is tied, of course, to love of the law. The judicial process and its laws can be to thinking types absolutely sacrosanct. That the law of the Constitution could be so violated by public officials was what astonished and infuriated Chairman Sam Erwin (TR) during the Watergate hearings. At times, such people are inclined to take their belief in law to hairsplitting extremes; they can be, as a result, reductively legalistic. Sometimes stupidly so; sometimes brilliantly. Thomas More based his whole self-defense on the fact that while he had never said he approved of King Henry's claim to be head of the Church, nor his marriage to Anne Boleyn, he had never said he disapproved of them, either. Though everyone in England knew that he did most heartily disapprove, that fact was not a point of law. Legally, silence implies consent; then let the jury so rule. Finally, Henry had to offer Sir Richard Rich, one of the magistrates, the governorship of Wales to perjure himself. On the basis of that perjury, More was convicted. Turning to his accuser, he said, "I am more sorry for your perjury than for my peril. And for Wales, Richard!?" Only after his conviction did More openly state his complete opposition to Henry's assumption of religious supremacy. When his sentence (to be hanged, ripped open, burned, and quartered) was by the "merciful pardon" of his sovereign commuted to just being beheaded, More quipped, "God forbid that the King should show such mercy to any of my friends, and God preserve my posterity from such pardons."

In this sort of ironic response to imminent death we glimpse one of the typical ways in which thinking types protect themselves from their very real emotional vulnerability. Their personalities are made up of the only two areas not keyed into the feeling function. Sensation types share volcanic involvement, and intuitives participate in the personalness of the oceanic world. But thinking derives from the controlled, organized territorial and the detached, abstract aethereal settings. Of course, like everyone else, thinking types do have emotions. Their problem is often that in trying to make sure reason rules them, they can, on the one hand, lose ready access to those emotions; on the other, they may be unprepared to deal with feelings they don't know how to control. Hence, their special susceptibility to emotional arousal. The composer Brahms simply refused to settle arguments with friends because he could not bear what he called the "painful and morbid excitement" of such intense interchanges.

Besides avoidance, thinking types may protect themselves from being hurt by investing their energy in many different areas, by not putting all their emotional eggs in one psychological basket. If A fails, they can then quickly turn to B. Rejected in a romantic situation, they can throw themselves into their work. Their predisposition is, in any case, to create different channels to meet different needs; a way of organizing life in appropriate compartments, and in emotional situations, this capacity allows them (at least at times) to rule out problematic aspects from consideration. When Queen Elizabeth threatened to place her favorite, the Earl of Leicester, under house arrest for joining with the Lords and Commons in their plan to withhold financial subsidies from her until she named a successor, Leicester threw himself down, passionately exclaiming that he would gladly die at her feet. "That," she replied with exasperation, "has nothing to do with the matter."

Because they know they may be unable to control their feelings, thinking types are often unwilling to sustain a direct expression of them. Feeling types like to let emotional states extend as long as possible; thinking types do not. They want the matter settled quickly. Similarly, they sense their awkwardness in dealing with other people's feelings and therefore may choose to ignore the cues, that is, they realize someone is unhappy or angry, but they prefer not to acknowledge the fact so they won't have to cope with it. They will be happy to help the person figure out *why* he or she is upset; what makes them uncomfortable is not the problem but the expression. At other times, thinking types simply make mistakes in interactions because they don't perceive how other people feel about things. Their failure to notice when they have hurt or angered others comes out of their aethereality; their reluctance to deal with direct displays of emotionality derives from territorial control. Two thinking types in a relationship together are capable of going along in established structures for long periods without, so to speak, diving into their feelings and submerging themselves there until they reach bottom. Each is likely to need the other to activate his or her feeling function. However, neither is predisposed to initiate such arousals nor to comfortably permit them to continue any longer than necessary, for they shake the careful order with which (with the utmost objectivity possible) both have organized their lives. Those prolonged stretches of emotionality so natural to FVs and FOs are exhausting to thinking types; they tend to stop learning from them and will instead dig into a rigid and defensive position on whatever the issue is.

Consequently, people of this type are inclined to worry about whether or not they have enough feelings. Perhaps they're *too* dispassionate, cold, or distant. This concern about what Virginia Woolf called her "angularities" is more frequently expressed by TA and TR women than men, as would be expected since, according to cultural stereotypes, females are supposed to be expressive, sensitive, and warm. Time and time again, thinking-type women hear themselves accused of being "masculine," that is, intellectual and aggressive—that is, aethereal and territorial—when they should be emotional and passive—that is, volcanic and oceanic.

All thinking types are disposed to be self-critical, perhaps more so than the other psychetypes. They continually judge themselves, which may be one reason why others tend to find them extremely hard to comfort. For instance, Eleanor Roosevelt's family and friends knew better than to try to comfort her about the presumed infidelities of her husband, FDR. In fact, they knew better than even to acknowledge the matter in her presence. Thinking types do not like to "pour out their hearts" when distressed or discouraged; they best deal with disappointments by turning inward to "regroup," to refine their theories and principles to fit the new circumstances, to figure out an acceptable compromise, or to modify a plan. This process is a private and intellectual one. Those who long to be of some use at these times are apt to get their feelings hurt. The thinking type rejects their attempts, and they feel pained or unappreciated. To avoid making matters worse, TAs and TRs need to learn how to communicate their appreciation of other people's concern, while explaining why they need to work the problem out for themselves. Otherwise, they are liable to be thought "unfeeling," "self-involved," "remote," "walled off," and so on.

Territoriality and continuity combine to make structure crucial to thinking types—and, of course, in particular to TRs. "Plan the work and work the plan." It is essential to such individuals that, first, they make plans, and, second, they follow them. Throughout the Jimmy Carter campaign for the Presidency (a campaign meticulously planned for years), this TR vocabulary dominated staff discussions: purpose, deliberation, organization, structure, plan, plan, plan. Generally, thinking types are able to wait a long time to effect their plans: Florence Nightingale waited sixteen years to begin implementing her ideas about nursing. What they don't like is to be rushed into things without sufficient preparation to "set the stage" in the proper way. Unlike sensation types, for example, thinking types spend a great deal of time deliberating about events before they occur. Lenin worked twenty-five years with concentrated purpose (and, naturally, a highly efficient organization) to bring about Socialist Russia. He went on planning for its future in his will; in it, he warned the Party about two high-ranking (discontinuous) people: He predicted that Stalin (an SR) would prove too rough, impatient, disloyal, and capricious. Trotsky (an IA) he considered "the most able man on the committee" but nevertheless flawed by a "too far-reaching self-confidence." He was certainly right about the first case, and since Stalin had Trotsky exiled, then murdered, we can't know how far the latter's aethereal arrogance might have driven him.

To some thinking types, the plan may be more interesting, even more valuable than the people involved in it, who may get moved about like chess pieces on a board. If it costs a knight to take the queen, one does not hesitate to sacrifice the knight. Florence Nightingale's plan at the Scutari Hospital was to convince the antagonistic doctors there that they needed her and her nurses, and that they ought to allow her to put into effect innovations in hygiene, treatment, spatial arrangements, and so forth, which would greatly improve medical care. Since they would not listen to her, she forbade her nurses to treat individual patients. Men continued to die at an alarming rate in their cramped, filthy quarters. Finally the doctors yielded, and she went to work. Her reorganization greatly decreased the mortality rate among the wounded. Her plan had cost a score of lives and saved thousands. Some people, however, (say an FO) might not have been able to sit back while even *one* person died, even to protect the futures of many others. Some "chess moves" don't work as well as Nightingale's; Franklin D. Roosevelt got nowhere with his plan to add a few pawns to the Supreme Court in order to gain Constitutional legitimacy for programs he believed absolutely necessary for the country's well-being. He lost, but he fought hard, for once thinking types settle on a plan, they stick to it fiercely. At eighty-six, Susan B. Anthony was still fighting for women's rights. "Failure is impossible," she told a suffragette convention then. "The fight must not stop. You must see it does not stop." With equal dedication to the study of science Marie Curie traveled from a Russian-controlled Poland to Paris, where she could attend the university. Living in a miniscule, heatless room, she subsisted on tea, bread, and radishes, and on occasion fainted from hunger during lectures. She graduated first in her class.

Thinking types, then, need to act according to a plan and are as concerned with being on the right path, moving in the right direction, as they are with proceeding at the right pace. Nothing delights them more than when their plans prove effective, whether that plan be to win a Presidential nomination, to organize a surprise birthday party, to arrive on schedule at the end of a day's driving, or to have a physics theory proved by phenomena just as one had predicted—as happened to Einstein when four years after he published it, the general theory of relativity was verified within one-tenth of a second by observed star deflections.

Conversely, nothing distresses thinking types more than when their plans do not go as predicted, nothing annoys them more than when others don't understand their plans, and nothing infuriates them more than when their plans are ruined. Say a thinking-type lawyer plans to take an important client to a particular restaurant; he has made a reservation, he has thought about what to order, he has fantasized the conversation they will have there. The client is an hour late to their meeting place; they arrive at the restaurant where there is a "Closed For Vacation" sign on the door. In all probability the thinking type will still be furious even after they are eating in another, equally acceptable place, muttering (at least to himself) about why the owner of his original choice was so stupid and immoral as to accept his reservation when he knew all along he would be closed, and why his client was so inconsiderate as to be late, because now everything is ruined. To be sure, such inconveniences irritate us all; as always it is the experience, not the response, that determines typology. The thinking type is outraged not because he can't enjoy the food at the first restaurant, but because someone has ruined his plan.

The more serious the plan, the more profound the outrage. A luncheon mishap is one thing, a rejected proposal of marriage or the collapse of a projected career is another. Florence Nightingale's dearest friend, Sir Sidney Herbert, reluctantly told her he could not carry on battling the War Office for her medical reforms as he was quite ill and—literally—working himself to death. Her response was not sympathy but anger: "Beaten! Can't you see that you've simply thrown away the game?" Her life's plan was at stake. Herbert died shortly thereafter; his last words were: "Poor Florence, our joint work unfinished."

Thinking types care for and desire order. They possess structured, well-ordered minds, and they want structured, well-ordered lives. "If," said Bertrand Russell, "the intellectual has any function in society, it is to preserve a cool and unbiased judgement in the face of all solicitation to passion." One's life style should reflect that internal equilibrium. To maintain order in their daily lives, TAs and TRs try to establish consistent habits and regular routines. Work habits, family habits, cleaning and shopping routines. Brahms, who for years ate lunch in the same restaurant day in and day out, prided himself on the fact that in complete darkness he could instantly put his hand on any book in his library. Total order is never possible, but thinking types are very hierarchical; everything in their lives is ranked on a scale of ascending importance. So, they make decisions about what to concentrate on and allow less significant areas to go by. Brahms, for instance, produced immaculate composition sheets but was careless about his personal appearance. (The intuitive Beethoven, indifferent to both, wrote as sloppily as he dressed, splattering ink on his music as well as on his shirt.)

A TR housewife may choose to keep her living room in order but give the den over to the children. The chaos there may appall her (all thinking types are intolerant of any kind of chaos), but in this situation she is following a principle: I have a right to cleanliness. They have a right to play. We each get one room. I don't have to try to sit and think in the midst of Matel mayhem; they don't have to share my horror of a cluttered floor.

Another product of the need for order is the importance people of this type attach to the careful management of money. They are rarely extravagant about or indifferent to financial matters; instead, they tend to watch their expenses, plan budgets, put away savings, avoid debt (or if they do owe money, they are diligent about repaying it), compare prices, look for bargains, restrain themselves about purchases, invest wisely, and—in the old cliché—prepare for a rainy day. Of course, some nevertheless get caught in a shower. Thomas Jefferson did far better for his country (when, in the Louisiana Purchase, he bought from Napoleon a million square miles for two million dollars) than he did for himself, for he died nearly bankrupt. But few thinking types get themselves into the financial scrapes that occasionally befall discontinuous intuitives and sensation types, who, without planning ahead, sometimes borrow money without repaying it and spend money without having it—as did James Joyce and F. Scott Fitzgerald.

Thinking types are too sensible to be careless about money. One of the reasons Queen Elizabeth refused to support those militaristic enthusiasts in her court who wanted England to charge into international conflicts was simply because she thought war a great waste of money. She preferred negotiations, just as Jefferson, despite the clamors of his circling hawks, preferred to buy land from Napoleon rather than fight him for it.

Elizabeth's personal motto was *semper eadem,* always the same. Equilibrium in life, in thought, and in art are cherished values to most thinking types. The desire to construct principles or systems that contain (and resolve) apparent contradictions between other principles or systems, a trait we discussed earlier in a different connection, is one comprehensive way of achieving equilibrium, unity, and simplicity. The impulse is both theoretical and aesthetic. Few thinking-type writers, from Alexander Pope to Henry James and T. S. Eliot, have ever been charged by critics with losing control and giving way to emotional or imaginative excesses. Satisfaction in simplicity, and the proper proportions of things is not a trait limited to artists. It produces thinking-type mathematicians, physicists, architects, engineers, and designers—all the way to collectors of scale models. It produces a general interest among all such people in whatever is structured to fulfill its proper form: a building, a space capsule, a planned city, a sonnet, or a sonata.

Imperfection in such matters exasperates them; it violates order. Many thinking types call themselves "perfectionists." Others at times may see them as "persnickety" or "nit-picking." Some thinking types are compelled to correct misprintings in library books or mispronunciations of words, to straighten crooked pictures in other people's homes, to notify television stations about programming errors, to grade students down for irregular typing margins on their papers, or to ask neighbors to trim their shrubbery properly. Those thinking-type children who care a great deal about being neat and correct may hear their peers calling them "prissy" or whatever the elementary-school slang for "stick-in-the-mud" may be these days.

To TAs and TRs, ambiguity can seem a kind of intellectual chaos, and they are prone to have little tolerance for the ability to remain in open-ended suspension, empathetically responsive to everything, without any "irritable reaching" after facts and certainties. Thinking types want the certainty, and they want it as fast as possible. They both seek and require early closure on things. "What are you driving at?" "Come to the point!" "That's not clear; rephrase it." "Early closure" does not mean dropping the matter. If a TA male and an SV female, for instance, are arguing about who is more considerate of the other's rights, and the SV closes the conversation by saying, "Okay. Let's drop it," the TA is unlikely to do so, at least not happily.

"Closed" is not the same as "closure." "Closure" means settled, because resolved. Moreover, if the SV says, "Sure, have it your way. You are the most considerate," and her partner knows she hasn't understood his point, he will be even more angry. He wants her to see why he says what he does. At best, he wants her to agree that he is right. The best thing you can say to a thinking type is "You're right." One of the worst things you can say is "You're wrong." The point is, then, to *resolve* situations as quickly as possible, not simply to end them. Thus, while thinking types are careful and deliberative, they are also decisive. While no one could procrastinate and shilly-shally over decisions longer than Queen Elizabeth when it suited her, Napoleon himself could not have more rapidly mobilized England against the Spanish Armada than she did. Decisiveness in the midst of conflict is a quality highly valued by thinking types. In *Profiles in Courage* John F. Kennedy chose to honor men who exemplified the ability to make the right decisions in difficult situations. Decisiveness can lapse into brusqueness when, in their eagerness to reach conclusions, thinking types interrupt other people's statements as soon as they see what direction they're taking or finish sentences for them in order to make the point efficiently. A rambling, circumlocutory speaking style frustrates TAs and TRs. In their view, many sensation types avoid the point, intuitives float over and circle all around it, and feeling types swamp it.

From their territoriality come the excellent organizational abilities seen in most thinking types. They are usually good group leaders, and TRs, in particular, make good group members as well—from softball teams to student councils, protest marches, PTAs, and Presidencies. From continuity and aethereal intellectuality comes their capacity to create whole systems that can endure through time. Lenin's Russia was one; the America of Jefferson, Adams, Madison, and Marshall (to name only a few of the thinking types involved) is another. Interestingly, one of the reasons they make such excellent leaders is that they are willing to delegate authority, and they are responsible about choosing those to whom they give it. Jefferson wrote of his Presidency, "No duty the executive had to perform was so trying as to put the right man in the right place." Because they are willing to rely on the skills others can provide them, they are diligent in assembling workable groups; the "Brain Trusts" of FDR and JFK come immediately to mind. Political thinking types coordinate people the way intellectual thinking types (like Sigmund Freud and Margaret Mead) gather and synthesize information.

Coordination suggests cooperation; TRs, especially, know how to work inside the system to alter it. When Florence Nightingale was criticized for cultivating the very medical higher-ups whose callous system she wished to destroy, she retorted, "Do you think I should have succeeded in doing anything if I had kicked and resisted and resented?" She succeeded in revolutionizing our concepts of hospitals and nursing by a number of common thinking territorial traits combined in an uncommon individual: by brilliant organization, by a sensitivity to status, by gathering information, and by the careful dissemination of that knowledge in detailed, factual reports filled, like her mammoth *Notes on Nursing,* with irrefutable data—statistics, charts, cost accounting, and blueprints. Florence Nightingale was not the madonna with the lamp, angelically bending over the dying with a gentle smile that myth has made her. Though it is true that wounded soldiers kissed her shadow as she passed, she probably passed rather quickly on her way to find out what happened to those five hundred blankets she ordered a month ago or to fire off yet another written assault on the War Office. Employees were frightened to request time off for a brief vacation even if they hadn't had one in ten years, and it was said that if she could get God in her employ, she would kill him with overwork. Moreover, Florence Nightingale kept on succeeding even after she herself had become a bedridden invalid because she managed to establish a wide network of communication— another thinking-type inclination. The information went out to influential people; those people then came to her.

For the same reason that they prefer continuing episodes to chance encounters, TAs and TRs are usually not interested in learning isolated facts or skills. They are only willing to be taught facts that can be put to use in theories or plans. It is the whole, not the part; the way to the end, not the side roads, that matters most. It does not satisfy a five-year-old thinking type to be told that "vegetable" means "like a tomato, and things like that." "What other things? And what makes them all vegetables? And what's the difference between tomatoes and fruits?"

People of these psychetypes also like to organize and classify collections not only of ideas and facts but of objects. Among both young and adult members of this type are numerous enthusiastic collectors of stamps and coins, of first editions or antiques, many amateur bird watchers, or botanists, or geologists —each specimen carefully collated and correctly identified. FDR, for instance, assembled one of the major stamp collections in this country. Jefferson collected and classified almost every variety of phenomena imaginable, from books to moose bones. Similarly, thinking types enjoy untangling mix-ups, whether it be an improperly labeled butterfly, a misunderstanding between two friends, a lost driver in search of a street address, a garbled message that needs to be deciphered, an accounting error, or a befuddled governmental bureaucracy.

But if thinking types really enjoy figuring things out for other people, they very much expect those people to acknowledge that they have done so. They need to be what we may call "sapiential authorities," to be those who can give good advice, those who know the answers, those who can, like Jefferson, "scatter information" wherever they go. To know the answer is thrilling to young TAs and TRs. Their eagerness to provide it sometimes earns them approval, which thinking types of all ages seek, for they deeply want people to agree with them. Sometimes it earns them derision: "Mr. Know It All." "Miss Smarty Pants."

Conversely, not to know the answer, or to give the wrong answer, is horribly embarrassing, for both TAs and TRs take themselves quite seriously, particularly with regard to their "brains." Shaw declined the Order of Merit with a note to the sponsors: "It would be superfluous, as I have already bestowed it on myself." Coupled with aethereal arrogance, this sort of self-congratulation about one's achievements is occasionally a cause of chagrin, or amusement, to others. FO Churchill's epigram for his Commanding General Montgomery was: "In defeat, unthinkable; in victory, insufferable." TA Montgomery's need to be a sapiential authority included nightly lectures to his troops—two-hour expositions of his theories on the state of the war with concluding advice about the dangers of venereal disease.

Thinking types love to explain things and provide information. Rather than confess ignorance, they will *try* to answer any question asked of them. If they don't know the answer, they will offer a supposition based on facts or principles they do know. "I'm not certain, but your leg probably feels hot because the blood is rushing to the site of the cut so that the white blood corpuscles can attack the germs there." Now, intuitives are even less at a loss for a reply; in fact, they are completely unstumpable. However, the answers intuitives come up with are often so bizarrely imaginative (or become so as more and more possibilities occur to them) that no one takes them seriously. Thinking types, on the other hand, are known to give *sensible* answers, which can be relied on. Suppose two hikers come across a snake in their path. "Watch out! Oh, God, watch out!" says the intuitive. "No, never mind," he adds, as his friend huddles panicked on the ground. "I know that snake, it's like the snake in *The Jungle Book*. It won't hurt you. It's an Appalachian copper foot, or copper something. If you're wearing rubber shoes, they won't bite you. Maybe we should wear rubber shoes on our hands. What if we had rubber feet, lightning would never strike us." This response is, like intuitives themselves, exaggerated and in any case, most of them would never have noticed the snake first. But the thinking type says, "Stop! I *think* that's a black snake, and they're nonvenomous. Let it pass." Here, neither type knows the answer, but the thinking type inspires confidence, the intuitive, further inspirations.

Consequently, TRs and TAs acquire reputations as people who are able to give good advice because they have "common sense." From her girlhood Eleanor Roosevelt performed this function for friends and relatives. "Ask Eleanor." "See what Eleanor thinks about it." "Did Eleanor agree it was a good plan?" Such is their respect for knowledge and "knowhow" that thinking types themselves are usually perfectly willing to acknowledge the sapiential authority of others, too. If, on that hypothetical hike, a third person had said, "No I used to keep snakes for a hobby. That looks like a black snake, but it isn't. And it *is* poisonous," the thinking type might ask, "Are you sure?" but wouldn't refuse to listen. They will accord experts a deferential hearing—doctors, lawyers, and teachers are treated with respect if they "know their business." His or her respect is the highest tribute a thinking type can give someone else. Even an absolute monarch like Queen Elizabeth listened well to good counsel; her lifelong closeness (in fact, collaboration) with her Secretary of State, Lord Burghley, was founded in his oath of office when Elizabeth had him swear that "without respect of [her] private will," he would always give "that counsel that [he] thought best."

To desire acknowledgment of one's sapiential authority is to desire to have impact on the world. And that is one of the most readily evident personality traits of the thinking type. We have spoken before of their high success rate in world affairs; one reason they have it is because they want it. TA Milton called ambition the last infirmity of a noble mind. TAs and TRs are ambitious people. They want power—not necessarily power to impose their wills on others but power to implement their ideas in whatever arena those ideas operate: politics, art, education, community affairs. Power to have impact. In itself, power is neutral; its uses may be deemed moral or immoral depending on our perspective. To those who approved the uses to which Lenin or FDR put their power, the two men were dynamic, aggressive leaders. To those who disapproved, they were dictatorial tyrants.

Likewise, thinking types are inclined to be very competitive. They hate to lose and are, in fact, rather unwilling to accept failure. As a result, they may occasionally have trouble doing so gracefully. Young thinking types, in particular (since maturation teaches us all to at least appear to accept defeat with poise), can be so upset by losing a card game or a spelling match, or missing the answers on homework assignments that they will challenge the rules, become emotionally defensive, or even collapse into a temper tantrum of frustration. Most adults have learned better. But the competitiveness with which John F. Kennedy or Franklin D. Roosevelt played a family ball game, the way Billie Jean King plays tennis, is the way Florence Nightingale fought, and Susan B. Anthony fought, and Abraham Lincoln fought for what mattered to them. The worse way for thinking types to lose is by making what they themselves consider to be a stupid mistake; that's when Mrs. King throws her racket in the air.

Another arena of competitiveness is argument, and thinking types love to argue—not only to prove a point but as an intellectual exercise, "a twenty brain-bends before supper" sort of thing. Debating societies are one format for this propensity, but there are others. TA William F. Buckley, Jr., has made a television career out of the trait. Watching a thinking-type couple try to verbally knock each other out in the first round, a third party may offer to intercede in order to save their marriage, only to discover that they are having a marvelous time fighting over the rights of the CIA. Verbal gamesmanship, with a sexual undertone, is particularly congenial to territorials and provided one of the staples of battling courtships in 1940s' movies, where TR women (Katharine Hepburn, Rosalind Russell, and Lauren Bacall) went a few witty rounds with SR men (Spencer Tracy, Clark Gable, and Humphrey Bogart) before throwing in the towel marked "Hers." The successful verbalist is one who can "score points." Few things delight a thinking type more than delivering a richly deserved thrust of wit. Cicero, Lincoln, and Jane Austen were, of course, masters at the riposte; so are Buckley and Vidal.

Like Lincoln, most people of this type have a strong reforming drive. While they are also attracted to the grandness and majesty that power bestows, its ultimate purpose is its use as a lever to move the world, or some specific part of it, to another (improved) position. Billie Jean King was not content to win tennis matches; she wanted to win for all women athletes the right to equal respect, and equal earnings, with men—a principle that has led her into fields other than the one at Wimbleton, for example, publishing and television. Ideas are power. Virginia Woolf wrote of her books, "This little pitterpatter of ideas is my wiff of shot in the cause of freedom." Similarly, Ibsen, Shaw, and Lillian Hellman wrote plays not to entertain people but to *teach* them; their works have messages. The message of *A Doll's House* is the cultural infantilization of women; Shaw's *Arms and the Man* laughs at our military romanticism.

The Little Foxes by Lillian Hellman warns us of our materialistic greed.

People who like to compete for power are disposed to be headstrong. People who wish to reform things (whether athletics, hospitals, governments, or religions) have the *potential* for fanaticism. These are both tendencies to which the thinking type is vulnerable. It is probably fair, for example, to speak of Martin Luther and Lawrence of Arabia in such terms. On the personal level, fanaticism translates into obsessive compulsion, usually about one's work (like Zelda Fitzgerald's determination to become a ballerina when in her late twenties) or in defense of principles so rigid as to be indistinguishable from prejudice —a thinking type, let's say, who lies awake all night and plans all day to dispose of the dogs who are digging holes on his territory, when they have no right to be there, and when their owners are clearly derelict in their responsibilities.

Reformers are not ready to stay home and cultivate their gardens, though that is the advice with which one of our great reformers, TA Voltaire, ended *Candide.* "Those who understand evil, pardon it; those who resent it, destroy it." Shaw, who wrote those words, fought with language. Some thinking types have fought more brutally—Savonarola with the torch, Robespierre with the guillotine. Those who are willing to be burned for their principles are unfortunately also usually willing to burn others for theirs. Particularly in cases when they have been disillusioned by the failure of a plan, or the betrayal of a principle, thinking types can be merciless in retaliation—even those who in normal circumstances are exempla of mildness and toleration. And the condemnation is often final. "I forgive," said Eleanor Roosevelt, "but I do not forget."

When feeling types have enemies, they want to hurt them, incapacitate them, as they have been hurt. But thinking types want their enemies totally annihilated. They are more likely to say, "I'd like to see a bomb dropped on him," than, "I'd like to choke him," for the emphasis is not, as it is with volcanics, on the physical or psychological process of punishing someone. They simply want their enemies not to be. They, as a TA put it, want to "blip" them out of existence.

The world of words is where, in a real sense, thinking types live. In all their relationships to life there is in TAs and TRs an intellectual quality that distinguishes them from the active/reactive quality of sensation, the imaginative quality of intuition, or the emotional quality of the feeling-type world. Within the framework of a shared intellectual base, Pierre and Marie Curie, TA and TR, met, courted, married, and loved. His first present to her was a monograph on the symmetry of electric fields. The laboratory in which they isolated polonium and radium was their universe. "It was in this miserable old shed," Madame Curie wrote, "that the best and happiest years of our lives were spent, entirely consecrated to work." Such a meeting of minds may be, if not the greatest pleasure, then one of the most cherished joys thinking types know. For them, mental intercourse can have as great an intensity as the other kind.

Intellectuality is not synonymous with intelligence. Thinking types can be stupid; they will still be intellectuals, but their conversation is likely to be boring and their ideas, clichés. Nor is a theoretical bent limited to the Platos, Curies, or Sartres of this world. What most interested Jefferson was "the essential principles of our government"; what may most interest a thinking-type bookkeeper is the essential principles of accounting. All TAs and TRs bring to bear deductive reason, apply the analytic process to whatever situation may face them, whether it be the art of painting portraits, the selection of a law partner, or the task of buying Christmas presents. Being hierarchical, they also reason comparatively and by a process of elimination. Thus, they are successful in screening out less significant considerations. Those often conclude the petty details and busy work of daily life, which is why so many TRs (and even more TAs) acquire reputations for being absentminded or—and despite the fact that they are always organizing everything—being unorganized. While planning what she's going to say at a city council meeting, a thinking type may forget where she left her key chain or that the coffeepot is now in flames on the stove, the kind of details that sensation types rarely neglect. Walking down the sidewalk with an imaginary conversation or the first page of a job report busily twirling in his head, a thinking type may walk a block past the grocery store he is now returning to because he forgot to pick up oregano when he went the first time. Those who participates in aethereality are inclined to resent being brought down from the level of abstraction on which they feel most at home, especially not to clutter up their brains with key chains or oregano.

Though not necessarily scholars, like Aquinas or Erasmus, most thinking types are scholarly; in other words, they like learning. "Thanks, I learned a lot." "That taught me something." Both sentences are high praise from such people. Nearly all enjoy being students; a great many go on to become teachers, for, as would be expected, their pedagogic abilities are considerable. In fact, the majority of our educators are probably TAs or TRs. Even more are "bookworms" whose vision of paradise might almost be to sit as long as they wished in an inexhaustible library. Marx, in fact, spent his life in one. Jefferson owned enough books to replace the Library of Congress when the British burned it down in 1812; he then bought himself an even larger collection than he had owned originally. And when he wasn't reading himself, he was writing down enormous lists of books he wanted other people to read. Queen Elizabeth, who told an ambassador she was more afraid of making a mistake in her Latin than of all the kings of Europe put together, almost never made such a mistake. She spoke Latin fluently, as well as many other languages, and spent her spare time translating the works of Horace and Plutarch. Generally, people of this type are excellent linguists. Significantly, Cleopatra was the first of the Ptolemies who bothered to learn Egyptian—their native tongue was Greek; she spoke over a dozen other languages as well and could converse with Caesar in Latin or Herod in Hebrew.

Almost all thinking types would agree with John Milton that "books are not absolutely dead things. . . . As good kill a man as kill a good book: who kills a man kills a reasonable creature, God's image; but he who destoys a good book, kills reason itself, kills the image of God, as it were in the eye." Hitler's gang, in their notorious book burnings, included the works of Freud. His response was to comment that he was proud to be burned in such good company.

Naturally, in all this emphasis on intellectualism there are those who slip over into pedantry and pomposity. The real "eggheads." But when a thinking type uses four polysyllabic words where one monosyllable would do, he or she is not necessarily trying to impress us. They just love words, and the complexity of large words fascinates them; the dictionary is one of their favorite books. TAs and TRs are the most highly verbal of all the psychetypes. They believe not only in the power but the responsibility of language, its moral responsibility. Words should always be chosen precisely, spoken grammatically, and pronounced correctly. One should mean the same thing by them in all places and at all times. The ethical imperative of verbal consistency can be a political liability, as Barry Goldwater discovered when he said the same things to very different interest groups during his (unsuccessful) Presidential campaign.

In the thinking-type world things need to be defined, with words. Emotions ought to be explained, with words. Deeds should be evaluated, with words. Everything has a name (the meaning of a movie, the quality of a sunset, the tension between two friends), and the right word that best describes everything should be found. With their great capacity for verbal statesmanship, TAs and TRs can also choose to use words as weapons against others; their ability to out-talk their adversaries means that they can attack not only through *what* they say but with the sheer barrage of language itself. People of other types may feel as if oppressed with the weight of all those words or mowed down by a machinegun firing sentences at them. Often sarcastic ones. It is very hard for a thinking type to resist a witty sarcasm if the occasion arises. Sir Thomas More asked his executioner to give him a hand up the steps of the scaffold. "I pray you, see me safe up; and my coming down, let me shift for myself." Even the quiet Brahms was noted for his satiric humor. He had a good friend who was a bad composer; passing the house once in which Beethoven had been born and commenting on the plaque commemorating that birth, the man expressed the wish that he might also be remembered by posterity. "Don't worry," replied Brahms. "There *will* be a plaque on your house after you die." Pause. "It will say, 'This House for Sale.' " This sort of "dig," even toward those whom they love, is typical of thinking types. And, of course, they love satire and parody, the former because it uses ideas to laugh at ideas, the latter because it uses language to laugh at language. The giants among our satirists and parodists have been thinking types: Voltaire, Swift, Pope, Austen, Lewis Carroll, Flannery O'Connor, are examples.

Reverence for language is one more manifestation of that reverence for truth with which we began our look at the thinking-type world. Censorship is abhorrent in such a world. "Constraint," said Jefferson, "may make a man worse by making him a hypocrite, but it will never make him a truer man. Reason and free inquiry are the only effectual agents against error." That is the most profound of the inalienable rights to them and one which we may in a sense consider the gift of thinking types to the consciousness of civilization: that "Almighty God hath created the mind free." In an essay defending the liberty of the press, John Milton expressed for all time this central touchstone of belief: "Give me liberty to know, to utter and to argue freely according to conscience, above all liberties." "So Truth be in the field," he said for every thinking type, "let her and Falsehood grapple; who ever knew Truth put to the worse, in a free and open encounter."

The TAs and TRs who have made their truths known, who have lived by valued principles and seen them brought successfully into the world, can come to old age with that assured serenity that is given to those who have fulfilled their own, and not the world's demands. Susan B. Anthony and Freud in their eighties. Shaw and Russell in their nineties. De Gaulle, Eleanor Roosevelt, Albert Einstein. Thinking types tend to age well. The dynamic, energizing force that makes these psychetypes attractive to others joins with a broadness of vision; their insightfulness about people joins with the kind of respect that makes others feel both understood and accepted. In youth, thinking types run the danger of being strident, defensive, emotionally brittle, restrictive, pompous, puritanical, or cold. As the rigidity of their principles loosens to incorporate larger principles, they learn to bend and accommodate. In so doing, they grow larger. Not all do, of course. There are narrow, inflexible thinking types who never change, shallow ones, and vicious ones. Not all learn, but most do. In his early twenties, Émile Zola, a TR, said that the world was so stupid and hideous he refused to "contemplate the dung heap" unless he held a flower to his nose. He had become by his death a champion of the poorest inhabitants of that dung heap: "I have one passion only —for light; in the name of humanity which has born so much and which has a right to happiness." He had become, as Anatole France said at his funeral, "a moment's embodiment of humanity's conscience."

There were thirty thousand people at Zola's funeral. There were probably no more than thirty at Annie Sullivan's. She and Zola are the same psychetype, and their accomplishments differ neither in motive, nor method, nor even in magnitude—only in breadth. Zola taught the world. Annie Sullivan taught Helen Keller; Annie was her "Miracle Worker." Just before her death another student begged Miss Sullivan to recover, for without her Helen Keller would be nothing. "Then," she replied, "then I have failed."

THINKING TYPES

Aristotle, TR	Plato, TA
Queen Cleopatra, TR	Cicero, TA
Martin Luther, TR	Augustus Caesar, TA
Erasmus, TR	Thomas Aquinas, TA
Sir Thomas More, TR	John Milton, TA
Elizabeth I, TR	Voltaire, TA
John Adams, TR	Alexander Pope, TA
James Madison, TR	Bishop Berkeley, TA
Thomas Jefferson, TR	Edward Gibbon, TA
Edmund Burke, TR	Henrik Ibsen, TA
James Watt, TR	Friedrich Nietzsche, TA
Sir Joshua Reynolds, TR	Lewis Carroll, TA
Jonathan Swift, TR	Jane Austen, TA
Johannes Brahms, TR	Henry James, TA
Florence Nightingale, TR	A. E. Housman, TA
Abraham Lincoln, TR	Bertrand Russell, TA
Gustave Flaubert, TR	Pierre Curie, TA
Anton Chekhov, TR	Virginia Woolf, TA
George Bernard Shaw, TR	Woodrow Wilson, TA
Susan B. Anthony, TR	Albert Einstein, TA
Karl Marx, TR	Franklin D. Roosevelt, TA
Madame Marie Curie, TR	Igor Stravinsky, TA
Nikolai Lenin, TR	T. S. Eliot, TA
Sigmund Freud, TR	Jean Paul Sartre, TA
Eleanor Roosevelt, TR	Bernard L. Montgomery, TA
Charles De Gaulle, TR	Flannery O'Connor, TA
Lillian Hellman, TR	W. H. Auden, TA
Katharine Hepburn, TR	Zelda Fitzgerald, TA
Lauren Bacall, TR	John F. Kennedy, TA
George McGovern, TR	William F. Buckley, Jr., TA
Margaret Mead, TR	Gore Vidal, TA
Barry Goldwater, TR	Ralph Nader, TA
Billie Jean King, TR	Frank Church, TA
Sissie Farenthold, TR	
Jimmy Carter, TR	
Barbara Jordan, TR	
Sam Erwin, TR	
Barbara Walters, TR	
Walter Cronkite, TR	

7.

The Feeling Type

"I feel a feeling which I feel you all feel." GEORGE RIDDING,
BISHOP OF SOUTHWELL, ENGLAND,
BEGINNING A SERMON IN 1885.

"Cogito, ergo sum." I think, therefore I am. Kant changed Descartes' axiom to "I ought, therefore I am." *Oughts* are moral, not intellectual, directives. And for feeling types the "oughts" come not from the head but from the heart. The heart, as Pascal knew, "has it reasons, that reason knows nothing about."

Jung defined thinking and feeling as the two rational or judgmental forms of psychic activity but pointed out that the two were "neither mutually relatable nor mutually reducible." By thinking, he meant objective conceptual connections; by feeling, subjective valuation. We have found this distinction to be true experientially. In the feeling type vocabulary, "true and false" usually translates as "right and wrong," "like and dislike," "good and evil." For them the intellect must be "wedded to this

136

goodly universe," as Wordsworth (an FV) wrote, "in love and holy passion." An earlier feeling-volcanic writer, Dr. Samuel Johnson, was always infuriated by those skeptical innovators like TAs Voltaire and the philosopher Hume, who divorced truth from what he considered its purpose: to ensure the full security of humankind by promoting mutual faith. Pointing out the logical weaknesses in Christianity, as both these men did, was not conducive to greater human happiness or security; it was therefore wrong to spend one's intelligence in such abstract (i.e., futile) queries.

FOs and FVs are the only two psychetypes without direct access to the thinking function. Intuitives share in aethereality, sensation types in the territorial world. Therefore, feeling types have less ability to detach themselves from emotional situations than intuitives and less ability to compartmentalize and control their emotions than sensation types. (Thinking types, of course, do both.) But the feeling function is composed of oceanic receptivity and volcanic engagement. It is subjective, concrete, unstructured, and involved; in other words, it is feelings. The third variable of their typology is temporal continuity, which they do share with thinking types, and because the perception of time is so pervasive an influence on all our attitudes, one may— simply on the basis of this commonality—confuse a thinking with a feeling type. For example, both are concerned with the incorporation of the past into the present. But for thinking types the past is useful insofar as it progresses toward the present and future or helps to explain them. Feeling types are also past-maintaining for the sake of the past itself. From their oceanic sense of unity and eternal flow comes that love of tradition and veneration of all enduring life typified in the romantic patriotism of a Mao Tse-tung, a Boris Pasternak, or a Winston Churchill. It was the latter's typological gift to make his readers and listeners feel the past, feel themselves a vital part of a living heritage, as century after century of English grandeur and valor rolled expansively outward from the past to merge with present communal hopes.

Feeling types experience on a personal level the emotional impact of past events in their lives. This does not mean merely that they acknowledge the significance of past emotional *crises.*

The feelings aroused by being blindfolded before a firing squad and then reprieved by a last second pardon, as happened to FV Dostoevski, are unlikely to ever leave the psyche of any type. But for FVs and FOs the mood of a walk along a beach at sunset, one's response to a child's smile, a moment of hurt, or anger or tenderness—these, as Wordsworth wrote about the joy a field of golden daffodils brought him, "flash upon that inward eye which is the bliss of solitude." And there they are felt again, just as they were first experienced. Feeling types do not simply remember emotions; they relive them. And they desire to so re-experience the same feelings. Wordsworth's definition of poetry was, in fact, that it is "the spontaneous overflow of powerful feelings: it takes its origin from emotion recollected in tranquility."

That is one reason why people of these two psychetypes love telling stories of the past, and why Shakespeare has his two feeling-type protagonists in *Othello* fall in love as Desdemona hears the warrior Othello tell her father the saga of his romantic past. A modern FV warrior, General Eisenhower, who entitled his autobiography *At Ease: Stories I Tell My Friends,* wrote that when something struck him as particularly interesting or amusing, his thought was "I simply must have a grandchild, or I'll never have the fun of telling this."

Thinking types, as we have learned, want closure on emotional situations but want it quickly. Feeling types reopen, re-explore, and react to events that other people have forgotten or finalized, or wish to do so if the feeling types would allow them to. For example, an FV says to his wife: "Remember how we felt that night when we came home from Arthur's party and sat together in front of the fire." The event he is referring to may have occurred three years ago, yet he goes on to ask, "What did you mean when you said . . ." Or, "What hurt me the most that night was . . ." Or, "Wasn't it wonderful? When since then have we felt that close? What's happened to us?"

It is fair to say that none of the other psychetypes has so intense or so accurate a memory of the past as FVs and FOs. It lies not so much in the ability to remember who won the World Series in 1924 or the equations in the Second Law of Thermodynamics; their "remembrance of things past" is human and per-

sonal. For intuitives, pastness rushes away like a landscape from
the window of a jet plane. Looking back is morbid to sensation
types; pastness intrudes on the full present moment like an
uninvited house guest. For thinking types the past has its own
file cabinet; full, yes, and carefully organized so that a memory
can be pulled and read over when needed. However, the cabi-
nets of time are separate, and when not in use, the drawers are
neatly shut. But feeling types carry their pasts with them, like
treasures in their pockets when the memories are happy ones,
like scars in the flesh when they are not.

Feeling types have a special sense of those things that will
remain important memories and may remark on that fact at the
time: "I'll remember and cherish this day always." Such was
Elizabeth Barrett Browning's response to her first meeting with
the poet Robert Browning, who came to pay his tribute to an
invalid fellow poet, and came again, and again, and fell in love
with her. Out of her felt remembrance of that first meeting and
what followed came her *Sonnets from the Portugese,* a poetic
recollection of their courtship which she gave to Browning after
their marriage and which he published after her death. Churchill was able to transmit his own sense of the vital importance
that Britain's fight against the forces of Nazism would have in
the memory of civilization to an entire nation, thereby inspiring
them to individual and private acts of self-sacrifice and heroism:
"Let us therefore brace ourselves to our duty and so bear ourselves that if the British Commonwealth and Empire last for a
thousand years, men will still say, 'This was their finest hour.'"

Among their most significant memories are those of their
childhoods, to which feeling types attach tremendous significance. Just as their involvement in the past often leads many
FO and FV writers to set their works back two or three generations to times less urban, sophisticated, or industrialized, so
their involvement in their own early years frequently makes
itself the focus of their creativity. James Fenimore Cooper's
Leatherstocking Tales, like *The Pathfinder* and *The Last of the
Mohicans,* or Washington Irving's *Knickerbocker* stories, or the
Wessex novels of Thomas Hardy *(The Return of the Native,* for
example, or *Far From the Madding Crowd)* all take place in
periods just preceding the writer's own. In the same way, child-

hood experiences form the substance of major feeling-type works like Wordsworth's epic on his boyhood, *The Prelude,* as they do Eugene O'Neill's family tragedies, George Eliot's *Mill on the Floss,* and Thomas Wolfe's *Look Homeward, Angel.* Of course, the majority of feeling types don't write novels exploring their childhoods, but all believe those years to be of crucial importance to their identities. Past actions explain present ones; what has happened once will happen again, and human consciousness grows like the seasons, returning upon itself in recurrent cycles. So few feeling types would say, as Napoleon did, that they were "born" only when, as adults, they achieved their aspirations, nor could they readily agree with Lindbergh's wish that people would stop talking about his transatlantic flight because "the boy" who flew that plane no longer existed. To intuitives and sensation types, "pastness" is virtually insignificant. Moreover, neither they nor thinking types have to the same degree the feeling type's ability to sustain emotions when the object of those emotions is no longer immediately present. It's not that everyone else is fickle or capricious in an "out of sight, out of mind" sort of way, but, that intensely and continually felt presence of any emotional relationship (whether the recipient be in the next room, across the country, or in the grave) is nevertheless a quality particular to feeling types; like Emily Dickinson, they consider love anterior to life, posterior to death: "Unable are the Loved to die, / For Love is Immortality. / Nay, it is Diety."

Because they cherish the past so deeply, feeling types may be slow to change, reluctant to accept the unfamiliar. They are therefore at something of a disadvantage when dealing with new situations. Having no instinctive territorial structure or aethereal theory that they can automatically apply to an original interaction, they must approach each encounter personally —one to one. Of course, all individuals can and do learn what roles are appropriate to what functions: "Wives of junior executives behave in this or that way when meeting wives of senior executives at company banquets." But feeling types don't *like* to compartmentalize themselves or others in that manner. Such social shorthand seems false to them. However, "getting to know" human beings takes time; it's hard to become emotionally intimate between shrimp cocktails and chocolate mousse.

So, generally, feeling types place a high value on those relationships that already have a history, those in which such intimacy has already been established. Like Mao and Eisenhower, both FOs and FVs prefer to be around old friends. Old faces and old places; for moving, too, can be especially difficult for feeling types. Emily Dickinson (who was, of course, highly introverted) went to the extreme of never leaving her Amherst house, but even the adventuresome Thomas Wolfe found a trip to Paris made him so horribly homesick that staying there caused "the most intolerable effort of memory and desire." Once they have established a home or a friendship, they are inclined to cling to it. Having gone through the agony of initiating a literary correspondence with a critic, Dickinson kept it alive for twenty years, though she had known from his first letter to her that Thomas Higginson was too limited and dull even to *understand* her poetry, much less appreciate it, and though she certainly never listened to any of his inane, as well as patronizing, advice on how she could "improve" her verses in order to make them publishable. Higginson never considered her a great poet, which she was; but he knew her to be the most loyal of friends, which (like most feeling types) she also was.

"Clinging" can develop into either passive dependency or stubborn tenacity: Oceanics are more vulnerable to the former tendency, volcanics to the latter. Similarly, depending on the attitude of the one clung to, it may be seen as an unfailing loyalty or as an unshakable albatross. And feeling types are very hard to shake. In *Wuthering Heights,* we watch Heathcliff (perhaps the most volcanic of all feeling volcanics in literature) relentlessly follow his beloved Catherine Earnshaw into the grave, first to dig her up for a final embrace, then to join her in death. Real FVs can be almost as persistent, particularly when they are in love, which in some cases is all the time.

The tenacity to stick to things can also be a tremendous asset not only in personal situations but in public ones as well. "We shall never surrender," Churchill told England, and England never did. Mao Tse-tung governed China until his death. Forty years ago, the journalist Agnes Smedley wrote of him, "I had the impression that he would wait and watch for years, but eventually have his way." She was right.

Conceptualization has primacy in the thinking-type world,

as we have seen. Obviously, what is primary to feeling types is their feelings. FOs and FVs are the most deeply and strongly emotional of the psychetypes, able to take great pleasure in simple emotional responses, the kind of pleasure a TA or TR takes in learning a new idea. And what holds true in private life holds true elsewhere. James Dean (an FV) was more emotional an actor than Clark Gable (an SR). The music of Tchaikovsky (an FO) is more emotional than the music of Brahms (a TR), and the paintings of Vincent van Gogh, also a feeling oceanic, are emotional in a way that perhaps *no* other artist has matched. He used color, he said, to express himself "more forcibly." He certainly succeeded; his very skies and stars and trees and fields are alive with overwhelming emotionality. In like manner, feeling-type writers are usually not interested in playing intricate games with language or in criticizing (with detached amusement) the foibles of humanity. It is doubtful that a feeling type could have written *Alice in Wonderland* or *Pride and Prejudice;* it is as doubtful that any TA could write *The Brothers Karamazov* or *An American Tragedy.*

D. H. Lawrence called himself "a kind of human bomb," and Emily Dickinson's personal metaphor was a "loaded gun." People who feel this way are writing because they want to explode moral complacency and falsehoods, and because they want to explore emotional truths, those profound truths of the heart that the heart of all the world feels. Love. Loss. Hate. Fear. Lust. Joy. Grief. "Is there more than Love and Death? Then tell me its name." So like Dickinson, who asked this question, and like most other feeling types, D. H. Lawrence could not bear to be around "head people" who denied, denigrated, trivialized, or avoided emotions—the art for art's sake or ideas for ideas' sake types. Such he considered Virginia Woolf's "Bloomsbury Group" to be, a group that was, in fact, largely comprised of thinking aethereals. "To hear these young people talk really fills me with black fury: they talk endlessly, but endlessly—and never, never a good thing said. . . . There is never for one second any outgoing of feeling and no reverence, not a crumb or grain of reverence."

Don't talk, said the volcanic Lawrence; feel. Don't think, experience. He wanted to throw out all the "ideal" values of our

mental consciousness so we could get back to our "blood consciousness." Take sex out of the head and give it back to the
body, he yelled. Blood and feelings never lie. Lawrence ir-
ritated people. He was too intense, intemperate, too passionate
for some to feel comfortable with. Most people need to distance
themselves from their emotions, but FOs and FVs need to be
experiencing them. That's how they know they are alive; that's
how they learn who they are. When they "grasp the soul at
white heat," then they feel most real. "The shore may be safer,"
Dickinson wrote a friend, "but I love to buffet the sea." People
found her too intense also. To the other psychetypes, feeling
types seem moody, seem to always be in one intense emotional
state or another, seem rarely to "let up."

But for an FO or FV the presence of a strong emotion is
likely to obliterate completely all other considerations, including the tranquility of those around at the time. There are no
extinct volcanos, we have discovered, only quiescent ones.
Even the combination of public position and our chauvinistic
condemnation of open affect in men may be insufficient deter-
rents when a feeling-type male is caught up in an overwhelming emotion. The bulldog Churchill wept while making an official inspection of bombed areas in London. The stately and
reserved Robert E. Lee (also an FO) was found sobbing in his
tent on learning of his daughter's death, and he was often unable to keep himself from weeping at the displays of affection
offered him by his troops. George Washington (an FV), usually
as stiff as one of his statues, was reported to have "wept una-
shamedly at his dinner table when describing his affection for
Lafayette." Washington understood his own typology; he
wrote: "In the composition of the human frame there is a great
deal of inflammable matter, however dormant it may lie for a
time, and when . . . the torch is put to it, *that* which is *within*
you must burst into a blaze." Our first President's blaze, like his
depression, was evidently awesome. According to Jefferson,
Washington's "temper was naturally irritable and high-toned,"
and when it did "break its bonds, he was most tremendous in
his wrath." Perhaps it was on such an occasion that he chopped
down his father's cherry tree.

Feeling types experience emotional arousal so intensely

that they can become frightened of being stirred *too* deeply, being swept away or flooded by their feelings; this is particularly true of those who are introverted and more a problem for receptive and passive feeling oceanics. Such people may just withdraw from, or avoid, encounters rather than endure the accompanying strain. It was for this reason that the composer Schubert refused to attend the opening-night performances of his music, while Emily Dickinson reached the point at which even *seeing* people was too wrenching for her sensibilities to deal with.

Once an emotion is ongoing, it is extremely difficult for a feeling type to interrupt its progress. They lack the discontinuous capacity to leap up from a painful argument and welcome an approaching visitor with a genuinely cheerful smile, the new situation having displaced the old. Powerful emotions develop an uncontrollable life of their own, one that is not responsive to a person's will or reason. Feeling types, therefore, must carry those sentiments within them until they exhaust or resolve themselves. In so doing, FOs and FVs occasionally get lost within such emotional states and become fixated there. At that point, a desire to sustain the feeling leads them to allow it to continue longer than is really necessary or congenial to others, and this is true of both positive expressions like love and negative ones like disappointment. A bad dynamic can result. An FV, say, is upset because his fiancée's former lover is in town. Assume his fiancée is an intuitive aethereal; his "endless gloom" will soon begin to oppress her. She will start to feel crowded, swamped, and even bored. So she pulls back and becomes very detached. In her view, he is running the thing into the ground. The FV senses her withdrawal, which only makes him churn up the situation more in order to arouse her again to his level of emotionality. If allowed to continue, this cycle becomes increasingly painful to both of them. It is, naturally, territorials and aethereals who are especially impatient with such prolongations of intense feeling. The TA Nietzsche was, in fact, bluntly contemptuous of Dostoevski's "degrading prostration" and "morbid moral tortures." He suspected the highly emotional Russian novelist of sinning "to enjoy the luxury of confession." Types to whom control or rationality are important are prone to accuse feeling types of "wallowing in their emotions," "milking" the feelings of others, or washing their souls in public laundromats.

But FOs and FVs have to explore their own feelings, and they have to find out what is going on inside those they care about. They want their lives to have emotional unity; that is their version of thinking-type order and structure. For there to be dissension between themselves and people they love is therefore unbearably painful, as are divisions among friends or internal emotional conflicts; these are to them what conflicts of principles are to TAs and TRs. Fidelity to the self is vital, but so is harmony with others. The novelist George Eliot faced this most traumatic of feeling-type problems when her father threatened to stop living in the same house with her if she refused to attend a church in whose doctrine she had ceased to believe. She finally decided that because it was important to him, she would attend the church services. To sit there need not violate her integrity; she could continue to think as she chose. But why, for a principle, violate a relationship? She based her decision on what she called "the truth of feeling."

> *Are we to remain aloof from our fellow-creatures when we may fully sympathize with the feelings exercised, although our own have been melted into another mould? Ought we not on every opportunity to seek to have our feelings in harmony, though not in union, with those who are often richer in the fruits of faith, though not in reason, than ourselves.*

The emotional sensitivity that Eliot displays here is typical of FOs and FVs generally. Except in cases when they are totally overwhelmed by their own feelings, these two psychetypes are instinctively the most emotionally aware and affectively versatile of all the types, including the two closest to them, SVs and IOs. SVs may be as volatile and engaged, but their territoriality controls them, and their discontinuity distracts them from their feelings. IOs, in addition to being discontinuous, have aethereality to distance them from their oceanic tendency to absorb emotions. So while obviously everybody feels things, it is feeling types who spend the most time coming to understand feelings and the process by which they become actions; it is they who best know how to integrate their emotions with their lives and put them to use there. Unlike the other three basic types, they neither disregard their feelings, nor wait for them to evaporate, nor forget about them. Consequently, they are likely to be more able accurately to express their own feelings (through their acts or words, through music or dancing) than individuals with different typological makeups. Perhaps no two English-speaking poets have revealed more refinement and versatility in delineating the most subtle shade of personal emotion than William Wordsworth or Emily Dickinson, both feeling volcanics; nor is there a novelist more intent on tracking down each nuance of even the most fleeting human feeling than the urgent, excessive, and always nakedly honest Dostoevski.

In the same way, successful feeling-type actors like Marlon Brando, James Dean, or Elizabeth Taylor can funnel their own charged emotionality into performances that pulse with tension and power. Taylor, as one critic has noticed, is at her best when playing women out of control—roles like Martha in *Who's Afraid of Virginia Woolf* or Maggie in *Cat On a Hot Tin Roof*: "women under obsessive and uncontrollable stress, who are pushed beyond limits of endurance."

Feeling-type sensitivity to emotional climates gives them a delicacy in dealing with others that substitutes for their disregard of formal societal customs. Rather than rely on pre-learned rituals of behavior, feeling types guide themselves by subtle social cues picked up from the reactions of others, generally on a nonverbal level. These cues are gathered by an almost seismographic sensitivity to what is appropriate or acceptable behavior; but to be correctly interpreted, the feeling type must have an ingrained knowledge of the culture by which the cues are generalized. In other words, in an unfamiliar situation, if a feeling type suspects (or is told) that he is *misreading* the cues, he feels completely vulnerable, for he has less access to those impersonal codes of conduct that people of other types rely on. Suppose, for example, that after a pleasant and compatible dinner with her employer and his six other guests, an FV picks up her plate and offers to help do the dishes. Her offer is politely refused, but she persists in wanting to help. Because she has liked the people there, the FV is assuming an intimacy that violates the social code that at dinner parties dishes do not have to be washed by the guests.

However, since cultural customs are fairly standard and easily perceived, most feeling types not only do not make such mistakes very often but demonstrate a high degree of social diplomacy, an attribute that makes many of them eminently successful in careers that involve therapeutic or diplomatic abilities, such as psychology, public relations, or social work— anything, in fact, that involves the capacity to work well with other people and to make other people work well together. That was George Washington's role in the founding of this country and the reason why he was the inevitable choice for the first Presidency. Only he could soothe and mediate and coordinate those diverse factions whose incompatibility threatened to split apart the Republic before it could be realized. Dwight D. Eisenhower played the same part in World War II. His tact and moral strength enabled him to resolve opposing views; that is why General Montgomery considered him the best choice as Commander of the Allied Forces. His accessible, easygoing personality was such that all the "warring generals, admirals, and air marshalls" would work with him harmoniously despite rampant jealousies and conflicting ambitions. In fact, his gifts as a peace maker may have transcended his talents as a war maker.

Their deep familiarity and rapport with emotions often gives feeling types a mastery over them that other types, caught suddenly in an unexpected trauma, may be unable to sustain. In situations in which a TR or an SV or an IA may be paralyzed by sudden upsurges of feeling—in times of pain, great sorrow, or deaths—FOs and FVs bear up with dignity and such inner strength that they are able to comfort the distressed, encourage the hopeless, care for and sympathize with those suffering both with patience and with sensitivity. Their quiet calm on such occasions may surprise friends who are accustomed to seeing them go to pieces over far less momentous events. But it is precisely because they are always sounding the depths of every variety of human feeling, including small rivulets, that feeling types are prepared to cope with the most profound. And it is also why, under strained circumstances, they are usually able to

maintain their social presence. Though he had wept before he
went to the courthouse at Appomattox, and though he had said
that he "would rather die a thousand deaths" than go there,
when Robert E. Lee surrendered the Army of the Confederacy,
he was so magnificently composed that General Grant was himself shaken by the man's unapproachable dignity.

The same heightened sensitivity that keeps them in touch
with their own feelings makes individuals of this type almost
equally sensitive to the feelings of others, even when the latter
are, themselves, still unconscious of the fact that they are feeling anything at all. But before emotions are strong enough to
be recognized by, say, a TA, an FO will "feel" them through the
person's body language or tone of voice, a sigh, an averted
glance. It is partly this capacity that makes these psychetypes
such excellent therapists, whether across a kitchen table or
across a professional desk. They know when to talk and when
to listen, and their facility with words used in emotional interactions enables them to "say the right thing at the right time." As
a result, they are rarely tactless in the way that, for instance, an
intuitive aethereal can be. Recall our hypothetical FV who
jumped up to wash the dishes. The instant she sensed from the
look on her host's face that she had made a social gaff, she would
put her plate down and change the subject as smoothly as possible. She would not, as a thinking type might, keep insisting on
principle that everybody troop into the kitchen and do their
share, nor would she fail, as some intuitives do, even to notice
that disapproving look.

In public life, their sensibility helps feeling types "read"
political moods and possibilities. Though they lack the sheer
tactical flair for politicking common among sensation types,
still, FOs like Churchill or FVs like the current Senator Lowell
Weicker can possess finely tuned antennae for picking up the
tone or atmosphere, the "Gestalt," of a parliamentary session or
a Congressional hearing. Yet, as a rule, feeling types are not
especially intrigued with power struggles. *Any* kind of social
conflict is likely, in fact, to exhaust or bore most FOs. Of course,
there are feeling types ambitious for pre-eminence; it is hard to
think of anyone more desirous to govern than Winston Churchill. Nevertheless, we find time and again with people of this type

a genuine reluctance to jump into the world's dusty arena and start slugging it out with all the territorial gladiators in there. What feeling types cannot resist, however, is responding to the needs of others. Having refused the command of the Northern army, General Lee was *pressed* to accept, and retain, that of the Confederacy. He did so because he was convinced that it was his moral duty to help his native state. There is no reason to suspect Eisenhower of being disingenuous when he protested that he was not interested in politics, when he insisted in 1948 that he "would refuse the nomination even if offered," or when he said that he allowed his name to be entered in 1952 only because public demand for his services was so compelling. Nor should we doubt General Washington's sincerity when he wrote to his wife:

> *So far from seeking this appointment, I have used every endeavor in my power to avoid it, not only from my unwillingness to part with you and the family, but from a consciousness of its being a trust too great for my capacity, and that I should enjoy more real happiness in one month with you at home than I have the most distant prospect of finding abroad.*

He agreed to accept the Presidency with the same reluctance he here expresses with regard to the command of the Revolutionary Army and was persuaded to continue for a second term only when convinced that without his tempering influence the two government parties would rip the colonies apart.

On a private level, too, their responsiveness to others makes it extremely hard for feeling types to refuse aid to those who ask it. For one thing, they are disposed to blame themselves for other people's unhappiness, and even if they avoid the impulse to assume that responsibility, their oceanic receptivity is such that they very easily feel sorry for others; almost, in fact, feel their unhappiness themselves. If, for example, an FO is in the room while a TR and an SR are having a marital spat, he will sense the tension and hurt that lies beneath their territorial control and is apt to become more outwardly upset than his friends are; their very control upsets him even more. Finally, he may get up and say, "Excuse me, this is too painful. Can I help in any way?" The couple assures him that "it's no big thing," and they may actually find it less *experientially* upsetting than he. It is certainly less upsetting than the equivalent situation would be to him and, say, an FV wife.

Feeling types want very much to avoid hurting other people's feelings. They know how it affects them to be hurt, and they assume it is equally distressing to others. In the way "being wrong" pains thinking types, so misperceiving someone else's feelings genuinely mortifies FOs and FVs. Their emotional sensitivity is the compass by which they guide their lives; if it isn't working properly, they feel disoriented. If the misperception is serious enough, it may even threaten their sense of the solidity of their own identities. How does it happen that feeling types, with all their perceptivity in this area, can occasionally be so completely mistaken in interpreting the emotions of others? Most commonly, such errors occur when their own feelings are aroused to the point that they drown out less intense cues coming at them, or when the cues are so painful that, in self-defense, the feeling type deliberately ignores them. It can also happen when a feeling type has received so much reinforcement and praise for his or her ability to "read" other people that an attitude of emotional infallibility develops. Though another person persists in denying that he is feeling any such thing, the FO or FV insists that he cannot be wrong, that he never makes mistakes about feelings.

Because error in this area is so devastating, feeling types are infuriated when they sense (and they sense it quickly) that people are self-consciously and manipulatively trying to play on their feelings. They hate emotional "phonies" because, to them, feelings are sacred. Marlon Brando's sister remarked that the actor was so upset by this kind of dishonesty in others that "he couldn't talk, he couldn't cope, he was too emotional." Brando himself attributes his famous mumble to the same reaction: "If I didn't trust or like somebody, I would either say nothing or mumble. I got to be awfully good at mumbling." One reason why feeling types are as comfortable as they are with powerful emotional states is that they can *trust* them. It's hard to fake overwhelming passion, fury, or grief. "I like a look of Agony, /

Because I know it's true. / Men do not sham Convulsion, / Nor Simulate a Throe."

Sometimes, though, the problem is not that people are, in Dickinson's term, "shamming," but that the feeling type, like everyone else, assumes that if someone else behaves in a certain way, he or she must be having the same kind of emotions that the feeling type knows he would have under those circumstances. And this, as we have been learning, is not true. It is easy to understand, however, why people of this particular type can fall into such errors. When greatly moved by strong emotion, intuitives and thinking and sensation types all act for a time like feeling types, that is, they are drawing on their feeling function when in the throes of love, hatred, jealousy, or anguish. When someone moves into a function that does not usually dominate his personality, he feels slightly ill at ease and may actually, in compensation, exaggerate that typological behavior. So, as feeling types on "thinking trips" are apt at times to become dogmatic, so thinking types, say, or sensation types who are "into their feelings" may appear sloppily sentimental or overwrought. Moreover, everyone in love is in direct contact with his or her feeling function. Usually detached, abstracted TAs become absorbed and devoted; freedom-loving, manipulative SRs act submissively adoring. When a feeling type (take, for example, an FV male) falls in love with such a person, he assumes that she loves him as he loves her, with the same intensity of emotional commitment, the same omnipresent involvement. However, after the first romantic enchantment has passed, the TA or SR is likely to revert to her basic typological attitudes. This does not necessarily mean that she no longer loves the FV, but for him that fact in itself is insufficient. Feeling types frequently accuse not only lovers but relatives and friends of "not loving them" when what they mean is not loving them in a feeling-type way. The happiness of these two psychetypes depends to a large degree on the quality of response they receive from others. The love must be a close and total reciprocity, one that understands and accepts and matches their own unique qualities as individuals. Now, no doubt we should all prefer to be loved like that, but persons of other types often allow their love to slip into a reliable functional slot in their lives. ("Of course, I love you, you're my wife, husband, child, best friend, and so forth.") Feeling types want it up front and center stage. Such was the relationship the FO composer Frédéric Chopin thought he had with Georges Sand, an IA. He never really recovered from her leaving him, and his last words were, "She promised I should die in her arms." She was apparently off, at the time, having her portrait painted.

When feeling types discover that love does not seem to mean the same thing to IAs or TRs or SVs as it does to them, they feel painfully disillusioned and may assume that they have been misled. Depending on their personalities, their response may be to grieve—or to retaliate; volcanics are more inclined to the second response, oceanics to the first. Feeling types have the potential to be vindictive, to hold grudges against others for long periods of time—neither forgetting or forgiving. When they have been hurt, they want to punish those who have hurt them. One method they choose when someone has ignored their feelings is to refuse to help him when *he* is emotionally distressed, not only not to help but deliberately to frustrate his attempts to resolve a dilemma by not answering him or by not allowing him to talk about the problem.

In more extreme situations they may even seek active revenge, as Heathcliff does when he marries Catherine Earnshaw's sister-in-law and torments her in order to hurt Catherine. If some thinking types want to see their enemies annihilated, some feeling types want to punish theirs so deeply as to permanently incapacitate them. Not, of course, by breaking their legs (though in a few highly volcanic cultures revenge does take the form of physical maiming); rather, the feeling type may be driven to inflict a kind of psychological damage. One motive for the suicides of two literary FVs (Anna Karenina and Madame Bovary) is to ensure that the men who have betrayed them will never recover from their guilt.

Obviously, not many real feeling types behave as excessively as Heathcliff or Anna Karenina, just as not many are as angelic as Melanie in *Gone with the Wind*, but all do have the potential for strong *negative* emotions, as well as the happier ones. Few insist they are as unrelievedly miserable as Thomas De Quincey or Dr. Johnson, who claimed his "vile melancholy" had made him "mad" all his life, but most have fairly persistent periods of depression, during which they are apt to complain a great deal. Being continuous and oceanically carried along by whatever state they are currently in, it is rather hard for them to pull themselves out of these moods. In addition, they are easily hurt. Albert Schweitzer said of those who did not tease him about his decision to leave music in order to become a medical missionary, "I felt as a real kindness the action of persons who made no attempt to dig their fists into my heart." That is how having their feelings hurt seems to FOs and FVs, a fist in the heart. So, a slight, which an intuitive might not even notice, and a thinking type would promptly dismiss, can deeply pain them. Dr. Johnson was kept waiting an hour by Lord Chesterfield and absolutely refused, thereafter, to accept his patronage.

The depressions of feeling types are also prolonged because they are already predisposed to self-blame and reproach. When they believe that they have done something wrong, have failed in some way that matters to them, they cannot accept condolences or reassurances. It does no good to try to comfort a young FO who has angered his best friend by a callous action by telling him to "let bygones be bygones. Cheer up and forget about it." He won't. Moreover, feeling types, lacking emotional detachment, are vulnerable to being flooded with great waves of self-pity now and then. Many have a rich enough sense of humor to make jokes about their own tendency to feel sorry for themselves. A few, like Thomas Wolfe, can, at times, become almost paranoid, assuming not only that there is "no life in this world worth living, no air worth breathing, nothing but agony and the drawing of the breath in nausea and labor," but, worse, that other people are out to "get them," to stop them from writing their books, getting their promotions, or saving their marriages, or whatever.

It was part of the genius of FV Judy Garland that she was able to take this typological vulnerability to hurt and pain and transform it, during her performances, into art. "I mean every word of every song," she said. Audiences felt that to be true. No one else, with the possible exception of Edith Piaf, ever made listeners respond so empathetically, ever stirred them to such loving pity and solicitious affection, as Judy Garland singing "Somewhere Over the Rainbow."

Feeling types can be hurt in relationships to the degree we have been describing because human relationships are perhaps the most important thing in life to them, so much so that without them life may seem to have no meaning at all. "I want to paint humanity, humanity, and again humanity," said van Gogh. For feeling types, no man can be an island unto himself. "Everyone shares the guilt of every crime, of everything that happens on earth." Dostoevski's statement is one way of expressing what Albert Schweitzer called "the ethics of reverence for life," that moral imperative that forces us "without cessation to be concerned with all the other human destinies which are going through their life-course around" us. Thus, FOs and FVs believe that all situations gain and grow in the process of interaction with other people, as they themselves blossom when, in such interactions, they feel others respond to them emotionally.

Feeling types love to have friends and enjoy a happy talent for making them. "How I like to be liked, and what I do to be liked," said the affable Charles Lamb, who was liked very much by Wordsworth and Coleridge and innumerable others who met him. But Lamb did not share his Romantic friends' obsession with solitary rambles over mountains and around lakes; he liked to be in London where the people were. So did Dr. Johnson, who remarked, "I look upon everyday to be lost in which I do not make a new acquaintance." "Friendship," he said rather gruffly, "is the cordial drop to make the nauseous draft of life go down," and he formed the Literary Club so he could meet with his everyday. Emily Dickinson's vision of heaven was a huge blue sky full of her friends: "My friends are my estate. Forgive me the avarice to hoard them."

Around their friends, FOs and FVs come alive and sparkle. They love talking about people, and being with people, and sharing with people. As a consequence, they tend to get along well in communal living arrangements, whereas (unless everyone's boundaries are clearly marked and respected) territorials feel crowded and invaded in such situations. But feeling types enjoy being close to their friends; they will also take a great deal of trouble for them—for example, learning things that would please them. If an FO has a friend who is interested in archeology, she will watch a television program on that subject with the friend constantly in mind almost as if she were watching it for him, in his place; and she will look foward to sharing what she learned when she sees her friend next. For all these reasons, most feeling types inspire great loyalty from those who know them.

If there is anything feeling types value more than friendship, it is relationships in which there is an even higher degree of intimacy—family or romantic love attachments. Many of the great lovers of literature and history have been feeling types: Phaedra, Dido, Romeo, Antony, Othello, Jane Eyre, Heathcliff, Gatsby. Nearly everyone falls in love, of course, and many are willing to renounce position or wealth or friends for love, but there come to mind no thinking or sensation types or intuitives who have given up a kingdom for love, as did FO Edward VIII. Despite the pleas of a sympathetic fellow feeling oceanic, Winston Churchill, who was trying to work out a compromise with Parliament, Edward abdicated to marry Mrs. Wallis Simpson, telling a shocked nation, "I have found it impossible to carry the heavy burden of responsibility and to discharge my duties as King as I would wish to do without the help and support of the woman I love." His TR predecessor, Elizabeth, gave up Leicester; the Duke of Windsor gave up England. Even the shiest, most circumspect feeling type is made daring by love. George Eliot (an FV) renounced reputation and the regard of her family to live with a married man whom she devotedly loved until his death twenty years later. Admiral Nelson (an FV), hero of the Napoleonic Wars, scandalized his country by deserting his wife to live with the "notorious" Lady Hamilton. He even left a will saying that he felt assured that in return for his services to his nation England would provide for Lady Hamilton after his death. England did no such thing; she was placed in debtors' prison and died a pauper. The poet, FO Elizabeth Barrett, judged to be a helpless invalid with only a few years to live, escaped from her dictatorial father's house and eloped with Robert Browning, a sensation volcanic. The only thing she regretted leaving behind was her dog, which her FV father, in a rage, threatened to murder. Browning, she wrote, moved between her "and the dreadful outer brink of obvious death, where I, who thought to sink, was caught up into love, and taught the whole of life in a new rhythm." She lived to raise a son with him. "My business is to love." "That love is all we know, is all we know of love." "I never lived till I had loved enough." These lines of Emily Dickinson's echo the beliefs of nearly all feeling types.

Because of its centrality, an FO or even an FV is likely to leave a love relationship only when it has entirely exhausted its emotional content or when it is supplanted by a greater emotional attachment. They are therefore more willing than other types to stay in a "bad marriage" or an unhappy affair, patiently trying to patch things up, to hold on to the past, to avoid so absolute a break with their continuity, to stay there as long as there is any shred of feeling left or unless they fall deeply in love with someone else.

Being this passionate, feeling types are also apt to be intemperate. Perhaps, to love, like Othello, "not wisely, but too well." They are, for example, prone to be jealous and intolerant of any kind of suspense in a love relationship. It maddens them to have to wait to find out whether their love is returned; they are impatient whenever they cannot be around the person they love; consequently, they are totally uninterested in the sort of chess game of sexual maneuvering that territorials enjoy playing. Love between two volcanics can generate such intense satisfaction that it becomes a totally engrossing and consuming passion before which the rest of the world fades to nothingness. Shakespeare's Romeo and Juliet or Antony and Cleopatra and Emily Brontë's Heathcliff and Catherine all are volcanics. For the most part, people of the other types simply do not have either the energy or the inclination to sustain so concentrated an emotional intensity, and the feeling type must learn to allow them their respites.

We have looked at several examples of feeling types who, with an "all for love and the world well lost" attitude, have been attacked by that world rather sharply. If at times there seems to be a stronger reaction to what feeling types do or say than to the other three basic types, the reason is probably that feeling types do or say things more strongly. They are so open and intense about their emotions that they on some level *invite* other people to become involved in them, as Norman Mailer asks us to do. A famous territorial may renounce reputation for illicit love, but she isn't usually required to renounce it so *publicly* as Ingrid Bergman was when she eloped with Roberto Rossellini. Consequently, the territorial is not subjected to the sort of attacks that were made on Miss Bergman, who was condemned in the U.S. Congress as "Hollywood's apostle of degradation" and "a powerful influence for evil." Similarly, TR film actresses like Bette Davis or Katharine Hepburn have never allowed the public to share in their private lives in the curious way the actions and attitudes of FO Elizabeth Taylor have involved her fans emotionally, either toward sympathy or anger, giving her, too, the honor of having a Congressman propose that she (and Richard Burton) be prohibited on moral grounds from re-entering the country. Like Judy Garland's songs, somehow the lives of feeling types belong to other people as well as to themselves.

Unfortunately, the very psychetypes who are willing to throw up the world for love are the two likely to be most pained by its loss, for feeling types have a deep and lasting desire to "belong." Though George Eliot never faltered in her courageous decision to live with Henry Lewes, that courage cost her bitterly—as, in Victorian England, she knew it must. The couple were not received by "decent people," her friends derided her, even her own brother never spoke to her again. But in her mind she and Lewes were morally married; those who would not call her Mrs. Lewes must renounce her friendship as they denounced her morality. In the end, by sheer triumph of character (and talent), George Eliot won back her place in the corporate whole, but the trial separation hurt her more than, say, society's attacks on IA Isadora Duncan ever troubled the independent spirit of that unorthodox lady—in fact, she rejoiced in them.

A secondary aspect of this desire to belong is the concern most feeling types, both men and women, take with their appearance. Being physically unattractive—"the only Kangaroo among the Beauty," as Emily Dickinson called herself—is especially dismaying to them. They dress as fashionably as they can to please others as well as themselves, and they are inclined to worry about growing old and losing their looks.

Of course, feeling types want to belong to some *one* as much as to a community. All need demonstrations of other people's feelings for them; many are, in a more general way, susceptible to emotional dependency on others. Elizabeth Taylor once said, "I need strength in a man more than any other quality," remarking that in the hiatus between two strong emotional attachments, she felt a kind of panic. To the SV Juliet, parting might be "such sweet sorrow," but to FVs, "Parting is all we know of heaven, and all we need of hell." Leave-takings and separations are very hard on feeling types. As volcanics, they need present involvement, not the sort of future possibility so attractive to intuitives that they may actually enjoy separations since a person just over the horizon may be more interesting than a person sitting in front of the fireplace next to them.

FOs and FVs have a great capacity for devotion. Clara Schumann's willingness, after her husband's death, to give the rest of her life to performing his music in order to bring it to the world's attention is not so unusual a loyalty for individuals of her type. For they are, in general, intensely loyal; ferocious, in fact, in defending those they love. Not only are feeling types themselves able to disregard any undesirable personality traits the people they care about may possess, they will not sit by while anyone else attacks those people. Falseness or faithlessness to a loved one they consider an unpardonable sin. Falseness to the self (dishonor) is an equal sin. In public realms feeling types are likely to define loyalty as "duty," which Robert E. Lee called "the sublimest word in our language." A feeling type performs his duty out of personal loyalty to his country and private loyalty to his honor. Asked at the battle of Trafalgar to remove his medals lest the French identify and kill him, Admiral Lord Nelson replied, "In honor I gained them, and in honor I will die with them." He died that day wearing those medals; his final words were "Thank God I have done my duty."

The quality of devotion is bound up with a nexus of personality traits that our culture traditionally has defined as "feminine." However, it is characteristic of all feeling types, men as well as women, to be trusting, nurturing, self-sacrificing, sympathetic, and tenderhearted. Even the "Great Bear" Dr. Johnson, who loved to "toss and gore" his opponents in debates, and whose temper was compared to earthquakes and thunderstorms, "nursed a whole nest of people in his house," including (for more than twenty years) an elderly blind woman whom he took care of and a young black man whom he had educated. Of his 300 pounds a year income, he gave 200 away in charity, and though, as his friend Goldsmith said, he had "a roughness of manner, no man alive had a more tender heart."

But since, particularly in the twentieth century, men are not supposed to reveal tender hearts, not supposed to be emotionally expressive and nurturing and warm and romantic and sentimental, young feeling-type males (especially FOs) have run up against the same problem as young thinking-type females: Their natural typology is in direct conflict with sex-role expectations. If an FO boy is criticized or ridiculed by his peers or never reinforced by his parents for being himself—for being intensely sensitive, open, responsive to beauty, passively receptive, physically affectionate but perhaps not physically competitive—he is likely to try to repress his psychetype or to be forced to express it in what society considers negative or aberrant ways. He may become moody or sullen or sluggishly apathetic since the energy required to stifle the self is exhausting. There is certainly nothing "unmanly" about the lives or the interests of men like St. Francis of Assisi or Lee and Churchill, or William Penn, founder of Philadelphia, or the American philosophers, William James and John Dewey; nothing weak in van Gogh's nursing of Belgium miners or Schweitzer's caring for African natives—just as there is nothing "unfeminine" about the intellects of Virginia Woolf or Margaret Mead. We place constrictive bars around human potential whenever we assume otherwise.

The importance of the past. The primacy of emotions. The centrality of relationships. The fourth major attribute of feeling types is their sense of involvement in the eternal life cycles of man and nature, the sense they have that we all, past, present, and future, coexist, "rolled round in earth's diurnal course, with rocks and stones and trees." That is why they love to hear other people tell the stories of their pasts, for the human emotions behind those experiences are universal. Tales of love and hate, joy and sorrow recreate those primal feelings that join all times and places in the circle of human existence. That is also why the empathetic closeness that feeling types, like Wordsworth and Dickinson, have with nature is one rarely approached by the other psychetypes. "To hear an Oriole sing may be a common thing, or only a divine." To FVs and FOs, common things like orioles *are* divine; to be surrounded by such beauty teaches us "more of man, more of moral evil and of good, than all the sages can." Therefore, feeling types share with Schweitzer that reverence for all life out of which one can live a part of the natural process simply, unrushed, in harmony—so that "living itself is ecstasy." "For man," wrote D. H. Lawrence, "as for flower and beast and bird, the supreme triumph is to be intensely alive." As children are.

For the most part, feeling types are people who can endure and accept, who can reconcile the inevitability of death with the process of living, who can comfort others by reminding them that our brief moments of gain or loss are just that— ephemeral. They are people who try not to judge others. "See everything," wrote Pope John XXIII, "turn a blind eye to many things. Correct a little." John did not consider himself infallible: "The Pope is only infallible when he speaks *ex cathedra,* and I will never speak *ex cathedra.* "

Clearly for such people, their hearts must rule their heads. What we characterized as the "intellectual quality" of the thinking-type world, we might call here an "engaged quality." FOs and FVs guide their intellects by their emotions. Thus, they are prone to lack a detached, analytical view of things. The impersonal theorizing of thinking-types Montaigne and Hume about death and immortality thoroughly amazed, as well as outraged, feeling-types Pascal and Johnson: Those men, they said, must either be lying or mad to act so indifferent to their own destinies. "Are you a theologian?" Pope John once asked an Anglican bishop. "No," the man replied. "I'm so glad," the Pope said, "for I'm not, either." William James (no theologian, either) told philosophers to damn the absolute; all is relative and particular.

The pragmatism, immediacy, and practicality of feeling

types comes out of the combination of volcanic involvement and oceanic subjectiveness. And so "learning by doing," as John Dewey put it, is more congenial to them than abstracting theories. To those who personalize things, the best teacher is intense emotion, "the hot blood's blindfold art," and not philosophical formulae. Feeling types therefore learn not by deriving the principle from a situation but by deriving the "moral." They grow not by expanding their ideas but by extending their empathy, by learning how to put themselves inside the feelings of those who are unlike them. For both FOs and FVs (especially those who are introverted), the private, internal exploration of emotion is a self-fertilizing experience; because it is a continuing process, and because the oceanic world is more centered on a whole state of being than a given incident, feeling types are probably less easily bored than any of the other psychetypes.

"Head talk" does not usually engage such individuals; Albert Schweitzer once remarked that one of the reasons he wanted to be a doctor was so he could "work without having to talk," work at putting his religion into "actual practice." A meeting of minds is not so much shared ideas as shared feelings: "I never met with so many of my feelings expressed just as I should like them," George Eliot wrote to praise Wordsworth's poetry. And, in fact, rather than have to articulate their emotions in "talk," many feeling types prefer to write them down. *Sonnets from the Portugese* is really a long letter from Elizabeth Barrett Browning to her husband, one she shyly slipped into his pocket one day. "How do I love thee? Let me count the ways" may have been too intensely felt for her to speak it. Of course, very few feeling types write letters like that, or like the three hundred poems Emily Dickinson dropped in the next-door mailbox of her sister-in-law, but all want to clarify exactly how they feel for those they care about and often find it easier to write the person a letter than, say, make a phone call.

Because it is so important that they not jeopardize relationships, FOs and FVs, unless they are deeply upset, are likely to try to avoid direct confrontations with their friends or loved ones. So, to express their hostility or hurt feelings, they tend to tease people or to be ironical. Winston Churchill was profoundly pained when the British people failed to return him to office following World War II; he expressed that pain through irony:

> *At the outset of this mighty battle, I acquired the chief power in the State, which henceforth I wielded in ever-growing measure for five years and three months of world war, at the end of which time, all our enemies having surrendered unconditionally or being about to do so, I was immediately dismissed by the British electorate from all further conduct of their affairs.*

Like most feeling types, Churchill was a romantic. His dashing exploits as a young cavalry officer and war correspondent in Cuba, India, Egypt, and South Africa caught the imagination of the world, as war caught his. War, because on that vast stage the most vital of morality plays would be performed, a drama in which the feeling-type virtues of honor, glory, loyalty, and communal self-sacrifice can shine forth like splendid banners as the white knights of freedom (America and England) join ranks to charge the dark forces of Axis tyranny. In Mao Tse-tung's fascination with all the brigand-heroes of ancient China, we glimpse another variety of the same military romanticism.

A more ordinary focus for romanticism than the heroics of war lies in romance itself. FOs and FVs of all ages feel a special closeness to children (because in them the miraculous process of life growing is so visible) and to youth because it is in youth that we allow ourselves to feel most intensely. Adolescents are characteristically the most romantic lovers of all; that is why Romeo and Juliet are so young.

The failure of romanticism is disenchantment; that, to a feeling type, may entail an absolute collapse of one's personal identity. When innocence, when faith, when honor is lost, "Chaos is come." Suffering such loss, Shakespeare's Othello and his Antony kill themselves, pausing only to remind the world of those contributions to the corporate whole so centrally important to feeling volcanics: "I have done the state some service, and they know it."

A common attribute of the romantic sensibility is a belief in fate, and we find this attitude general among feeling types.

It may find a focus in a fascination with gambling—which was Dostoevski's obsession—or an interest in fortunetelling techniques like tarot cards, or in a more general philosophical stance, as in the "fatalism" that pervades Thomas Hardy's novels. Fatalism usually informs a vision of life more tragic than comedic; significantly, the heroes and heroines of literary tragedies are almost invariably feeling types. In life, as in literature, individuals of these two psychetypes are often inclined to agree with Johnson that "human life is everywhere a state in which much is to be endured and little to be enjoyed." Hence, when told that an acquaintance was a perenially happy man, the Great Bear growled, "It is all cant; the dog knows he is miserable all the time!" After all, if to *think* about the world is to laugh, and to *feel* about it is to weep, FVs and FOs may be expected to share a certain pessimism with regard to what Lawrence called our essentially tragic age. Nor is it surprising that Dostoevski's favorite reading was the Book of Job.

These negative expectations evolve, on one level, from the fact that feeling types spend so little psychic time in the future. TRs and TAs plan and theorize in order to control eventualities. Feeling types do not. Consequently, when they need to make predictions, their typological unease with all those unknown future possibilities leads them to make pessimistic ones. Rather than attempt to analyze or manipulate what may happen, they are inclined to worry about it and, more often than not, to assume the worst. If they are feeling happy, no doubt Fate will come along with her account book and collect her payment: "For each ecstatic instant, / We must an anguish pay / In keen and quivering ratio / To the ecstasy."

At an even deeper level, feeling types believe that happiness does not enrich one as much as sorrow does. "Action is transitory, / Suffering is permanent," said Wordsworth. Sadness and pain, they understand. They know how to live with those: "I can wade Grief, but the least push of Joy breaks up my feet, / And I tip—drunken." And so with their intense emotional sensibility, feeling types see everywhere the tragic potential of life, even in moments of joy, even in triumph. From his victory over Napoleon at the Battle of Waterloo, the Duke of Wellington sent a dispatch that Napoleon could never have written:

"Nothing except a battle lost can be half so melancholy as a battle won. A victory is the greatest tragedy in the world, except a defeat."

The personal warmth of feeling types, their responsiveness and sensitivity to others, their care and their kindness, rise in their finest moments to a sublimity of spirit in which goodness becomes greatness. We often hear said of these people that their character transcends even their accomplishments, that Washington and Eisenhower were better than their Presidencies, William Jennings Bryan better than the Presidency he never won, that in General Lee, who lost a war, "moral qualities rose to the height of genius." A young man wrote of George Eliot once, "She appeared much greater than her books. Her ability seemed to shrink beside her moral grandeur. She was not only the cleverest, but the best woman I had ever met." To be loved for who you are and not for what you achieve in this world is no slight, and certainly no universal, tribute.

Dr. David Livingstone, a missionary in Africa, never found the source of the Nile that he was seeking. Henry Stanley did. He discovered it after coming there to search for Dr. Livingstone, and we remember Stanley not because he found the source of the Nile, but because he found a man who was devoting his life, amid awesome hardships, to the welfare of mistreated people. Livingstone was a warrior; his war was against slavery, and his weapons were the journals he sent out to tell the civilized world that to imprison their fellow creatures was to be more than uncivilized; it was to be less than human. Livingstone chose to stay at his mission rather than return with Stanley to England. When he died, the natives wrapped him in barks and carried him, on foot, through the virgin jungles and mountains of central Africa, across the continent to the eastern shore where he could be taken home to his family. It took them a year. They did it because they loved him.

FEELING TYPES

St. Francis of Assisi, FV
George Washington, FV
Dr. Samuel Johnson, FV
William Wordsworth, FV
The Duke of Wellington, FV
Admiral Lord Nelson, FV
George Eliot, FV
Emily Dickinson, FV
James Fenimore Cooper, FV
Thomas Hardy, FV
William James, FV
Theodore Dreiser, FV
D. H. Lawrence, FV
Eugene O'Neill, FV
Sergei Rachmaninoff, FV
Feodor Dostoevski, FV
Albert Schweitzer, FV
John Dewey, FV
Dwight D. Eisenhower, FV
Pope John XXIII, FV
Judy Garland, FV
Marlon Brando, FV
James Dean, FV
Senator Lowell Weicker, FV
Norman Mailer, FV

Blaise Pascal, FO
Charles Lamb, FO
Thomas De Quincey, FO
Lawrence Sterne, FO
Louis XVI of France, FO
Washington Irving, FO
Oliver Goldsmith, FO
Franz Schubert, FO
Frédéric Chopin, FO
Clara Schumann, FO
Vincent van Gogh, FO
Robert E. Lee, FO
Elizabeth Barrett Browning, FO
Dr. David Livingstone, FO
Peter Ilyitch Tchaikovsky, FO
Thomas Wolfe, FO
William Jennings Bryan, FO
Mao Tse-tung, FO
Edward VIII, Duke of Windsor, FO
Winston Churchill, FO
Ingrid Bergman, FO
Edith Piaf, FO
Elizabeth Taylor, FO

The Sensation Type

"Easy, easy, old girl. I wish you would realize there is a real art in getting this close to calamity."
— HUMPHREY BOGART TO
LAUREN BACALL

"Dr. Livingstone, I presume. I am Henry M. Stanley." With these famous words, a sensation territorial ended an adventure that had begun with the simple receipt of a telegram from an editor then in Paris, who asked if the two could speak together. Stanley, just returned from covering wars in Abyssinia and Spain, left immediately for France and arrived in the startled editor's house before the man had gotten out of bed. "I am Stanley, and I have come to answer your message." Asked if he would consider going to Africa to search for Livingstone, Stanley agreed at once. Meeting such challenges was nothing new to this veteran war correspondent. From age fourteen, when he left his native Wales to go to sea as a cabin boy, to his service,

166

first in the Confederate Army, then (after release from a Federal prison camp) in the U.S. Navy, Stanley had been irresistibly drawn to action and excitement. Now he set out to locate a man for two years lost to the world, somewhere in the thousands of square miles of unexplored, disease-ridden, and hostile wilderness of central Africa. In six months he found the missionary near Lake Tanganyika, led there not by any geographical expertise or exploratory training but by following signs, listening to native rumors, and by what he called simply instincts. Why on so momentous, in fact miraculous, an occasion did Stanley speak in such a polite and emotionless way? Because, he explained later, his feelings were so stirred by seeing Livingstone alive that in order to maintain control, it was necessary for him to be as formal as possible. What Stanley did and the fact that he was there to do it are what sensation types are all about.

Like thinking types, sensation types are territorial; like feeling types, they are volcanic. So while SRs and SVs are active and involved people, they want to organize their actions and control their involvement. Theirs is a world in which the physical has primacy over the conceptual or the emotional, in which peak experiences are prized and self-sufficiency struggled for. It is also a discontinuous world in which the feeling-type desire to maintain the past and the thinking-type need to construct time in a linear progression have little meaning. Insofar as the traits of discontinuity affect personality, sensation types will *seem* like intuitives in their total involvement with situations, their attempts to intensify the moment, their impulsiveness and changeableness, and in their discomfort with continuity. But beneath these similarities always lies a crucial experiential difference. Intuition and sensation are as mutually exclusive as thinking and feeling, for intuitives *project* onto the world, and sensation types *react* to it. Intuitives reject the past and present for an infinite future full of possibilities; sensation types disregard the future as well as the past in favor of an eternal present filled with actualities.

In fact, their absolutely primary involvement in the present, their orientation toward the here and now, is perhaps the most distinctive characteristic of sensation types. SR Jacques Cousteau called it "the philosophy of the wind," as opposed to "the philosophy of the stone," which attempts to stop time by building and acquiring things "in the hope that they will last and make you immortal." Instead, why not "just blow wherever you want," taking "full advantage of the instant, trying to make each instant beautiful and fruitful?" Focusing all their attention on the present moment, people like this are not very involved in projecting future desires or needs. They don't worry about tomorrow; they're too busy experiencing today. When Scarlet O'Hara (an SV) says, "I won't think about that now. I'll think about it tomorrow," she means she won't think about it at all. For as Lady Bird Johnson once remarked about her SV husband Lyndon, sensation types act as if there is never going to be a tomorrow. Actually, it may be difficult for them even to imagine such theoretical possibilities. This quality makes these people very spontaneous; it also makes them unpredictable. Mussolini was in 1914 a pacifist, in 1915 an advocate of Italy's entering World War I on the side of the Allies, next a socialist, then a Fascist. Journalists said his views were simply "those of the last book he happened to have read," and one warned, "I don't know where he is going, but he is certainly going somewhere." Their openness to the moment gives SRs and SVs the flexibility to act quickly. "None goes so far as he who knows not whither he is going," as Oliver Cromwell put it. However, if carried to an extreme, it can lead to the opposite: a narrowed perspective in which the limited horizon of the present shuts the person off from anything he has not already experienced and makes him very resistant to change. Thus, unless new situations are put in his path (and by their presence absorb his attention), the sensation type can get "caught" in things, for the sufficiency of the present precludes any motivation to alter it. Individuals of this type tend not to know what they want until they have experienced it—a vicious circle obviously. Saying, "Try it, you'll like it," to a six-year-old SV is apt to provoke a "How do you know?" response or, more simply, a stubborn shake of the head.

So sensation types can just drift into things. Caesar did not consider himself a military man until he saw himself in the process of conquering Spain. The writer Bret Harte suggested to SR Mark Twain that he try writing books, too; another friend persuaded this great performer that lecture tours would be a good opportunity for him. SV Leo Tolstoy wrote to his aunt: "You recall the advice you once gave me—to write novels. Well, I've followed it. I don't know whether what I write will ever see the light of day, but it is work that amuses me." No one ever had to *advise* intuitive James Joyce to become a writer, or Marilyn Monroe to become a movie star; these were visions cherished since adolescence. SV Robert Frost said he taught school "to find out whether I had it in me to think and write," but such a question would never have occurred to TA John Milton. Sensation volcanics (with all their immediacy and engagement) are more susceptible to this danger than their territorial counterparts, for they lack the purposeful, effective goal-directedness that the latter gain from the primacy of territoriality. When SR Cousteau compared his life style to the wind, he added, "But I'm a very organized wind."

In a person of this type disregard of the future may be joined to an equally pervasive rejection of the past. In fact, looking back is considered morbid, and "turning back" viewed with distaste. "The past for me is absolutely disgusting," said Cousteau. "When very rarely I have recurrences of feeling, I'm overwhelmed with a desire to vomit." Nor does such an individual accept with equanimity the intrusion of the past on the present. When it's over, it's over: "Frankly, my dear, I don't give a damn." At eighty-two, Tolstoy decided he really could not abide his wife, and with the same sort of finality as Rhett Butler's inimitable remark, the Russian novelist walked out of his house and took off through the snow. He never returned home but died in the midst of his wanderings at a railway stationmaster's cabin.

Being cut loose from the rapidly fading past is no real loss to sensation types, and so they are often fairly unperturbed by past mistakes and failures. If each event is unique, and each discrete moment of time stands on its own merit, then to be "there" at the moment is more important than to present a consistent picture of the self, as the political policies of Cromwell or Stalin or Lyndon B. Johnson or Richard Nixon certainly indicate. "The most unhappy hours in our lives are those in which we recollect times past to our own blushing," wrote John Keats, an SV. Continuous people occasionally have been rather shocked by how little a few sensation types in particular have bothered to blush despite their total reversals of former positions or absolute denials of former acts.

Because of this temporal existentialism SRs, and even more so, SVs, have an intense sense of the transitory nature of life—the sense, as Frost said, that nothing gold can stay. The poetry of sensation types like John Donne and Robert Burns is filled with that theme, but probably no one expressed the fragility of life, caught the moment as it passed more immediately than John Keats, who himself died at twenty-five: "And joy, whose hand is ever at his lips / Bidding adieu; and aching Pleasure nigh, / Turning to poison as the bee mouth sips." One way of holding on to the reality of a past that is always "bidding adieu" is to preserve it in concrete ways; this is especially important for people who are reluctant to place much faith in the future, either. Sensation types, therefore, are prone to collect and save anything that can serve as a factual record of the past events of their lives: photos, notes, diaries, trophies, tapes. Richard Nixon's (self-destructive) proclivities in this regard are all too well known. The Johnson Library in Texas (with its exact replica of the Oval Office and its more than one million photographs of LBJ) is another example. Memorabilia of this kind are *concrete* evidence of one's prior experience, for unless captured in a concrete form, that past will slip away. In his book *Dandelion Wine,* sensation-type Ray Bradbury preserves each summer day in a bottle. Julius Caesar (SR) wrote his account of the Gallic War while he was fighting the Gallic War, a scribe sitting beside him in the chariot taking dictation.

With their profound awareness of the brevity and mutability of all created things, many sensation types think of time as an enemy to be combated by living life at its fullest, right on the edge of the peak. Since "plucking and withering are inseparable," Charles Lindbergh said he wanted to spend his life flying, for that way each moment was "crowded with beauty, pierced with danger." Seasonal reminders of time's passage, like birthdays, are consequently often depressing. They force the SR or SV to the perception—one natural to continuous types—that life is constantly moving through a continuum of time, and nothing can halt it, not marble nor the gilded monuments of men, not love, not intensity of experience. Time will ultimately be the victor, and its booty is death. Death thus holds a special fascination for most people of this type; Keats for one; Ingmar Bergman, the film director of *The Seventh Seal,* for another. Hemingway courted death, personally and vicariously, through wars, bull rings, big-game safaris, airplane crashes, and numerous other dangerous tests of courage, and finally married it with a suicide.

To those "half in love with easeful death," like Keats or Hemingway, making love may seem the paradigm of the life experience; completely absorbing, completely focused and immediate, the sex act is also soon ended. What may be the instant of fullest life is just that—an instant. A fragile moment. If one could only reach the edge of orgasm, where time is obliterated, and "Awake for ever in a sweet unrest, / Still, still to hear her tender-taken breath, / And so live ever," that, to Keats, would be perfection. But one cannot. The half-wished-for alternative is then "or else swoon to death."

Faced with the enemy of time and a need to intensify life, sensation types place a high value on variety; they seek for new experiences the way SR Louis Pasteur explored neighborhood junk piles for "hidden treasure." People like this want to be mobile. The wanderlust of Henry Stanley was shared not only by professional adventurers like SV Sir Francis Drake, who circumnavigated the globe and ranged the seas to capture Spanish gold for Queen Elizabeth but also by writers like Hemingway, or Walt Whitman, or Mark Twain (the river-boat pilot, soldier, prospector, foreign correspondent, world traveler). Charles Lindbergh, who estimated he had flown across the Atlantic hundreds of time since his original trip, is another obvious example of this propensity—as was Amelia Earhart. Variety means not simply change of scene but change of people and change of work. Cousteau has been a gunnery officer, an agent for the French resistance, a testdiver for minisubmarines, a deep-sea diver, the author of some half-dozen best sellers, a television director and producer, an underwater photographer, the designer of sea-floor labs, and the co-inventor of the Aqua-Lung. He said he originally chose a seaman's life because it was the "toughest" and would provide the most variety and excitement. So it has proved.

Given their discontinuity, it is easy for sensation types to assume that something new will be available; in fact, it may be desired because it is new. Since people of this type are not bound by the past, they find it less difficult than continuous types to ignore prior or conflicting situations, and since they are so totally absorbed in the present, they can actually forget the past. As a consequence, when they do make a long-term commitment to something, or someplace, or someone (and, of course, most people will at some point), their capacity to do so may surprise them, as Mark Antony—and everyone in Rome— was startled by his unshakable fascination with Cleopatra.

What the conceptual world is to thinking types, the physical world is to sensation types. They delight in it, and they learn from it. Out of their volcanic engagement with life comes this type's heightened sensory awareness and an appreciation of sensual pleasures unrivaled by persons with other leading functions. From Dickens's and Tolstoy's love of good food, good wine, foppish clothes, and beautiful surroundings, to the diverse physicality that crowds the poetry of Chaucer, Keats, Burns, Whitman, and Frost, there can be in SRs and SVs almost an envelopment of the self in the senses. Such people really enjoy physical comfort: a chair before a fire, a cool drink, a comfortable bed, a relaxing massage. And they usually like to perform physical tasks—tending a garden or mending a fence or cooking a meal or building a cabinet—chores often unappealing to intuitives who are less interested in working with their hands.

Sensation types perceive through their senses, not through their ideas or their emotional responses. They communicate through their senses, and in the last analysis they really trust only the evidence of their senses. Those who, as Keats said, "delight in sensation rather than hunger after truth," believe in what they have seen, heard, or felt; "axioms of philosophy are not axioms until they are proved upon our pulses." Robert Frost did not name his poems "Thoughts During an Air-Raid" or "And Death Shall Have No Dominion," but rather "Blueberries," "Birches," "The Wood-pile," "West-running Brook," "Mending Wall," and "The White-tailed Hornet." He is, of course, talking about general truths of life in these poems, but he is communicating those truths, as they were communicated to him, through engagement with particular objects in the physical world around him.

The ability to focus total sensory awareness on one immediate experience has produced from among members of these two psychetypes many of our eminent painters, including Renoir, Modigliani, and Picasso. Interestingly, the sensation-type scientists, Samuel Morse, Robert Fulton, and Louis Pasteur, also began careers in painting. For some people of their type, the most fully alive experience possible is one that totally involves them sensually. This tends to be more true of SVs than SRs. In the latter, aesthetic sensibility and sensuality may revolve simply around a desire to structure and organize their surroundings so that they will be both functional and pleasing. Introverted SRs, who don't require as much stimulus from the physical world, are even less apt to be swept off their goals by "hedonism" or sensual awe. It is unlikely that Henry Ford was ever made late to the factory by the beauty of a rose. And the perceptivity of this type about personal aesthetics, which includes the aesthetics of behavior, is prone to formalize itself into a code of proper dress and proper manners rather than the grace of a gesture or the charm of a dress.

In the sensation volcanic, aesthetic appreciation is less centered on structure and more involved with direct engagement in immediate experience. They are, consequently, more easily absorbed by any given particular of the sensate world—are, in a way, more broadly sensual. A territorial's relationship to his environment is generally not that close; his self-discipline and objectivity do not allow him to "let go," to sink into nature the way sensation volcanics can. He would rather control his environment than fuse with it. The difference in the two is exemplied by their attitudes toward sex.

Sexual prowess is a trait common to both SVs and SRs. For example, the male SR personality has found its way into popular culture, compressed and exaggerated into the myth of the man's man who is irresistible to women—cool, competent, fearless in action, self-assured, self-controlled, and sexually-charged. This is not only the male of popular historical romances and American detective fiction but one that Hemingway idealized. The kind of male popular in the movies: James Bond, Bullitt,

Hud, and the epitome of all sensation territorial myths, Rhett Butler. Never flustered, never weak, and probably never real. But the sexual magnetism of SRs Clark Gable and Humphrey Bogart *was* real, as is the appeal of their female counterpart, Marlene Dietrich (also an SR), equally cool, controlled, self-assured, and absolutely competent. So is the apparently time-less vitality of Elvis Presley. Of all the types, those with sensa-tion as their leading function are probably the most interested in sex. But for SRs, sex tends to be just that, sex; they differenti-ate its energy from other energy. When it's over, they go on to the next arena, outwitting Goldfinger or looking for the Maltese Falcon. Volcanics are less structured, less forcefully competi-tive, and have less need to insist on their distinctness. If sexual play between territorials (like Bogart and Bacall) is like an ag-gressive chess game, sexual play between volcanics (like James Cagney and Jean Harlow) is more like a pillow fight. The combi-nation of the two, at least fictionally, seems to be the most exciting of all—Rhett Butler (SR) and Scarlet O'Hara (SV) or Gable and Harlow in the steamingly erotic *Red Dust*.

For SVs, sexuality can become a pervasive sensuality that absorbs the whole personality. As Keats wrote to Fanny Brawne: "A few more moments thoughts of you would uncrys-tallize and dissolve me. You always concentrate my whole senses." SV Gandhi considered his overwhelming sexual desire for his wife dangerous; he blamed it for the death of their first child, and rather than let his appetite master him, he gave up sex entirely. SV Tolstoy reached the same conclusion, became celibate, and went about advising the rest of the world to do likewise. (His appeal met with little success.) From being a libertine and a gourmand, he became a chaste vegetarian. He gave up smoking as well and took to wearing peasant clothes. Visitors were escorted into the mansion by a butler to find the Count seated at a little bench making shoes. Only someone who felt the pull of sensuality intensely would need to go to such extremes to escape it. Disciplined territorials are better able to control those aspects of their discontinuity that interfere with the self-defined structures of their lives.

Tolstoy quit the university he was attending, where his grades were, in any case, extremely low. F. Scott Fitzgerald was thrown out of Princeton. William Faulkner and Robert Frost never finished college, either, and Hemingway chose never to go. The schooling of Benjamin Franklin and of Burns, Dickens, and Twain was even more haphazard. The point, naturally, is not that sensation types are unintelligent; rather, they *tend* to be uninterested in formal intellectual structures. In fact, discontinuity and volcanic physicality operate in such a major way in their personalities that many have a directly negative attitude toward thinking. Abstract thinking, that is. Hemingway somewhat viciously derided intellectuals as weak, cowardly "eggheads." Faulkner, another Nobel Prize winner, always insisted, "I'm just a farmer who sometimes writes stories." His remark may well be disingenuous, but the underlying attitude is typical.

Nor do sensation types trust abstractions; as scientists, they are empiricists. "The greatest aberration of the mind consists," said SR Louis Pasteur, "in believing a thing because it is desirable." To prove that altitude affects germs, he climbed the Alps; to understand electricity, Franklin (also an SR) flew a kite; to explore the moral and amoral impulses within a human being, SV Robert Lewis Stevenson gave us Dr. Jeckyll and Mr. Hyde. Similarly, such people do not like to generalize, and their references are almost always specific. Keats did not write to his sister, "As a boy, I loved fish and animals." He said, "How fond I used to be of Goldfinches, Tomtits, Minnows, Mice, Ticklebacks, Dace, Cock Salmon and the whole tribe of the Bushes and Brooks." Moreover, he confessed, "I haven't one Idea of the truth of any of my speculations—I shall never be a Reasoner because I care not to be in the right." In his view, and that of most sensation types, "Nothing in this world is proveable. . . . Probably every mental pursuit takes its reality and worth from the ardour of the pursuer, being in itself a nothing." We learn, he said, not by "law and precept," not by "irritable reaching after fact and reason" but by "sensation and watchfulness." He himself had "never yet been able to perceive how anything can be known for truth by consecutive reasoning." "O for a life of Sensations rather than of Thoughts."

Those who are reluctant to generalize, and who remember best what they have learned through their senses, may run into problems since they are often unwilling (or unable) to profit from knowledge gained out of past experiences. Instead, they must by trial and error learn everything new every time. Were it not for their great physical competence, sensation types probably would not survive as well as they do in the active lives they prefer to live because they are prone to refuse to be taught things, preferring to trust their instincts, or as Lindbergh said, to play it by ear. "Lucky Lindy" (so-called because he survived innumerable near-fatal accidents) was in a canoe for the first time when he took a solo trip down the Yellowstone River rapids and first flew a plane alone when he took off in the one he had just bought.

Intuitives rely on inspiration; sensation types trust to trial and error, to skill, and to chance. "Genius is 1 percent inspiration and 99 percent perspiration," claimed SR Thomas Edison, whose perspiration is reputed to have had the greatest cash value in history; at the time of his death, the money earned by the 1,098 patents he had taken out on his inventions was estimated at almost 26 billion dollars. Edison said he was lucky as well as perservering, and Alexander Fleming (another SR), in his Nobel Prize speech, called his discovery of penicillin "a triumph of accident, a fortunate occurrence which happened while I was working on a purely academic bacteriological problem."

To some degree, distrusting abstractions makes sensation types distrust language itself. Words can change their meaning, can be manipulated to do so, or so these psychetypes assume. Thus, they prefer to base their actions on facts, on data, on deeds. In their experiential world, the purpose of knowledge is to provide a basis for action. "Why this routine repetition of abstract rules?" a young sensation type may ask about classwork. "What's it *for?*" Facts, on the other hand, matter absolutely, because if your facts are wrong, your actions will be wrong. "Your experiment works, or it doesn't," Lindbergh bluntly summarized. "Every aviator knows that if mechanics are inaccurate, aircraft crash."

"The fact is the sweetest dream that labor knows," wrote Robert Frost, who despite his profession once remarked:

Sometimes I have my doubts of words altogether, and I ask myself what is the place of them? They are worse than nothing unless they do something, unless they amount to deeds, as in ultimatums and war cries. They must be flat and final like the show-down in poker from which there is no appeal. My definition of literature would be just this: words that have become deeds.

One way to keep language accurate is to put all your verbal cards on the table—to call a spade a spade. However, for all their touted preference for verbal directness, at least a few sensation types have been known to keep a couple of their cards up their sleeves. "A diplomat's word," commented Stalin cynically, "must have no relation to action. Good words are a mask for the concealment of bad deeds. 'Sincere diplomacy' is no more possible than 'dry water' or 'iron wood.'" He knew that; he also did it.

Abstract principles of behavior are not easily internalized by those who distrust any sort of generalization. And so, sensation types are less likely to be motivated by logic or plans than by powerful desires. Such individuals do not really operate out of any ethical theory or a system of moral values in the way thinking and feeling types do; their morality is, instead, "situational." Feeling types rarely revise their moral positions and then usually do so under duress and with considerable internal struggle, even anguish. But what sensation types consider "right" depends very much on the specific circumstances of a given situation. What is right changes as events change. They feel no obligation to adhere to a moral edict deriving from a past situation nor a willingness to impose it on the present. That, in fact, they would consider "wrong." The new circumstance inevitably differs from all previous ones, and such a rigid approach would lead to inappropriate judgments. Now, since civilized lives are fairly circumscribed and consistent, a sensation type may seem to be applying an ethical system not unlike that of a thinking type. But experientially he or she is making individual decisions about specific occurrences. It is not that SV Scarlet O'Hara considered it right to cheat and shoot people; she considered it right to cheat and shoot the particular Yankees who were invading her world. A sensation type might turn over to the police a wanted man he found intruding on his territory but might lie to harbor a friend from justice or to protect even a stranger who had asked for his help. He would not, on principle, turn in a lawbreaker, friend or stranger, as a thinking type might. Thus, what one does when one is poor and hungry will be different from what one would do wealthy and well fed. "Prosperity" wrote SR Mark Twain, "is a great protector of principle." Nor are prospects of eternity likely to have much effect on such people. Living as they do in the physical present, SRs and SVs have little of the aethereal's impulse to "shuffle off this mortal coil" and become pure spirit. What was to the intuitive Hamlet "too too solid flesh," the living body, is the center of their experiential world. Roman emperors were considered deities, but the SR emperor Vespasian did not believe it for an instant. Dying, he joked, "Well, I think I am about to become immortal," and Julius Caesar was no more serious about his own godhead.

For sensation types, "Death is the great divorcer for ever." So synonymous do they consider the life of the body and life itself that if the body goes wrong, nothing will seem right. As Cousteau said, "When the body is functioning well, the most simply physical acts can give you the greatest pleasure. But if the body is not well, it's impossible for you to be happy. Just a little headache, a small pain, and your whole being is off balance." Hemingway's body, aged and ill, would no longer perform for him with the superb resiliency and skill it once had. Its weakening was, to the novelist, too insupportable a loss to be borne.

Sensation types place tremendous faith in their bodies' competence. They constantly want to learn and perfect new physical skills; sports appeal to them particularly, and their athletic abilities are likely to be considerable—not simply those of professionals like Jack Dempsey, Joe DiMaggio, Joe Namath, or Chris Evert but those of people whose professions are completely unrelated to physical abilities. Sir Alexander Fleming was an outstanding athlete. Benjamin Franklin, whom we tend to think of as sitting by his stove with his bifocals on, once swam the Thames River from Chelsea to Blackfriars, "performing on the way," he said, "many feats of activity both upon and under water that surprised those to whom they were novelties." In fact, he even set up a swimming school in London to supplement his income.

Tolstoy (who deeply lamented his small size) spent his young manhood regaling companions with such feats as simultaneously lifting two men off the floor. Keats was only five feet tall, but his "fine flow of animal spirits" was such that his friends might have been less surprised had he become a boxer than a poet: "He would fight anyone, morning, noon, and night. It was meat and drink to him." Robert Kennedy's mountain climbing, Lyndon Johnson's deer hunting, and the equestrian skills of Jacqueline Onassis all derived from these three SVs' strong sense of their bodies' competence to meet and master physical challenges.

This delight in body skills includes not simply athletics but any manual tasks. It is interesting that three sensation-type writers should enter that profession though its *physical* manifestation: Franklin, Twain, and Walt Whitman were all printers' apprentices. They first learned how to set type; they went on to create the words that others would set into print. Generally, SRs and SVs tend to be successful at solving technological problems (as Morse, Pasteur, and Edison indicate), to be good at the domestic arts, good in surgical branches of medicine—at any work, in fact, that requires observation and dexterity. This does not mean that anyone who cannot fix a Ferrari engine with a hairpin or make a banquet out of leftover hash and potato peels is no sensation type. As always, individuals choose to develop certain traits that lie within the potential of their psychetypes to the exclusion of others. Obviously, Stalin and Picasso or Gandhi and Jack Dempsey did not live their lives in the same way.

The optimism based on their sense of physical competence gives many sensation types a kind of courage that earns them reputations for fearlessness. Stalin became a hero when forced in prison to "run the gauntlet"—that is, to rush through two lines of soldiers who would beat him with their rifle butts. He refused to run, but walked slowly and unflinchingly to the end of the line, blood pouring from his head. He had given himself the name "Stalin"—steel—and apparently he deserved it.

Though Hemingway has been accused of having an air of "fake hair on the chest," it should be remembered, as one of many possible examples of his courage, that while serving as an ambulance driver in World War I, he carried an unconscious comrade to safety after he himself had been wounded, and during which rescue he received 273 fragments of machine gun fire in his leg. Sometimes, with Hemingway, and particularly with young sensation types, fearlessness in the face of any obstacle turns into precipitous acts of bravado, feats of daring, and flamboyant heroics of the sort that made Twain remember himself as a "swaggering boy," or that led the young Julius Ceasar to tell the pirates who had kidnaped him that he was worth more ransom money than they were asking and to order them about while in captivity, assuring them that someday he would come back and have them all executed—which he did. This is a type of "I can dive off a higher cliff than you" or "I can jump my motorcycle over more cars than you" cockiness. "Why shouldn't I fly from New York to Paris? I'm almost twenty-five," wonders Lindbergh and does so. "Why shouldn't I hit the fans a homerun in the World Series exactly where I'm pointing my bat?" Babe Ruth asks himself, and hits it.

Another aspect of this type's confidence in physical agility is their concern with efficiency, whether it be to build a bridge across the Rhine in ten days, as Caesar did, or to vacuum a room in ten minutes. No one has demonstrated this trait on a more successful scale than SR Henry Ford, inventor of the industrial assembly line, whereby through precise standardization of parts, organized specialization of workers, and continuous-motion quantity manufacturing, Ford was able to put a "Tin Lizzie" within the price range of most Americans. Like Ford, all sensation types usually have very specific notions of how to go about performing a physical task. To watch someone dreamily and sloppily pack, unpack, and repack the trunk of a car is apt to drive an SR or SV mad with frustration. They need to act, and act quickly. One way of ensuring their ability to do so is by having their own assembly-line efficiency procedures; another is by being prepared for any eventuality. "Chance favors only the mind which is prepared," wrote Pasteur of his scientific successes. This is different from thinking-type "planning ahead." A TR going on a trip might sit down and carefully decide what she should take with her; an SR would at the last minute pack everything she could possibly need, as Stanley did when he went into Africa: He had more supplies, more ammunition, more offerings for the natives, more of everything than any previous explorer in that area; he even brought a dismantled boat, the *Lady Alice,* which enabled him to circumnavigate the great lakes at the Nile source. Confidence comes not from plans and theories but from always being poised for action and, as Bogart said, "from knowing the ropes."

If their territoriality offers sensation types a great sense of competence with their physical environment, their volcanic involvement puts them into a very close relationship with it. Many people of these psychetypes are conservationists, like Lindbergh; others, particularly those who are introverted, become forest rangers, ranchers, cowboys, or sailors. Camping, fishing, and hunting can be favorite pastimes. Their closeness to the natural world also gives them tremendous respect for its powers. Just as, despite their bravado, the well-being of their bodies means too much to SRs and SVs for them to jeopardize it recklessly, so their reverent awe before the extrapersonal forces of nature prohibits them from being foolhardy. "To appreciate fully," Lindbergh wrote, "you must have intercourse with the elements themselves, know their whims, their beauties and their dangers. Then every tissue of your being sees and feels, then body, mind, and spirit are one." Sensation types will take risks (Lindbergh was, after all, a stunt flyer who would dive his plane under bridges, stand on his head on its wings, or land it in the middle of town squares), but they will not endanger themselves by disregarding or violating the forces of nature. They are careful to adjudicate what is possible and what would be disastrous.

In addition, they have excellent tolerance for physical discomfort. This is one reason why men like Caesar or Cromwell or Andrew Jackson were so loved by their soldiers; it was said that Mark Antony would go for days on campaigns without food or sleep and could drink the urine of horses. However, as we have mentioned, sensation types are far too much "into" their bodies not to dislike having to be uncomfortable. In order to avoid that, a sensation type on a camping trip, for instance, will make use of whatever natural resources come to hand in order to create a pleasing physical environment. He or she will observe the best spot to pitch a tent, will stack leaves under the sleeping bags, arrange a neat circle of stones around a fire, use a hat to gather blueberries along the way. If this person happens on an unexpected lake, having brought no fishing equipment along (which is unlikely), he will make a rod and line from a branch, an unraveled string, and a ball-point pen clip. Robinson Crusoe is the fictional paradigm of this aspect of sensation typology.

Next to their focus on the present and their physicality, the third area of importance to sensation types is being self-sufficient. They want to be able to do things without relying on other people; for one thing, they have difficulty trusting in the abilities of others, or in the accuracy of anything they have not personally observed. Seeing is believing. Even after he achieved eminence in his late years and therefore had the means to delegate responsibilities, Pasteur went himself into slaughterhouses to inoculate sheep for anthrax, sucked out, himself, the foam from the mouths of rabid dogs in order to prepare a serum, then sat beside his patient all night to be sure his treatment was working.

One way to be self-sufficient is to be orderly. Naturally, this comes easier to SRs, who know what they want, than to SVs, who are more apt to know what they *don't* want and to lack the objectivity to pull themselves out of such negative emotions. Order demands precision of the sort that Lindbergh insisted on when preparing for his solo trip across the Atlantic Ocean. Nothing inessential was to be taken along, nothing wasted, and no detail too small to be ignored. Unneeded areas of his navigation charts and extra pages of his log book were cut out. The heavy soles of his aviator boots were removed and thin ones substituted. He took no night-flying equipment, no gas-tank gauges, no sextant, no radio, no parachute. What mattered most was gas—earlier pilots had crashed because they had run out of fuel. So whatever he didn't absolutely require was sacrificed for the precious amount of extra gasoline he knew he needed. Only gas could get him to Paris. To eat during the thirty-three hours, he took five sandwiches and one quart of water: "If I get to Paris, I won't need anymore, and if I don't get to Paris, I won't need anymore, either."

Because of their insistence on precision and efficiency, and their impatience with slowness, sensation types are prone to be rather bossy. They like to be directors, to take charge and give orders so that they can "get the thing done." Nagging people and being fussy about details are two resulting traits likely to irritate others. But SRs and SVs believe it important to have exactly the right tool for the right job: the right cooking spice, the right airplane, the right power saw. Since they enjoy working with their hands so much, they want their instruments to be as accurate as possible. "It has ever been a pleasure for me," Franklin commented, "to see good workmen handle their tools, and it has been useful to me, having learnt so much by it as to be able to do little jobs myself in my house, and to construct little machines for my experiments." Their refusal to tolerate substitution extends to likes and dislikes as well. A five-year-old SR may be perfectly content to sit for hours painting with water colors, but if she asks for water colors and is given pastels instead, she may stubbornly refuse to use them, especially if she has never used them before.

When sensation types, who have been trained in our thinking-type culture, start being directive, they will probably talk about their "plans." Experientially, however, such people do not make plans in the way TRs and TAs do. Plans include steps and details deployed in time, one event following another in logical sequence. To decide beforehand what ideas or actions should be imposed on future situations is completely antagonistic both to the sensation type's sense of reality and to his or her values. What they do instead is sketch in an outline of what they'd like to see happen; for the rest, they wait upon events to decide. We may call these tactics "battle plans," and, in fact, they rather resemble the sketchy strategies laid out by generals such as SR Erwin Rommel. Under "RESULTS" in Lindbergh's "plan of action" for his transatlantic crossing there were only two entries: "1. Successful completion, winning $25,000 prize. 2. Complete failure."

In order to succeed without planning, sensation types rely

on their ability to act swiftly, on the kind of immediate recognition of necessity that distinguished Caesar's military genius or Lyndon Johnson's political maneuvering, and on a capacity to work with great speed and economy of effort. Such people not only act quickly, they act in the most expedient way possible. The best method is one that works. The best code is the one that can be effectively (and rapidly) put into practice; the best ideas are those that are useful. SRs and SVs are extremely practical people. After being told that his first patent was too innovative to succeed on the market, Thomas Edison never again invented anything that was not imminently salable. Often expediency applies to ideals and moral considerations as well. Principles must bend before facts. When a popular preacher in Philadelphia was fired because he had plagiarized his sermons, Benjamin Franklin was the only parishioner to stick by him: "I rather approved his giving us good sermons composed by others than bad ones of his own manufacture." With regard to pacifism, he noted: "Common sense, aided by present danger, will sometimes be too strong for whimsical opinions." Deism, "though it might be true, was not very useful." Franklin said he once "conceived the bold and arduous project of arriving at moral perfection." He made a little book with seven columns for the days and thirteen lines for the virtues; the idea was to check off each moral slip, gradually correcting them until he produced a clean sheet. However, he soon abandoned the idea, deciding that his achievement "if it were known, would make me ridiculous; that perfect character might be attended with the inconvenience of being envied and hated; and that a benevolent man should allow a few faults in himself to keep his friends in countenance." As with most sensation types, it is difficult to determine how much Franklin is engaging here in what Robert Frost called "my kind of fooling." But we need only recall the actions of a Henry VIII or a Bismarck to realize how expedient a few sensation types are willing to be.

As they demand order, so sensation types insist on control; control of themselves, primarily; control of others, if need be. Since control is a territorial characteristic, sensation volcanics naturally have more trouble maintaining their objectivity at all times. Keats had "fits of violent passion" on some occasions and "would freeze into reticence before calamity" on others. Participating as they do in the feeling function, SVs (like Lyndon B. Johnson or Robert F. Kennedy) are far more volatile, personal, and warmly expressive than SRs like Lindbergh, whose self-control never broke once throughout the tragedy of his son's kidnaping and murder nor the relentless invasion of his privacy that followed.

Sensation types (and particularly SRs) are the most controlled and the most private of all types. "An enigma wrapped in a mystery," Churchill called Stalin. Such people have an absolute horror of intrusion into their personal affairs. The private lives of William Faulkner or Marlene Dietrich are just that —private. One suspects that Garbo may be an introverted SR, precisely because it is impossible to know what type she is. The unrevealed love affairs of Benjamin Franklin and Charles Dickens, the disarming pose of Mark Twain, the gates around Picasso's villa, the security measures of Henry Ford, the Presidency of Richard Nixon, all are evidence of this impulse toward secretiveness. One way to maintain privacy is never to lose control; self-revelatory urges are therefore suppressed, while the revelations offered by others may be bothersome, even distasteful, as FO van Gogh's emotionality was to SR Gauguin. Losing control they consider a "weakness," as failing to act when you know you should act is a weakness; and to be weak in these ways— "to lose one's cool"—is intolerable.

Another way to stay in control is to stay independent, to be like Robert Frost's "Lone Striker." All sensation types have a strong "don't fence me in" attitude toward life, one that includes both people and places. Bogart loved the sea because it was "the last free place on earth." The Lone Eagle, Lindbergh loved to fly because it made him "independent of the world" with its millions of people cooped up in strips of brick and concrete. "Why return to that moss? Why submerge myself in brick-walled human problems?" Faulkner and Hemingway loved to hunt because in the forests of Mississippi or mountains of Africa there was a little wilderness left to them, indomitable and incorruptible, solitary and free. Limitations on their freedom frustrate sensation types; the intrusions of other people's wills on their lives enrage them. Lauren Bacall said that the way she persuaded Humphrey Bogart to stop drinking was never to nag him which he found distasteful; instead, she simply ignored him, which sensation types cannot bear.

People of this typology may have a rather vague sense of the past, but there is one thing they vividly remember, and that is anything, or anyone, that ever threatened them. Dickens's father was imprisoned for debt, and the boy was forced to work in a factory for a year. Afterward, even when he had to work at four jobs simultaneously, he never allowed what had happened to his father to happen to him. Cicero once wrote a series of pamphlets making fun of SV Mark Antony. Years later, when Antony seized control of Rome, he had the orator's head chopped off and his tongue and hands nailed up in the Forum. There is nothing worse you can do to a sensation type than to humiliate him. That he will never forgive. Mozart was once impatiently kicked by a count; it made him physically ill for days. He never forgot it.

To defend his or her own individuality, the people of these two psychetypes will go to considerable lengths. They will do the same for those who "belong" to them. Anyone indiscreet enough to say a dishonorable word about Andrew Jackson's wife Rachel found himself in a duel with "Old Hickory." If they are apt to take revenge on those who threaten them, sensation types are also deeply loyal to and appreciative of those who meet their needs. Lindbergh named "The Spirit of St. Louis" after the town whose citizens had given him financial support. Warren G. Harding, in a less happy example, gave cabinet posts to some of the friends who had helped him into the Presidency; those friends subsequently gave national oil deposits at Teapot Dome to private businesses. Harding's volcanic loyalty to men who abused his trust destroyed him publicly and distressed him personally: "I can handle my enemies; it's my friends that keep me up walking all night."

Sensation types also derive a great deal of self-confidence from their control. It can be expressed in a kind of affable cockiness (like that of Joe Namath or Burt Reynolds) or in an unyielding determination never to quit until a total victory is won. "When the going gets tough, the tough get going." Control and will, of course, may be used to good ends or bad. Stalin used it to enslave Russia; Gandhi used it to free India. It had been another SV, Tolstoy, who—responding to Gandhi's letter praising his book, *The Kingdom of God Is Within You*—had given him the term "passive resistance." But Gandhi explained that there was nothing passive about that teaching of love. The tactic, *satyagrada,* which he used to free his country from British domination, was an active force, the force of the soul. Those who are passive, he said, may break under pressure. Gandhi was fighting with all the skills and strengths of his typology; nothing could more dramatically illustrate the unmovable self-control of a sensation type than that small, frail man sitting quietly on a railroad track as a train roared toward him, or continuing a "fast unto death" until his demands were met. But Gandhi was fighting for peace with the power of the human soul and not the power of tanks. He won.

Another way sensation types maintain control is to accept the need for social restrictions. Here we come across what may appear to be a typological contradiction. Why should those with so strong an impulse to free themselves from all restrictions so frequently be the ones to adhere most fervently to "law and order"? However, it is precisely because they tend not to internalize ethical systems that they rely more heavily than other types on external ones. For some assume that unless codes of conduct are imposed from the outside, they and everyone else may feel free to act out their aggressive impulses, and all chaos will break loose, trampling civilization. "If the desire to kill and the opportunity to kill came always together, who," wondered Mark Twain, "would ever escape hanging?" Thus, by understanding social rules, by accepting some restrictions, and by staying in control, sensation types feel that they are ensuring their own freedom. As a result of this typological compensation, they may, despite their discontinuity, grow to be quite conservative and resistant to innovations. Back to the "good old days," said Twain and Frost and Faulkner. Henry Ford went so far as to collect handicrafts of older, better times, to build replicas of an old red-brick schoolhouse and Longfellow's Wayside Inn, and finally an entire town recreated just as it had been when he was a boy—no electricity, no telephones, and no cars.

Being territorial, people of these two psychetypes both

understand how social structures work and respect them deeply. "Caesar's wife must be above suspicion." Being volcanic, they are highly sensitive to other people. The combination has two results. First, status matters enormously to sensation types. F. Scott Fitzgerald, for example, resented bitterly "being a poor boy in a rich boy's school" and confessed to his mother that he volunteered in World War I "coldbloodedly and purely for social reasons." Fascination with the rich and therefore powerful is the perennial theme of his writings: "The rich are very different from you and me." Hemingway said that was a stupid remark, but Hemingway simply cared about a different area of status: He carried around with him always a Presidential citation he had received for wartime services. The second result is that sensation types are probably the most unfailingly polite of all the types. They place a very high value on good manners, respect for elders, proper social behavior, and sensitivity to protocol. Lindbergh and Bogart were considered old-fashioned "gentlemen." Their chivalry was a modern version of that Renaissance emblem of courtesy, SR Sir Philip Sidney, warrior, poet, and courtier, who, mortally wounded on a battlefield, gave his only water to a dying peasant soldier, saying, "Have this. Thy need is greater than mine."

Many sensation types want to bond with a group, join with others who share their activities or social roles. They like team sports and teamwork in formal structures such as clubs, fraternities and sororities, military services, company organizations, and political parties. When referring to past events in their lives, such people may use the indefinite corporate "we" rather than "I." "We always wore gray loafers in high school." "When we were in Korea . . ." Baron von Richthofen's immediate group was his fellow German fliers, his "Flying Circus," as they were called; his larger group included Allied fliers as well; that is why, having shot down a British pilot, he flew into enemy range in order to drop flowers in tribute over the grave of a valiant adversary.

Because they like to control situations, sensation types are capable of being manipulative both in interpersonal relations and in broader power situations. Perhaps the most evil instance of this characteristic in literature is the SR Iago, who manipulates Othello into murdering his wife—and does it out of what Coleridge called "motiveless malignity." Some members of this type may find it difficult to restrain themselves from manipulating those whom they consider "weak," and whom they therefore do not respect. It can, of course, just be a harmless desire to stir things up, as Bogart liked to do at parties, in order to "get some action started" and have a good time; on the other hand, it can be the sort of Machiavellian intrigues in which, according to Trotsky, Stalin involved others: "tying a man to him not by winning his admiration but by forcing him into complicity in heinous and unforgivable crimes." People of all the types may try to manipulate others; oceanics, for example, do it by being so passive that someone else ends up taking charge of their lives for them. The way sensation types tend to do it is the way SR Mark Twain has Tom Sawyer trick all his friends into whitewashing his fence. He makes them think they *want* to do it. Benjamin Franklin said he dropped direct argumentation in debates and adopted an air of "modest diffidence" instead.

> *I found this method safest for myself and very embarrassing for those against whom I used it. Therefore I took delight in it, practised it continually, and grew very artful and expert in drawing people, even of superior knowledge, into concessions the consequences of which they did not foresee, entangling them in difficulties out of which they could not extricate themselves, and so obtaining victories neither myself nor my cause always deserved.*

Because they are discontinuous, sensation types want life to be a series of peak experiences; manipulating people is one way to achieve that. Because they are volcanic, they want those experiences to be active ones. No one is more action-oriented than these two psychetypes. *Veni, vidi, vici.* I came, I saw, I conquered. That is how they want life to be. Whether busting trusts, charging up San Juan Hill, or shooting elephants, Teddy Roosevelt was always in action. For such people, not to be able to act, or to have to delay acting, is extremely difficult. If they cannot assertively take charge of situations, they are at a loss. When Louis Pasteur's son was reported missing in action during the War of 1870, the old scientist just started walking, located the battle site, and searched among the three hundred survivors of a troop of twelve hundred men until he discovered his son, nursed him, and brought him home. When the seventy-eight-year-old Queen Eleanor of Aquitaine heard that her son King John was in trouble, she got on a horse and rode a thousand miles in the heat of summer to rescue him.

Crises bring out the best in sensation types, and they tend to evaluate themselves on the basis of how quickly and courageously they can respond to a crisis. That is why they have received so many medals for military valor, some of them awarded posthumously. That is why so many are courtroom lawyers, like F. Lee Bailey, or surgeons, or politicians. These fields call for an ability to respond directly, to meet challenges, and to act swiftly; they also require immediate solutions, which is much more appealing to people of this type than any kind of suspended or prolonged problem. So they love crises not only because they are exhilarating peak experiences that call for bold and decisive action, but because they are over quickly, leaving one free to move on to the next event. SRs and SVs are at their worst when they are forced into a position in which they cannot take direct action. Sometimes, in such situations, they will deliberately turn things into a crisis so that they *can* move. Bogart seemed to enjoy pushing relationships like that with his boss, Jack Warner, to a breaking point; having endangered an acquaintanceship and created a crisis, he would then take steps to smooth things over. Nunnally Johnson called it Bogie's social brinksmanship; Bogart called it the art of coming close to calamity.

Like Bogart, many sensation types view life as a game. Some, like him, wish to play the game gracefully, with wit and style. Some, like Bismarck, prefer "blood and iron." But fortunately the latter are in the minority.For the most part, individuals of this type are congenial, fun-loving people. They enjoy playing games devised by others, they like practical jokes. Even the stern Bismarck was called the "mad Junker," and once let a fox loose in a formal drawing-room party. Benjamin Franklin was always putting hoaxes in his newspapers and, on one occasion sent into the scientific Royal Society a proposal for making flatus aromatic so that breaking wind in public would perfume the air. Sensation types also enjoy playing roles and taking on different ones to fit different social functions or occasions. For the same reason (and because it is a physical emblem of bonding) they love uniforms. Picasso, who saw himself as something of an adventurer as well as a ladies man and a painter of genius, sported a Browning automatic in the streets of bohemian Paris. Keats and Whitman dressed the way they thought poets ought to dress, just as a sensation-type girl at a dance will be dressed exactly as she *should* be dressed for that event.

In this connection, we might stop to consider for a moment why there seem to be relatively fewer sensation type women who have come to historical prominence than women of other types. One would think that women so active, competitive, and pragmatic would have achieved higher status in greater numbers. However, the typological concern for the importance of roles tends to make SR women accept the legitimacy of society's traditional definition of their domestic "place," and the volcanic engagement of the SV makes motherhood and family more enduringly attractive to her than to her thinking or intuitive counterparts. Marlene Dietrich resisted the blandishments of Hollywood, sincerely preferring to stay in Germany and mother her new daughter, until her old friend von Sternberg arrived, requesting that she join with him in a new project.

Living as they do so fully in the present, these people need some method of incorporating the separate moments of their lives. One way that they do this is by mythologizing experience. When individual events and attitudes are seen as part of a myth, they gain tremendously in power, become transpersonal, and serve to mitigate discontinuity. Heroism in war is one very powerful myth to them. Dietrich, whom Hemingway always called "the champ," received the American Medal of Freedom and the French Legion of Honor for her bravery "in support of military operations in North Africa, Sicily and Italy" as well as in England, France, Belgium, Czechoslovakia, Labrador, Greenland—in all of which she had entertained allied combat troops on the front line. Such myths serve the same purpose for sensation types that visions serve for intuitives, or theories for thinking types, or emotional commitments for feeling types. Stories of their pasts as told by Bogart or Lyndon B. Johnson may not have always been literally true; they were, however, mythically true—true to the felt memory. Charles Dickens's mythic truth about his boyhood's misery became, through the magic of his art, *Oliver Twist* and *David Copperfield.*

There are other aspects to this tendency to mythologize. Sensation types are very susceptible to magic. Poetry is written, said Keats, with "the magic hand of chance." Their interest in conjuring and magicians gives many a facility with "sorcery," from medieval alchemy to modern card tricks. They love mysteries and may be superstitious. There are, they believe, forces and powers in life that express themselves in certain signs and synchronicities. Mark Twain was born on the day Halley's comet appeared; desperately ill, he held on to life until he could go out with it when it returned seventy-five years later. The comet was in the sky again the night he died. People of this type have a feeling that if you wait for the inner moment, some signal to begin an act will be given you. "It's less a decision of logic than of feeling," Lindbergh said of his faith that his immensely overweighted plane would clear ground obstacles. "Something within you disengages itself from your body and travels ahead. . . . Sitting in the cockpit, the conviction surges through me that the wheels *will* leave the ground, that the wings *will* rise above the wires, that it is time to start the flight." When he took off in *The Spirit of St. Louis,* he let his wheels touch ground once more, "lightly, a last bow to earth, a gesture of humility before it." Sensation types are so closely tuned to physical things that they actually sense a communication with them. Lindbergh's biography bears his plane's name, for his plane was his partner: "From now on, the explosion of the engine will be inseparable from the beat of my heart. As I trust one, I'll trust the other." For this reason, many SRs and SVs keep with them totem objects that symbolize their territory when they are away from it; for Keats this object was a small picture of Shakespeare that had been in his room when, on Shakespeare's birthday, he began his first major poem.

It was Keats who gave the most fitting term to the last major rubric of sensation-type traits. The term is "negative capability," and the poet meant by it an ability to empathetically respond to whatever is outside oneself; Keats loved

Shakespeare because (unlike Wordsworth's "egotistical sublime" way of expressing his own feeling) Shakespeare never gives us himself; he gives us instead Hamlet and Lear and Falstaff and Juliet. Most sensation types have this kind of ability to negate the self and become their surroundings, to be "there" wherever they are. "Most people," said Hemingway, "don't know how to listen." He did, and that was a great part of his charm.

SRs and SVs are the most *reactive* of the types; they require the most stimulus because they need things to react to, bounce off, respond to. Similarly, they need immediate impact from others in order to know whether they have gotten through and to sense how others are responding to them. It was not enough for Dickens and Twain to write books. Both went on the stage and read their books aloud so they could *see* the faces and *hear* their listeners' laughter or fright or tears. Sensation types define themselves as the result of their experiences, and the pleasure they take in those experiences is greatly intensified by the participation of other people.

That "thereness" is why people of this type can be so extraordinarily magnetic. Intuitives throw the self out at others; that is charisma. Sensation types draw others into them; that is magnetism. Like mirrors, they reflect back to those around them a heightened sense of their own beauty or intelligence or charm. No one ever had so many friends as John Keats or the "Good Count" Tolstoy; few politicians have ever been so warmly embraced by such different kinds of people as Robert F. Kennedy or Andrew Jackson. No man ever gained an entire nation its freedom without a war except Gandhi.

Sensation types do not usually think of themselves as carving with their deeds statues in the halls of history. Dying at twenty-five in a small room in a foreign land, John Keats, who knew that he would not live to marry the woman he so passionately loved, nor to write the poems that he knew were within him, gave his last words to try to comfort and protect a distraught friend terrified by the young poet's suffering. "Now you must be firm for it will not last long—I shall die easy. Don't be frightened." On his tombstone the poet asked that they carve the words: "Here lies one whose name was writ in water." He was wrong. The name of John Keats is written in the marble of poetry, as eternal as his Grecian urn because it is as alive as his nightingale. When the phenomenal world is sensed that intensely, as through a burning glass, it takes fire and transcends its own particularity, becoming universal. That's how close Keats was to sheaves of autumn wheat; that's how close Charles Lindbergh, setting out in his small silver plane to cross the Atlantic alone, felt to the sea, down toward whose waves he dived, to tip his wings once in homage and supplication.

SENSATION TYPES

Mark Antony, SV	Julius Caesar, SR
Geoffrey Chaucer, SV	Emperor Vespasian, SR
Sir Francis Drake, SV	Eleanor of Aquitane, SR
Robert Burns, SV	Henry VIII, SR
John Keats, SV	Sir Philip Sidney, SR
Walt Whitman, SV	John Donne, SR
Leo Tolstoy, SV	Thomas Hobbes, SR
Robert Louis Stevenson, SV	Oliver Cromwell, SR
Andrew Jackson, SV	Wolfgang Mozart, SR
Warren G. Harding, SV	Benjamin Franklin, SR
Teddy Roosevelt, SV	Mark Twain, SR
Auguste Renoir, SV	Sir Henry Stanley, SR
Amedeo Modigliani, SV	Louis Pasteur, SR
F. Scott Fitzgerald, SV	Gauguin, SR
Jean Harlow, SV	Sir Alexander Fleming, SR
Ernest Hemingway, SV	Thomas Edison, SR
Babe Ruth, SV	Charles Dickens, SR
Jack Dempsey, SV	Otto von Bismarck, SR
Benito Mussolini, SV	Henry Ford, SR
James Cagney, SV	Baron von Richthofen, SR
Mohandas Gandhi, SV	Charles Lindbergh, SR
Lyndon B. Johnson, SV	Pablo Picasso, SR
Robert Frost, SV	Joseph Stalin, SR
Robert F. Kennedy, SV	William Faulkner, SR
Joe Namath, SV	Amelia Earhart, SR
Jacqueline Onassis, SV	Humphrey Bogart, SR
Burt Reynolds, SV	Marlene Dietrich, SR
F. Lee Bailey, SV	Jacques Cousteau, SR
	Richard Nixon, SR
	Chris Evert, SR
	Elvis Presley, SR

The Intuitive

"I intend to be the greatest architect that ever lived."
—FRANK LLOYD WRIGHT, IA,
BEGINNING HIS CAREER

"I want the whole world to see my body."
—MARILYN MONROE, IO,
BEGINNING HER CAREER

"It was only on the evening after Lodi that I realized I was a superior being. I was only twenty-six, but I foresaw what I might become. It was as if I were being lifted up into the air, and the world were dissolving beneath my feet!"
—NAPOLEON BONAPARTE, IA,
BEGINNING HIS CAREER

"Today Germany! Tomorrow the World!"
—ADOLPH HITLER, IO,
BEGINNING HIS CAREER

In the world of intuition there are only four things that deeply matter: the future, the vision, the imagination, and charisma. Intuitives are people who wish, through the creative power of their imagination and the effective power of their charisma, to bring a vision into being that will alter the future. "I am destined to change the face of the world; at any rate that is my belief." Few intuitives have visions as grandiose as Napoleon's, and few succeed so remarkably in bridging the chasm of a resistant world that lies between vision and reality. But the happiness of all intuitives depends on their ability to do just that.

If for sensation types tomorrow never comes, for intuitives tomorrow never ends. SVs and SRs say they are too busy living for today to worry about the future. IAs and IOs can't be bothered with today at all; they are too busy dreaming about next week, next year, a thousand years, unending eternities of infinite time. "You're dying from overwork, you have no life of your own," Napoleon's mother told him. "You live only for posterity." "Well," he replied, "do you call that dying?" Napoleon lived, it was said, for what people would think of him "ten centuries hence." All intuitives would like the opportunity to do so. "These are not for you," said Beethoven to a musician who claimed his compositions were unplayable. "These are for a later age."

Those who are discontinuous disregard the past; those who are aethereal concern themselves with open-ended possibilities; those who are oceanic recognize no boundaries of space or time. Because the combination of these three perceptual sets produces intuition, it should scarcely be surprising that intuitives experience the boundless future as more intensely real than the present, so real that it seems to *be* the present. When the beginning and completely unknown composer Beethoven told a shocked publisher that he expected to receive the same financial terms as Goethe and Handel, clearly he already considered himself the equal of the two leading artists in Europe. When the fictional Mr. Macawber tells David Copperfield that something is bound to "turn up in coal," he is immediately, in his own mind, an enormously successful coal merchant, and so cheered is he by this belief that the bill collectors yelling threats outside his door trouble him not at all.

Depending on their perspective, other types may find such attitudes amusing, misguided, stupid, insane, or inspiring. But the intuitive is neither rationalizing nor is he or she being facetious. Whatever is possible *is real*. The future cannot come fast enough for them, so they attempt to draw it into the present. Cecil Rhodes had already given Africa to the British before he even set foot on the continent. James Joyce considered himself the equal of Ibsen before he had written a book. Marilyn Monroe was a movie star when still a struggling contract player. Anyone managing to get through *Mein Kampf* would have realized that Hitler was already conquering the world while still sitting in a German prison. Intuitives are always prophesying; like Cassandra at Troy, they are not so often listened to. Napoleon, Kaiser Wilhelm II, and Hitler did exactly what they had always said they would do. Not all visionaries sit upstairs with William Blake, talking to God. Furthermore, the future relevant to intuitives cannot be circumscribed within a year or even necessarily within a lifetime; it is a far, far-reaching one. As the critic Hazlitt said of Samuel Taylor Coleridge (an IO), "He had a hunger for eternity." For all IOs and IAs, visions go on endlessly. Ezra Pound's inexhaustible *Cantos* grew, as he wrote them, to include his various views on democracy, capitalism, usury, Greek culture, Chinese ideograms, the Renaissance, and the First World War. There were to be a hundred "chapters"; the longest poem in history, had he completed it.

Perhaps because death itself is not perceived as an end, many intuitives are fascinated with the idea of suicide. We are not talking here about people who for imbalanced psychological (and not typological) reasons actually commit suicide. The deaths of Marilyn Monroe and Hitler are not explained by their having been intuitive oceanics. However, an interest in suicide, such as obsessed the fictional IO Hamlet, is the outgrowth of aethereal speculations about *all* future possibilities; in that sense, it is characteristic of these psychetypes. Napoleon wrote about committing suicide, thought about it, constantly played with the idea; he certainly never did it.

Participating in aethereality with its impulse toward theoretical generalizing, intuitives prefer to move in a cosmic realm, to operate always on a level of universal significance. "In 1886 I discovered the Christ Science, or Divine Laws of Life, Truth, and Love, and named my discovery Christian Science," wrote Mary Baker Eddy; a more cosmic vision would be hard to come by. A sensation type might be thrilled by discovering a nightingale outside the window or the headwaters of the Nile, but an intuitive is likely to be dissatisfied with less than cosmic thrills, like discovering divine laws or transcendentalism. Ralph Waldo Emerson's first sermon was entitled "On the Relation of Man to the Globe." Sir Walter Raleigh's *magnum opus* was called *The History of the World*. As a volcanic, Wordsworth was awed by his intuitive friend Coleridge's originality of mind and the way it could discover and express the "connections of things" by "throwing out in profusion grand central truths from which might be evolved the most comprehensive systems." All intuitives will try to expand everything to cosmic dimensions; a minor car accident becomes a saga of unique peril and flashing thoughts of union with the eternal. A $100 stock investment becomes a career of wheeling and dealing à la Howard Hughes.

Their faith in the future and their discontinuous indifference to the past can give these psychetypes tremendous optimism. In fact, the past flies away from them even more quickly than it does for sensation types. SV F. Scott Fitzgerald in the first flash of success and marriage, rode down Fifth Avenue and "bawled because I had everything I wanted and knew I would never be so happy again." It is doubtful that many intuitives ever think they have everything they desire; something else may always beckon. Having Italy, Napoleon wanted Spain; ruling Europe, he dreamed of conquering the east. "Europe is a molehill."

This optimism gives intuitives great resiliency. The inimitable intuitives of literature, for example, are all irrepressibly unstumpable. That is the basis of their appeal. Having been beaten nearly to death, Don Quixote charges off at the next windmill. Having been tossed into prison for debt, Mr. Macawber throws a party to celebrate his expectations of being released. Mr. Toad in *Wind in the Willows* rushes out to buy another motorcar to replace the one he has just crashed. And Falstaff, the most extraordinary of all these intuitive oceanics, leaps up from the eulogy Prince Hal has spoken over his body and has another drink, another joke. Real IAs and IOs can be just as exuberantly undefeatable, as the dauntless (if futile) escapes of the imprisoned Mary Queen of Scots or Napoleon, the political effervescence of Hubert Humphrey, and the final triumph of Sarah Caldwell's Boston Opera Company make clear.

One reason that intuitives are able to be so optimistic is that their minds leap naturally to the successful perfection the future will bring. They don't spend a great deal of time laboriously working out the logical details. Darwin confessed that if he had ever foreseen what a chore *The Origin of Species* would turn out to be, he "never would have undertaken it." Moreover, an intuitive (say a ten-year-old girl who has announced to her friends that they will put on a play that evening with costumes and lights and popcorn and music) does not appreciate being told that her scheme is impractical, precipitous, or—worst of all—uninteresting. As to impractical and precipitous, she will be glad to write the play that afternoon and assume most of the parts herself (like Bottom in Shakespeare's *Midsummer Night's Dream*); as to "uninteresting," they are all a bunch of boring deadheads if they don't want to try.

Intuitives are very concerned about safeguarding the future that so concerns them. First of all, they want to keep it "open" as long as they can. No possibility can be comfortably closed off. Persons of this type prefer beginnings to resolutions, the emergent to the already arrived. Sensation types, who metaphorically live on earth, cannot bear to be fenced *in;* an intuitive, like Shelley's skylark, "a scorner of the ground," cannot bear to be pinned *down.* As Blake said, "He who can be bound down is no genius." Thus, they hate closure; long arguments that have to be resolved, clothes that are too constrictive, the routine of jobs or marriages—anything that is closed and goes on too long. The architectural dictum of Frank Lloyd Wright (an IA) was: "Break open the box!" Get rid of all these "boxes on sticks" and open space into free-floating designs. In the second place, intuitives attempt to mold the future even after their death. Napoleon spent his years on St. Helena trying to decide what would have been the best ending for his romance with posterity.

I ought to have died in Moscow. 'Til then my fame was undiminished. My dynasty would have been established; history would have compared me with Alexander and Caesar, whereas as things have turned out, I am practically nothing. No, no, at Waterloo would have been best. The love of the people, their mourning!

The last time Marilyn Monroe left her house before her death, she took over to the publicity department a package of the subsequently famous nude photographs to which she attached a note: "These should go to *Playboy.*" Mary Queen of Scots prepared to the last detail the religious martyrdom she perceived her execution to be—the clothes and rosaries she would wear, the farewell letters, the tokens. Queen Elizabeth (fearing that people would indeed try to staunch handkerchiefs in Mary's blood and save them for holy relics) would allow no observers at the beheading, and that seems to have more immediately distressed Mary than her own imminent death.

In the vocabulary of experiential typology, being a visionary does not necessarily mean being a mystic (though Blake was) nor fantastic (though we could see "The Fiddler on the Roof" by Marc Chagall in that way), nor unearthly (though D. W. Griffith dismissed sexuality from his myth of the female and Mary Baker Eddy summarily denied the very existence of the material world). A vision is the desire of the imagination and the will that becomes synonymous with the personhood of the believer and is therefore perceived as reality. The vision of Isadora Duncan was to revolutionize the world through dance. The visions of Orson Welles, Federico Fellini, D. W. Griffith, and Mel Brooks are their uniquely individual concepts of the motion-picture art. The vision of Queen Victoria was her love for her consort, Prince Albert, to whose memory she dedicated endless memorials, including a half century of mourning.

An intuitive, then, may have a vision about anything, even one as simple as Mr. Toad's infatuation with motorcars. So limited a perspective, however, is unlikely to be satisfying for long, for all intuitives have at least some impulse toward a far-reaching, bigger-than-life vision, be it God, humanity, art, progress, psychology, politics, business, whatever, in addition to a series of what might be called "minivisions" about current events, career prospects, or personal relationships. Moreover, these visions change, generally becoming larger and larger when they are successful or tossed aside for a fresh start when they are not. Particularly with young intuitives, enthusiasms often predominate over, and sometimes even exclude, skill. The ratio of exuberance to skill is one way of distinguishing the discontinuity of intuitives and sensation types. Intuitives simply do not take into account that they may be totally unprepared to fulfill the vision; and if they fail more often, they also attempt more. Monroe first wanted to get into modeling, then to be a movie star, then to be a great (and serious) actress. Her expanding vision should not be confused with a thinking-type plan such as, "If I get into modeling, then perhaps I can use the portfolio to get a screen test; if I work hard, perhaps eventually I'll be able to get a good part." When Monroe entered films, she had had no training, no encouragement, no education, no financial support; she could not sing or dance, she had never even acted in a school play, and compared to what she was later to achieve, she was not even particularly attractive. All she had was her vision of herself as a "movie star," the will never to abandon that vision, and the charisma ultimately to make it a reality. Walt Disney's comic strip about Mickey Mouse eventually grew into a world of films and television series, and eventually Disney*land,* then Disney *world,* and then the City of the Future, and then—who knows what dreams he left behind in memoranda? He said Disneyworld would never be finished.

An intuitive, caught in the rapture of a new vision, will be totally committed and absolutely absorbed. Inspiration has struck, and while the passion lasts, it will control his or her existence. Unlike thinking aethereals, they cannot put a new theory aside. So it is futile to try to dissuade these psychetypes by pointing out insurmountable difficulties, disruptions, or even hazards to life or the complete opposition of everyone involved. "If 100 percent of the critics told me I could never make it," Monroe told a roommate at the Studio Club, "they would all be wrong." Eventually, the intuitive may forget about the vision, or it may dissolve or be replaced with a new one; until that happens, however, its reality is absolute. To others, the energy and activity of expectation that an intuitive generates at such times may be either inspiring or, if it happens constantly, exhausting. If that enthusiasm allows other people no room for their *own* ideas, so much absorbed intensity becomes a strain.

IOs and IAs, in fact, are apt to have trouble remembering anything (including, in some cases, friends, family, sleep, when they ate last, what they are wearing, where they parked the car, even where they live) that is unrelated to the all-consuming vision. Conversely, they have excellent memories for things that are connected with it. Too drugged to focus her eyes, during the filming of *The Misfits*, Marilyn Monroe would turn instinctively to face a movie camera. Too drunk to walk, John Barrymore could recite Hamlet's soliloquies. Napoleon once asked for an artillery report on a foreign country. Examining the maps, he pointed to a clump of trees near one particular village: "There was a cannon emplacement behind these trees ten years ago. Is it still there?"

Napoleon confessed, "My memory goes back only to the time when I began to be somebody." Similarly, it was with the performance of his first opera that IA Richard Wagner could say, "Life has only now begun to have true meaning." Until they discover a vision, intuitives genuinely have no center to their lives and may wander about from interest to interest in a purposeless, ineffective way. Talents not yet propelled by the imagination are often obscured. Wagner's first music teacher considered him the worst pupil he had ever had. Charles Darwin's father despaired that his playful, lazy son, who had failed to get through either medical or divinity school, would ever amount to anything; so he allowed him to take a trip to South America on the *Beagle* as an amateur naturalist. Darwin then got his vision: "As yet I have only indulged in hypotheses, but they are such powerful ones that I suppose, if they were put in action but for one day, the world would come to an end." Ever after, the celebrated the day the *Beagle* sailed as the birthday of his "second life."

Charles Darwin had the good fortune (the highest fortune for someone of his psychetype) to effect a vision universal in scope; he set out to discover "what we have come from and to what we tend . . . to guide our speculations with respect to the past and future." His theory of evolution did indeed change the future. Not all IOs and IAs are, of course, that successful; genius is rare among all the types. Not all aspiring intuitive actresses can become a Marilyn Monroe, nor all conductors a Toscanini, nor all writers a Joyce. Nothing is more horrible to such people than the failure of a crucial vision. Hamlet's world turns to dust; Don Quixote, made "sane," dies of grief. Suppose Victoria had learned thirty years after his death that her dearest Albert had never cared for her at all? Sometimes such failure is so insupportable that the intuitive simply refuses to admit it. A neurotically extreme example is Hitler's claim, while Allied troops were storming Berlin, that victory was still possible, and that regardless of "all setbacks," his six years of war "would go down in history as the most glorious and valiant demonstration of a nation's life-purpose." Hitler shot himself, but the final announcement to the German people was: "The Führer has died in battle at the head of his troops."

So absorbed are they in their visions that intuitives, with their aethereal asceticism, are relatively indifferent to the "real," utilitarian world. When other pupils went home for the holidays, Toscanini stayed in the conservatory library studying scores. Socializing meant nothing to George Gershwin; he was married to his piano. Alexander, Napoleon, and Patton were Spartan in their personal habits; Hitler neither smoked, drank, nor ate meat; he apparently cared very little about sex and had almost no outside interests. On first meeting, SV Mussolini dismissed the future Führer as "a garrulous monk." As would be expected, such indifference to the world often leads to rather unrealistic attitudes and behavior. Nero, Mary Queen of Scots, Charles I—none of these ever grasped the reality of their political situations, and all suffered the consequences. Perhaps the most memorable instance of this kind of indifference was Marie Antoinette's presumed reply to the report that the starving French peasants had no bread: "Then let them eat cake." At nineteen, in a more charitable though hardly more realistic impulse, Percy Shelley sought to emancipate the Irish peasantry by sealing copies of his *Declaration of Rights* in green bottles and in miniature balloons and floating or flying them across the Irish Sea from Wales. But the limits imposed by mundane reality are actively oppressive to IOs and IAs. "Matter is evil," said Mary Baker Eddy, who then added that truly, there was no such thing as matter. Her philosophy so exasperated SR Mark Twain that he wrote an angry, satirical book to expose her. Despite their shared discontinuity, the perceptual worlds of intuitives and sensation types are as mutually exclusive as thinking and feeling. That physicality so compelling to SRs and SVs, that orderly continuity so necessary to thinking and feeling types, both keep pulling the intuitive back to earth where he doesn't want to be, doesn't want, as Shelley put it, "to fall upon the thorns of life" where a "heavy weight of hours" will chain and bow him. Those who are happy are those who, "singing, still soar, and soaring, ever sing." Intuitives want to take off, to fly higher and higher into a world of absolute perfection. The demands of daily life make that difficult. "Domesticity bore down heavily," commented Frank Lloyd Wright of his first marriage.

That passion for Albert and family that absorbed Victoria's imagination did not stop her from warning her daughter, "Believe me, Children are a terrible anxiety and the sorrow they cause is far greater than the pleasure they give. . . . I am equally shy of marriages and large families." Loving Albert did not stop the idea of sex from being to her "too dreadful." In general, intuitives find it difficult to believe that other people can be so strongly motivated by something that is merely physical—like sex. Thus, Albert's reality, as with the visions of all intuitives, did not reside in the tangible, material world at all, but in "Albert" as the objective manifestation of Victoria's imaginative commitment.

Because intuitives fail to test out empirically a great many aspects of the outside world, they run the risk of uncritical acceptance, of taking up untenable positions or inaccurate facts, as happened to the poet Ezra Pound when, with far more enthusiasm than realistic understanding of politics, he began broadcasting propaganda for Mussolini's fascism, a movement in which he thought he saw an Italy revitalized as it had been during the Roman Empire and Renaissance. With their aethereal detachment, intuitives are prone to lack a great deal of insight into other people's motivations; though normally very trusting, their vulnerability in this regard sometimes causes them to have unwarranted suspicions about the motives of others. Because, being oceanic, they are quite easily swayed by people, they worry that someone, if given the chance, will try to use them, manipulate them, or "do them in." When Marilyn Monroe's former in-laws said they would love to have her come visit them, her response was, "How much is it going to cost me?"

Impracticality in one's daily life is another product of the same aethereal indifference to the volcanic world. Intuitives, for example, are often impulsive and extravagant buyers, though the things they buy (like Monroe's jewelry) may be soon afterward lost or forgotten. As happened to her, John Barrymore, and Valentino, these psychetypes—despite great wealth—may get themselves into hopeless debt. Wagner owed money all over Europe and had to be supported by others; so did Blake, Coleridge, Isadora Duncan, Dylan Thomas, and James Joyce. But persons of this type are not as upset by such insolvency as a thinking type would be; many share IA Frank Lloyd Wright's belief: "God give me the luxuries of life, and I will willingly do without the necessities."

Their disinterest in the practical aspects of tasks also makes intuitives (and especially IOs) the least efficient of the psychetypes at what are to them unimaginative chores: shopping, household furnishing and repairs, sewing, cooking, planning trips, paying bills, taking care of the car, or, for that matter, taking care of the baby. Feeling unable to cope with motherhood, Mary Baker Eddy gave away her baby son to be cared for by others; she made no effort to reclaim him and never saw him again until he was thirty-four. Similarly, these individuals are rather indifferent to their surroundings; some may live in an apartment for months without bothering to unpack completely —if they never settle in, they are always ready for flight. They tend, too, not to be especially *au courant* with what is going on in the world except in those areas in which their imaginations are engaged. An intuitive musician once glanced at a Nixon news conference on television a year after he was inaugurated, and asked, "Whatever happened to Lyndon Johnson?"

Likewise, many members of this type, having poorly developed sensation functions, may be clumsy. Obviously, when the vision concerns the body, as with such intuitives as Isadora

Duncan, Rudolph Nureyev, or Olga Corbett, this is not the case. Beethoven apparently could not pick up a glass without breaking it or put on his clothes without tearing them, but he *could* play the piano as well as anyone alive. As always, primary consideration should be given to the experience and not the behavior: Most intuitives are simply not interested in working with their bodies; therefore, they tend to be poor at athletics and mechanics. Even Darwin, who strove to be scientifically accurate, had "no sense of mechanics or instruments" and relied completely on "instrument-makers whose whole trade was a mystery" to him. Neither are these two psychetypes especially good at spatial arrangements or spatial directions: Intuitives have been known not only to walk past their house but to drive past their town. They can get lost easily and have trouble following directions.

Being oceanic, IAs and IOs do not consider at all meaningful the social roles and status differences so perceptible to territorials. In fact, they may not even see them. Thus, as we mentioned earlier, Queen Victoria felt no compunction about sending sentimental valentines to her "best friend" the coachman, John Brown. Such people choose their friends wherever they wish without regard to status or function. And since they don't pay attention to social customs, they may not perceive (or care) when they have violated the rules. Now, the zany antics of Mel Brooks and the flamboyant bohemianism of Isadora Duncan are *deliberate* violations of decorum; we may assume, as well, that when Dylan Thomas smoked cigarettes through his nose at parties, he suspected Emily Post would not be amused. That is different from Marilyn Monroe's puzzlement at her studio's horror when they discovered she had posed for a nude photograph. They asked her to deny it; she refused to do so. Why should she? She wanted the whole world to see her body. George Patton's military career was almost terminated when he publicly slapped an enlisted man for cowardice; he seemed surprised by the uproar. Intuitives, then, have a certain propensity to be socially awkward, and what may seem to them simply openness and honesty make strike others as tactless. Beethoven and Toscanini expressed astonishment that their orchestra members felt hurt and humilated by the two conductors' insults and criticism. But the maestros cared only to make the music perfect; they assumed everyone else felt the same. Young thinking types and sensation types learn the rules of social behavior quickly; feeling types sensitize themselves to unspoken cues. But young intuitives often run into trouble by saying or doing things unacceptable to others; they have to make a special effort to memorize the rules of the game, and they are occasionally unwilling to do that.

When people are under stress, they turn to the strengths of their primary functions. Thinking types plan, feeling types explore their emotions, and sensation types act. At such times, intuitives turn to their imaginations. At *all* times, that is where they place their greatest trust, in that inner vision compared to which the phenomenal world is, as Blake put it, "dirt under my feet." It is significant that while the Age of Enlightenment produced so many eminent thinking types, the age of the imagination (which became known as the Romantic period) was hospitable to the contributions of discontinuous types—and, in particular, to intuitives. It was one of those intuitives, Coleridge, who defined the artists of his age as those who "revere the infinite," hence "their wandering through the unknown, their grander moral feelings, their more august conception of man as man, their future rather than their past—in a word, their sublimity." To Coleridge, as to all intuitives, the imagination was an active, shaping spirit, "the living power and prime agent of all human perception." Through the imagination we create a symbolic language that gives meaning to nature; through the imagination we idealize and unify the world. Coleridge believed, and his fellow intuitives would agree, that the imagination "is essentially *vital,* even as all objects (*as* objects) are essentially dead and fixed."

Intuitives are the most imaginative of the psychetypes. "Imaginative" is not the same as "creative"; creativity is transtypological. Nor does it refer only to creative endeavors like painting or composing. Queen Victoria wanted the title "Empress of India" not because it gave her greater status, but because it stirred her imagination; that's why Napoleon decided to call himself "Emperor" and not king. And as he and Hitler knew better perhaps than any other two men in history, it is through their imaginations that men are governed: "The driving force which has brought about the most tremendous revolutions has never been a body of scientific teaching, but always a devotion which has inspired them." Hitler said this, but it could as easily be a quote from Alexander or Napoleon or Trotsky or Patton, all of whom *inspired* their followers rather than taught them.

Intuitives do not learn by formal study, by training, by rules or logic. "My business is to love," FV Emily Dickinson had said. "My business is to create," wrote IA William Blake, adding, "I will not Reason and Compare." Such people may seem to operate directly out of their unconscious, totally indifferent to factual or literal considerations or customary forms. Isadora Duncan had refused ever to take dancing lessons. Claude Debussy was ectastic when his teachers told him his compositions were "unworthy of a man of talent." "At last!" he exclaimed, "I have written something original." Intuitives are the great innovators. When humanity acknowledges their innovations, they are hailed as prophets, forerunners, and geniuses ahead of their times; when it does not, they are ignored (or, on occasion, institutionalized) and called idiosyncratic dreamers, zanies, "crazy inventors," mystical zealots, or even psychotics. As we said when comparing the sensation types Gandhi and Stalin, any typological proclivity may be applied for good or ill by healthy people or sick ones, by the talented or the mediocre. Alexander the Great is one thing; Charles Manson is another. Both are intuitives. One intuitive gives us the theory of evolution; another, a theory of human propulsion by means of miniature rockets attached under the arms. We know about Darwin; we rarely learn the names of the other people.

Some intuitives may become so controlled by their imaginations that, like Don Quixote, they cannot themselves distinguish between objective and subjective realities. This is different from their being *perceived* as extraordinarily, or excessively, imaginative by others—as intuitives usually are. Beethoven's music was dismissed as unplayable; Wright's buildings as impractical; Patton's tactics as impossible; Ezra Pound's poetry as incomprehensible; Isadora Duncan's dancing as immoral lunacy. If the sensation-type style sometimes makes peo-

ple think these psychetypes are more simplistic than they really
are (the works of Twain, Dickens, and Frost are, after all, read
by children), then intuitives are often assumed to be more difficult than they necessarily need be: it *is* possible to follow
Ulysses or a Fellini movie or a theoretical paragraph of Carl
Jung's. The result of this assumption is that many intuitives do
not enjoy the immediate fame that was given Twain, Dickens,
and Frost. Trotsky lost to Lenin; Jung lost to Freud; they are
only now, in the whirligig of time, coming into their own.

In response to the world's dismissal, some intuitives are apt
to dismiss their critics in return as unenlightened reactionaries;
and for those who lack imagination, IAs and IOs have a rather
snobbish contempt—Napoleon suggested that all persons who
did not realize that "imagination rules the world," should be
"tossed in a pond." In like manner, if told that they are unseri-
ous or scatterbrained, intuitives are apt to retaliate by taking a
cavalier attitude toward "serious thinking," in other words,
"slow literal-mindedness." Their own mental world is anything
but slow. In a radical series of rapid inspirations, one thought
leaps after another, not as bricks are laid but as a series of
pebbles are skipped across water, each one creating its own
expanding circle. "My soul," said Isadora Duncan, "was like a
battlefield where Apollo, Dionysus, Christ, Nietzsche, and Richard Wagner disputed the ground." In just such crowded eleva-
tors, most intuitives are always pushing the express button for
the top floor. When Wordsworth praised Coleridge's mind as
one that saw the connections of things, he added that it was
sometimes impossible to see how Coleridge's mind got from
one connection to the next. Intuitives leap, they don't walk; one
thought or image or idea immediately suggests another and
then another. This is the sort of "take it over the edge" style of
Jonathan Winters' or Mel Brooks' comedy. In so whirling an
imagination, quotations, metaphors, references, and colloquial-
isms are apt to be mixed up, and many intuitives are inimitable
in their malapropisms. "Hang on like grim death," Darwin ad-
vised. "You can't pull the wool under my carpet," another intuitive may warn. Or, "I'm not stretching my neck on a limb."
Neologisms appeal to them, and they enjoy making up new
words; some are serious contributions to the language, like

Coleridge's "esemplastic," or "coadunate," or his critical use of the terms "intuitive" and "organic." Others are the outgrowth of unstumpability. At a loss for a word, an intuitive may simply make one up.

No one could have more indefatigible a will than an IA or IO pursuing a vision, but from their perspective it is not so much an issue of will as of being "chosen." With their oceanic spirituality, intuitives are deep believers in forces beyond man's purview and particularly in those affecting their own destinies. "I go the way that providence dictates with the assurance of a sleepwalker," Hitler said. Mary Baker Eddy heard the voice of Christ call her to her destiny; it had already been predicted, she believed, in the Apocalypse of St. John. "To destiny" was engraved inside the wedding ring Napoleon gave to Josephine. "I have become great only through the influence of my star," he said. The deep interest these psychetypes have in religious and spiritual matters may take the form of an orthodox faith or something more eclectic—the mysticism of Blake, Emerson's transcendentalism, Valentino's belief in mediums and otherworldly guides, Hitler's fascination with occultism, yoga, and astrology. Plutarch tells us that "if the least unusual thing happened, Alexander thought it a prodigy or a presage, and his court was thronged with diviners and priests whose business was to sacrifice and purify and foretell the future."

We have called intuitives "high energy" people; that energy, however, is imaginative rather than active. This may seem a strange assumption to make about psychetypes, who include among their members people like William Randolph Hearst, Patton, and Hubert Humphrey—people who never seem to take time out to sleep—not to mention the Alexanders and Isadora Duncans. The term refers not to the results, however, but to the generating source of energy. IAs and IOs (and of course this is more true of introverted ones like Christina Rossetti or Emily Brontë than extraverts like Mary of Scotland) will delay or avoid taking action if the activity in question does not sufficiently activate their imaginations. Orson Welles, who can look like the blur of a comet when he is engaged in a project, can also wait for years to begin (or complete) one. For one thing, acting means having to choose one possibility and therefore having to close out the myriad others that flash so appealingly through the intuitive's mind. This process of elimination they find very painful, so much so that they may decide that the best thing to do is not to act at all but just to let things happen. "The same thing is not done twice in a century," explained Napoleon, who refused to work out his battle strategies in advance. "I have fought sixty battles and I can assure you I have learned nothing from any of them." Everything is possible, so let what will happen, happen. "I know not what I do, for everything depends upon events. The greater one is, the less one can have a will."

Sometimes (never, though, with Napolean) this attitude results in prolonged procrastination or a paralyzed passivity of the kind that affects the fictional IO Hamlet; his problem is that he cannot bring himself to act. If the volcanic Othello had been the hero of that play, he would have killed the king in the first scene. (And, of course, Hamlet would have never rushed into his wife's bedroom and smothered her to death on the suspicion of adultery, as Othello does.) Like other IOs, Coleridge has been penalized by history for never finishing anything, including his repeatedly promised *Opus Maximum* that would set forth a systematic account of his entire philosophy. After years of delay Darwin was only prodded into completing his *Origin of the Species* by the threat of imminent publication of his theory by another scientist who had independently come to the same conclusions. Nor was the subsequent debate on evolution waged by Darwin himself, but by the aggressive TR Thomas Huxley, who assumed the name "Darwin's bulldog."

When an intuitive's imaginative energy *has* been set in motion, he or she will literally leap into action, as Mary of Scotland did when she rode nearly a hundred miles on horseback without rest to recapture her throne. And since once the energy has been released to one area, it tends oceanically to spill over into others, the intuitive can maintain activity until the precipitating factor is resolved, dissipated, or displaced. One way of acting is by refusing to act, and these psychetypes often handle conflicts by simply removing themselves from situations or threatening to do so. Napoleon was always sending in an offer to resign in order to force concessions from the French war department. Marilyn Monroe was always walking off movie sets, or never showing up, or terminating commitments. Twentieth Century-Fox had finally fired her for failure to live up to her contract shortly before her death. Conflicts around them are distressing to intuitives; their own worlds are so changeable and imaginatively tempestuous that they can tolerate very little *external* change. Something or someone has to stay stable so they can spin, stay grounded so they can fly— this stability was part of the attraction that Prince Albert and Arthur Miller (both thinking aethereals) held for Queen Victoria and Marilyn Monroe (both intuitive oceanics).

The imaginative vision, then, is the center of an intuitive's life. Of equal importance is the means by which he or she implements that vision in such a way that the world responds to it. And that means is charisma. Of all the psychetypes, IAs and IOs are the most charismatic. Being the most inspired, they are generally the most inspirational; like catalysts, they change the people around them. The charismatic force of Adolph Hitler was absolutely devastating—and deadly. On its strength alone he mesmerized an entire nation, conquered most of Europe, and came terrifyingly near to conquering the world. Hitler's speeches were not reasoned arguments; as one observer noted, "He states the most astonishing and totally inaccurate things. He roars, he pleads; if need be, he weeps. But he never analyzes, discusses, or argues." No, he "inspired" for four hours at a time while thousands screamed "Heil Hitler!" back at him. Soldiers would rush to death at the command of Alexander and of Bonaparte, Custer, and Patton. Napoleon's troops would meet any demand their "little corporal" asked of them. He won the battle of Arcola by rushing to the enemy's bridge, raising his standard, and crying, "Follow me." When he escaped from Elba, a battalion of French troops was waiting at Grenoble to capture or kill him. Napoleon walked toward their bayonet points, threw open his cloak, and shouted, "Soldiers of the fifth army corps! Don't you know me? If there is one among you who wishes to kill his Emperor, let him come forward and do so! Here I am." Breaking ranks, cheering, "Vive l'Empereur!" every man fell in behind him. Gathering soldiers in this way at every town, he marched from the sea to Paris without firing a shot. "Before him," asked Balzac, "did ever a man gain an empire simply by showing his hat?" One young officer even dropped dead at his feet from excitement at seeing his Emperor return.

No film stars have ever had the overwhelming and personal impact on fans that Valentino and Monroe had. In moviedom, where legends come and go like quicksilver, their loss is still mourned, and their myths inimitable. There has never been another god or goddess like those two. No other film director ever inspired his actors or transformed the medium itself as did D. W. Griffith. Lillian Gish's own autobiography is dedicated to Griffith and is devoted to the story of his compelling power to raise whatever he touched (including her) into a manifestation of his personal vision.

An intuitive turns on charisma like a flash of light—or fireworks. The self and the inspiration become at those moments synonymous, and in responding to one, we are moved, sometimes even transformed, by the other. Feeling oceanics and thinking aethereals, because their primary areas are those that produce intuition, have access to this kind of charisma. Observing people like Churchill or like FDR, John Kennedy, Martin Luther King, Malcolm X, or Frank Church, we can notice the moment during their speeches when they "kick over" or "kick up" into intuitive charisma. At such times, the personality is no longer simply a vehicle for expressing ideas (as it is with thinking territorials); the personality *is* the idea. The distance between what is said and who is saying it falls away, and our response is usually a quickened heart, a chill down the spine. Of course, IA Patrick Henry's "Give me liberty or give me death" is a memorable example, "It was like listening to Homer talk," said TR Thomas Jefferson, who was awed by Henry's charismatic powers, but suspicious of his practical capability to govern. Significantly, those intuitives (in the vanguard, as always) who helped inspire the colonies to revolt—Henry and Samuel Adams, and Thomas Paine—were not called upon to help administer the new country.

Putting out charisma is extremely draining for intuitives; they feel that others expect it of them, that they must be "on" all the time to be accepted or appreciated—not only in social situations but in personal relations—that they must always be amusing or inspiring. The energy it costs them to do so can be debilitating and so may lead to periods of "charisma slump" during which they completely withdraw. It is also a very volatile and precarious possession. One may leap to a throne with it, but it is harder to keep a throne long purely on charm. Intuitives have a tendency either to succeed spectacularly or fail dismally—or both. Their careers are meteoric, a rapid rise being followed by a swift fall. Many intuitives have exactly this sense of their own lives. "Men who are truly great are like meteors," Napoleon said. "They shine and consume themselves, that they may lighten the darkness of earth." Therefore, he felt he must "mount higher and higher" lest he perish the moment he stopped climbing. Many intuitives have perished rather precipitously, Sir Walter Raleigh, Mary of Scotland, Charles I, and Marie Antoinette were beheaded. Alexander, Shelley, Valentino, and Gershwin died in their twenties or thirties. Nero, Hitler, and Monroe committed suicide. Trotsky was assassinated. Shelley drowned. Custer was massacred. Isadora Duncan was strangled by a scarf when it became caught in the hubcap of her car. Pound was institutionalized. D. W. Griffith died a pauper. Napoleon and Kaiser Wilhelm died in exile. John Barrymore and Dylan Thomas drank themselves to death. The problems of intuitive oceanics seem to be even more constant than those of aethereals, because they lack the latter's ego-protecting detachment and ability to structure life in an orderly way, but both these psychetypes lead very high-risk lives.

Intuitives feel fully alive only when they are inspiring others, as many others as possible. "I need 500 million men to love me," said Napoleon, adding that he would like each of them to love him exclusively. Having singlehandedly and purely by the force of his personality subdued a whole tribe of Matabele warriors, the African adventurer Cecil Rhodes returned to his followers (who were astonished to see him still alive) and remarked, "It's moments like this that make life worth living!" George Gershwin, when asked why he insisted on always playing the piano himself and never listening to anyone else, explained, "You see, when I'm playing everyone is happy, and when anyone else is playing, I'm miserable." Gershwin once asked Oscar Levant, "Do you think my music will be played a hundred years from now?" "It will be if *you* are around," Levant replied.

If an intuitive does not have an effective vision, has not yet focused on a meaningful interest that will also interest others, he or she will try to inspire others with his or her life itself—try to make people respond just to the charm of the personality. This may take the form of clowning, flirting, high-powered conversation, or preaching at others. Some intuitives and in particular IAs, have a propensity to play God; the egalitarian generosity of spirit in IOs helps to mitigate this type of arrogance. For example, the IO Debussy hated the "inhuman grandiloquence" of IA Richard Wagner, with his "goose-stepping, iron-helmeted music." "Had Wagner been a little more human," Debussy wrote, "he would have been more divine." It is not unfair to think the same could be said of several other intuitives.

Because they want to inspire others, intuitives may find the slow routine of teaching a frustrating and boring experience. Wagner despised his work as an instructor at Dresden, and Ezra Pound was fired from Wabash College for presumed eccentricities and a contemptuous attitude toward his colleagues. A contemporary said of Pound, "He was a drop of oil in a glass of water. The trouble was, I believe, that he had no wish to *mix*. He just wanted to impress." Intuitives simply cannot tolerate a denial of their charisma. To the publishers who would not treat him as if he were Handel, the young Beethoven snapped, "With men who will not believe and trust in me because I am as yet unknown to universal fame, I cannot hold intercourse." Such people will take any steps necessary to ensure that the potential of their charisma is not diminished. Mary Queen of Scots was very used to having people fall violently in love with her or otherwise come under her spell. The poets Ronsard and du Bellay had written impassioned poetry to her; men like the Seigneur de Dauville had left their wives to follow her; several had been executed for attempting to abduct or make advances to her. One of Mary's visions was to "charismize" Queen Elizabeth as well. Elizabeth had good reason, knowing of Mary's effect on people and seeing how the Scottish Queen's English jailor and the British ambassador Throckmorton had succumbed to her charms, to fear ever meeting Mary personally.

And that was increasingly what Mary desired. When the one scheduled meeting between the two queens was canceled, Mary took to her bed for days in a flood of tears. Through the long years of her captivity she kept believing that if Elizabeth only saw her, Elizabeth would love her. Perhaps she was right. Elizabeth never did.

IAs and IOs respond to stress situations by throwing out even more charisma. Isadora Duncan's best moment was when she turned on a Boston audience that was hissing and booing her avant-garde dance tribute to the Russian Revolution by baring her breasts and telling everyone there exactly what she thought of their values. Marilyn Monroe always said that the happiest moment in her life was when, in below zero weather with a temperature of 104 degrees, she entertained thousands of riotous American GIs in Korea. It was the most photographed event in the history of the world up to that time. Monroe's acting ability turned on when the camera turned on—and not before. Then, at times, as in *The Misfits* when the director and other actors were exhausted from dealing with her near nervous collapses, her drugs, and her marital problems, she would take off. As Montgomery Clift discovered: "Marilyn was an incredible person to act with . . . the most marvelous I ever worked with, and I've been working for twenty-nine years. But she went over the fringe. Playing a scene with her, it was like an escalator. You'd do something, and she'd catch it, and it would go like that, just right up."

Charisma is so important to intuitives that in the gap between having an inspiration and sharing it with others, they may become shy out of a sudden rush of anxiety that no one will respond to them. They also may feel competitive toward others over "who's got more charisma?" For that reason and because of their aethereal tendency toward emotional detachment, intuitives are often intolerant of showiness, exaggeration (unless it is successfully imaginative), or strong emotionalism in others. Having evoked sobs and tears from his concert audiences, Beethoven would burst into loud laughter at their response, sneering, "You are fools!" These sorts of attitudes make intuitives rather unwilling to listen to others. The young James Joyce was not interested in talking with his eminent countryman William

Butler Yeats and told him so: "We have met too late; you are
too old to be influenced by me."

Some intuitives may even become vicious if others deny
their charisma. The treason of Benedict Arnold (who had been
one of the early heroes of the Revolutionary War) was partially
caused by his sense that George Washington unjustly preferred
other young officers, like Alexander Hamilton, to him. It was
also said of the sweet, helpless, vulnerable Marilyn Monroe,
about whom everyone felt so protective, that she was the
"meanest woman in Hollywood," and that she had left behind
her a track of the broken spirits of all those Good Samaritans
who had befriended her.

Whether in positive or negative ways, there seems to be an
excessive quality in intuitives. All discontinuous people tend to
be exuberant, but sensation types are too controlled to allow
themselves to be carried away as IAs and IOs often are. "Prudence is a rich, ugly, old maid, courted by Incapacity," said
William Blake. "The road of excess leads to the palace of wisdom." There was certainly a lack of prudence in the behavior
of most of the intuitives we have been talking about, people like
Custer, for example. Such people have very swift and strong
reactions to people and events; these reactions may change just
as swiftly. Beethoven and Wagner, Dylan Thomas and Monroe,
went through their friends very rapidly. Mary of Scotland fell
passionately in love and passionately out of love with Henry
Darnley in a matter of months. William Randolph Hearst's opinions were apt to be as violent as they were ephemeral and as
numerous as his newspaper outlets. So carried away by the
moment's vision are intuitives that they may be unable to structure time at all and may completely disregard the probable
consequences of their actions. When Shelley fell in love with
Mary Godwin, he expected his current wife, Harriet, to believe
with him in an idealistic notion of free love between free spirits.
He assumed Mary would live with him as his spiritual wife,
Harriet as his spiritual sister. Harriet refused and subsequently
drowned herself.

Intuitive excess manifests itself in all areas of their lives.
They are prone, for example, to swamp others with communications. Monroe was on the telephone dozens of times a day;

Mary of Scotland wrote to Elizabeth, among others, incessantly and was, in fact, convicted of treasonable conspiracy on the basis of the indiscreet "casket letters." Napoleon wrote eighty thousand letters during his fifteen-year reign. Even when Prince Albert was in the next room, Queen Victoria could not resist dashing off a few lines to him or jotting down the day's events in her copious journal:

> *but ill or not,* I NEVER NEVER *spent such an evening!!! My* DEAR-EST DEAREST DEAR *Albert sat on a footstool by my side, & his excessive love and affection gave me feelings of heavenly love & happiness, I never could have* hoped *to have felt before!—really how can I ever be thankful enough to have such a* Husband.

If there is anything intuitives like more than writing letters, it's talking. They are the great talkers of the psychetypes, absolutely irrepressible and frequently irresistible conversationalists. Oscar Wilde and Coleridge were more famous for the genius of their talk than their written works. But as Coleridge said when asked why he spent more time talking than writing, "The stimulus of conversation suspends the terror that haunts my mind."

IAs and IOs can also be so playful at times and so whimsical that they strike others as being overgrown children. Even the tragic Napoleon of St. Helena enjoyed a quick game of hide-and-seek with the young daughters of his keeper. All discontinuous people seek a high level of excitement and are able to immerse themselves intensely in present happenings; both sensation types and intuitives tend to have imagistically rather than logically associative minds and are, therefore, dramatically imaginative. But there are differences between sensation-type role-playing (with its emphasis on gamesmanship, myth making, and fulfilling one's function in society) and intuitive play-acting, which seeks to express the symbolic truths that lie within given situations. Such play-acting can be dangerous for these psychetypes, for (unlike sensation types who nearly always are able to stand apart from a given role and control it) intuitives run the risk of being carried away and forgetting that their act (what Dylan Thomas called his charismatic "instant Dylan") *is* an act. Similarly, there is a difference between the intuitive's love of costume (like Alexander's Persian outfit that so upset his Greek officers, the Greek dresses Nero paraded about in to the horror of the Roman Senate, or the plumed Marmaduke regalia Napoleon wore back from Egypt) and the sensation-type love of those uniforms which are shared by all members of a bonding group. A young sensation type would not wear a cowgirl suit to a Girl Scout meeting; she would wear a Girl Scout uniform; a young intuitive, if she ever joined such a group, might conceivably, on bird-watching day, come dressed as a woodpecker.

The fun-loving intuitive, in what Queen Mary called her "merry mood" and Beethoven his "unbuttoned mood," will do nearly anything to cheer other people up. They will clown until they exhaust themselves. Out of their oceanic generosity they also love to give people presents. Alexander and Napoleon gave away entire countries to their families and friends. From all we've been saying in this chapter, it is obvious that IAs and IOs can be quite eccentric, as are their fictional characterizations, like Don Quixote, Nero Wolfe, and Mr. Macawber. For, like the painter Whistler's mannerisms, General Custer's flamboyant dress and hair, Sir Walter Raleigh in his black suit and one pearl earring, or Sarah Caldwell conducting her operas in her bare feet, these psychetypes *want* to be different. Censure from the corporate body of society so distressing to feeling types may at times be actually exhilarating to intuitives. "I shall not suffer anyone to insult me by treating me as if I were a king," said Napoleon. He would be an emperor and crown himself; that would be different! Intuitive eccentricity expresses itself not only in many of the traits already discussed but also in a number of specific ways associated with their excessiveness. They are drawn to improbable people (that is, people who, by virtue of their vastly different status or function, would seem improbable to a territorial) and to people who are similarly eccentric or, in the intuitive's view, "interesting." They also tend to have a certain rather bizarre fascination with cruelty as the "Gothic" poems and fictions of Shelley, Emily Brontë, and Christina Rossetti suggest. Likewise, the boasting and exaggeration typical of intuitives derive not only from their tendency to get so carried away with things but simply from an impulse to be as unique as possible.

For all these reasons intuitives are usually thought to be peculiar and even assumed to be "mad" by the other psychetypes. In the case of Nero and Hitler we may readily agree with such accusations, but the same was said of Brontë, Pound, Eddy, Wright, Duncan, Patton, and Monroe. Was Napoleon the "mightiest breath of spirit that ever animated human clay," or was he the unprincipled, tyrannical madman Jefferson judged him to be? Was Blake a genius or insane, or both? Naturally, with so many people accusing them of being imbalanced, and with their own imaginations so compellingly overactive, IAs and IOs worry if indeed they *are* normal. One of the benefits of psychetyping to intuitives in particular is that it reassures them that their experiential world is innately no less normal than any other; it has been our experience that most intuitives are comforted by this knowledge.

One of the primary reasons why other people consider intuitives so eccentric is that they are the most changeable and inconsistent of the psychetypes. With the past vanishing into ancient history behind them, the future opening simultaneous and infinite possibilities before them, and the oceanic world merging and dissolving around them, intuitives naturally see the world as one of constant change, a perpetually moving, shifting kaleidoscope of events and inspirations. With everything that unpredictable, they think it best to assume a "you never can tell" attitude toward life. And so with intuitives you never *can* tell. Their moods are likely to fluctuate abruptly from one extreme to another. Even the comparably mild Victoria expressed the hope that when she was "in a passion," Albert would "not believe the stupid things I say, like being miserable I ever married and so forth." Biographers have expressed astonishment that Beethoven could be in such profound despair one day and so serenely joyful the next, that John Barrymore could be wonderfully charming at noon and viciously impossible at supper, that General Patton could be at once a generous leader and an autocratic megalomaniac.

On the Macawber principle of "something is bound to turn up," intuitives are always turning over new leaves to see what that something might be. When Isadora Duncan lost her school in France, she went to Russia and opened one there. Coleridge tried to be a cobbler, a doctor, and a cavalry officer. He tried to found an ideal community called Pantisocracy on the banks of the Susquehanna River in Pennsylvania; after that failed, he thought of becoming a Unitarian minister. Finally, a lifelong annuity from the Wedgewood china millionaires enabled him to devote his time and talents to lecturing, poetry, philosophy, theology, criticism, and marvelous talking. When Hubert Humphrey lost the Presidency, he ran for the Senate. When Napoleon was imprisoned on the tiny island of Elba, he started a mulberry plantation to raise silkworms.

After the battle of Waterloo and his abdication, Napoleon made a grand gesture worthy of the Homeric heroes he admired. He voluntarily put himself in the custody of his conquerors: "I come, like Themosticles, to rest at the hearth of the British people." They imprisoned him. Brought captive to Plymouth Harbor, he walked out on the deck of the *Bellerophon*. Lining the docks were thousands of Britishers who had come to jeer a man whose very name they had been taught to despise for fifteen years. He stood there quietly and looked at them. In silent tribute, hat after hat after hat came off until the whole harbor fell as quiet as Napoleon Bonaparte, who had won and lost a world.

That is one of the gifts of intuition. The Ninth Symphony is another. And *Ulysses*. And *Birth of a Nation*. And *La Mer*, and *The Rime of the Ancient Mariner* and *Tristan and Isolde* and *Wuthering Heights* and *Rhapsody in Blue*. Much that is new and daring and innovative, that is willing to take the risk of leaping forward without praise or support or even understanding, much of modern poetry, music, dance, architecture, psychology, and philosophy are gifts intuitives have offered us. And so is Mickey Mouse, and so is *Blazing Saddles*, and that is wonderful, too.

INTUITIVES

Alexander the Great, IA	The Emperor Nero, IO
Sir Walter Raleigh, IA	Mary Queen of Scots, IO
Patrick Henry, IA	Charles I of England, IO
Benedict Arnold, IA	Marie Antoinette, IO
William Blake, IA	Samuel Taylor Coleridge, IO
Percy Shelley, IA	Christina Rossetti, IO
Ludwig von Beethoven, IA	Thomas De Quincey, IO
Emily Brontë, IA	Queen Victoria, IO
Richard Wagner, IA	Carl Jung, IO
Napoleon Bonaparte, IA	D. W. Griffith, IO
General George Custer, IA	Gerard Manley Hopkins, IO
James Whistler, IA	Claude Debussy, IO
Ralph Waldo Emerson, IA	Ezra Pound, IO
Cecil Rhodes, IA	Dylan Thomas, IO
Mary Baker Eddy, IA	Rudolph Valentino, IO
Leon Trotsky, IA	Adolf Hitler, IO
Frank Lloyd Wright, IA	Arturo Toscanini, IO
Kaiser Wilhelm, II, IA	Mark Chagall, IO
William Randolph Hearst, IA	Marilyn Monroe, IO
Isadora Duncan, IA	Hubert Humphrey, IO
John Barrymore, IA	Sarah Caldwell, IO
George Gershwin, IA	Mel Brooks, IO
James Joyce, IA	
Orson Welles, IA	
General George Patton, IA	
Walt Disney, IA	
Federico Fellini, IA	

10.

The Worlds of Time and Space

Marcel Proust said that the only true voyage of discovery would be one that set sail not to look at foreign lands but "to behold the universe through the eyes of another." If this book has had to be more an excursion boat than an ocean liner, it has at least ventured to touch upon eight very different shores. Far longer trips could be taken into each, exploring in more depth the major types, the more specific differences between the two psychetypes who share a leading function, the relationship of traits and the areas from which they derive, not to mention the uses to which experiential typology could be put in therapy, business, or education. This discussion has meant to be suggestive rather than exhaustive; there are many considerations yet to explore, always with the provisos that no individual will express all the characteristics of his or her type nor be contained by those they do manifest; that some aspects of our experiential worlds are better explained by other theories, by body type, by social conditions, or by psychological equilibrium; and that, in the last analysis, our individual personhood can be accounted for by *no* theory, nor should we try to squeeze it into one.

There are, however, two further elements of our psychetypes that the limits of this book's scope have not allowed us to develop but that ought, at least, to be sketched in briefly.

INTROVERSION AND EXTRAVERSION

Jung defined and amply analyzed introversion and extraversion in his germinal study, *Psychological Types*. For that reason, and because these attitudes do not alter the traits of a given type (both introverted and extraverted thinking types make plans, live by principles, and desire impact), we have not stressed them in our discussion. However, in actual life these dimensions are of enormous significance. This is particularly evident when the type is held constant, when, for example, we contrast the introverted F. Scott Fitzgerald with the extraverted Ernest Hemingway: both SVs, both twentieth-century American novelists, but vastly different in their choice of life styles. On the other hand, when we contrast dissimilar psychetypes, the introversion/extraversion factor is subordinated. Compared to an extraverted intuitive like Napoleon, Beethoven seems as quiet as the Mad Hatter's dormouse; but compared to an equally introverted thinking type (like Brahms), Beethoven looks like the Mad Hatter, the March Hare, and the Red Queen spun into one.

Introversion/extraversion affects one's continuity or discontinuity; broadly speaking, introverts appear to be more continuous, extraverts more discontinuous. A very approximate graph would move along the following path from continuity to discontinuity, using "e" for extraversion and "i" for introversion:

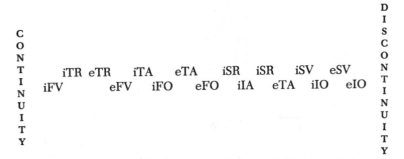

Extraversion is not another term for "gregariousness," nor is introversion a word for "shyness." The former basically means giving primacy to external stimuli; the latter means giving primacy to internal stimuli. Time moves more quickly, it feels faster, to extraverts. Introverts have a slower, steadier rhythm. Like continuity and discontinuity, these are not categorical states but a continuum along whose gradual scale people may place themselves. Nobody is completely extraverted; even Lyndon Johnson needed to be alone once in a while. And the introverted guru on the mountain top is likely to wish an occasional traveling salesman would drop by his hermitage. Nor is this rhythm of time permanently fixed in a given individual; it alters with different periods of life and with different situations. So while it may appear easy to categorize someone as introverted or extraverted on a first meeting, such judgments may prove to be invalid over a longer period of time.

A thinking type just observed in a heated intellectual argument on a topic of vital interest to him is likely to seem more extraverted than one would find him in the locker room of a roller derby team. An extraverted intuitive in a "charisma slump" is capable of sitting through an entire dinner party without opening his mouth once (but everyone would know that he was depressed). A sensation type you meet dancing on a table top at a dull gathering in order to get some action started is not *necessarily* an extravert. And a feeling type sitting at home absorbed in remembrances of an absent lover is not *ipso facto* an introvert: Nathaniel Hawthorne once spent several years of his life more or less locked up in his room at home;

afterward he returned to the normal social intercourse of his life. Nor, for example, are intuitives automatically more extraverted than feeling types or more introverted than sensation types, and so forth. Anyone of any type can be introverted or extraverted.

In general, the extravert's strength lies in the quickness and energy, the drive, with which he can set things in motion; the introvert's strength lies in the steadiness and profundity which which he can sustain his interest. And, of course, each is vulnerable to the defects grafted to their strengths. Extraverts may dissipate their energy in scattered starts and stops. Introverts may lack the necessary push to activate new arenas of endeavor.

It is probable that a majority of those men and women who have had a vital impact on active affairs of Western civilization —our political, military, and social leaders, our Alexanders, Caesars, Cleopatras, Elizabeths, Napoleons, Churchills, Lenins, Roosevelts—have been more extraverted than introverted. However, this is not inevitably so. Martin Luther King, for instance, was an introverted thinking aethereal. Nevertheless, the very nature of politics can place a psychological strain on introverts (like Woodrow Wilson or Richard Nixon) that extraverts would not feel.

Conversely, many of our intellectual and creative masters have been introverted, as were Freud, Marx, Einstein, Milton, Keats, and Beethoven. But again, like all such classifications, there are innumerable exceptions, from Mark Twain and Picasso to Walt Disney and Fellini. Extraverts who have chosen an occupation (like writing), which demands extended, sedentary periods of solitude, may seek release in outside activities of a more active nature; Hemingway with his enthusiasm for boxing, fishing, hunting, and bullfighting is a well-known example. The public performances of novelists like Twain, Dickens, or Norman Mailer are others.

Extraverts have the energy to sustain prolonged dealings with the external world; they can go from eight hours in a hectic office situation to a cocktail party, to a crowded restaurant, to three hours of television at home before they fall asleep. A constant schedule of this kind of neural bombardment is more likely to give the introvert a headache and the urge to lock himself, at least for a while, in a quiet bathroom, that last solitary refuge. But solitude makes the extravert uneasy. He may equate quietude with loneliness, or at least with boredom. It was said, for example, that the Sun King, Louis XIV, as well as Lyndon Johnson, even invited people to talk with them as they sat in their toilets.

Extraverted personalities require more stimulus from the outside world than introverted ones. The former get a great deal of pleasure from interactions; in fact, it is through them (rather than through exploration of inner thoughts and feelings) that they learn things. Jacques Cousteau is said to fill the few empty hours air travel imposes on him between one full encounter and another by voraciously tearing through magazines and newspapers to keep up with "what's going on." Napoleon left a wake of discarded books and reports behind the path of his galloping carriage; as soon as he finished one, he hurled it out the coach window and picked up another.

Such individuals are not especially comfortable with introspection and generally prefer being around other people to being alone. Somehow, it is almost as if things were not completely real to extraverts unless they are externalized. Someone like this, for instance, will be less happy attending a movie or watching television alone than will an introvert. He or she wants someone to talk or laugh with as they watch. If they do go alone, they will probably need to relate the plot to someone when they return home; they will need, in other words, to externalize it, to bring it out into the world and share it. Thus, extraverted children require more stimulus and usually demand more attention than the young introvert content for hours to play alone or sit quietly and read.

Introverts actually need such periods of solitude—time to sit alone or walk alone in nature, as was the daily habit of men like Einstein and Freud. When naturally introverted personalities find themselves caught in the whirling external demands of public life, the psychological toll can be high indeed. This was one (though, of course, only one) of Marilyn Monroe's problems. An introvert, she chose one of the most extraverted of all careers: movie stardom. Needing solitude ("I restore myself when I'm alone"), she was almost never alone. Similarly, the efforts of introvert F. Scott Fitzgerald to live the life of an extravert strained his self-sustenance to its uttermost limits, as he tried to explain in *The Crack Up:* His lifestyle was "an overextension of the flank, a burning of the candle at both ends; a call upon physical resources that I did not have." In "Pasting It Together," he added, "I only wanted absolute quiet to think out why I had developed a sad attitude towards sadness, a melancholy attitude towards melancholy, and a tragic attitude towards tragedy." For it is from inside the self, from explorations of one's heart and mind, that introverts learn, and from this inner life they gain their greatest pleasure.

And so, while such people's outer lives are likely to appear less "dramatic" than extraverts' (compare the "events" in the lives of iTR Karl Marx and eTR Nikolai Lenin, or eIO Dylan Thomas and iIO Samuel Taylor Coleridge), the *internal* life may be extraordinary indeed. Coleridge may have been sitting in his cottage, but he was imagining Kubla Khan. Such people may in fact feel that things lose something or change in indefinable ways when they are externalized. Any emotion is somehow altered when an introvert tries to articulate it; the paraphrased poem is not the same.

For introverts, new situations may be not so much invigorating challenges as intimidating prospects, for they tend to feel somewhat shy and inhibited under such circumstances and therefore to dislike large gatherings. Some, in fact, may have a sense of being invaded, actually bombarded by these intrusions of the outside world. The continual invasions of Lindbergh's privacy led him finally to leave America in complete secrecy (to avoid further publicity) and establish residency in England; only when he and his family were already in the Atlantic did he allow the news to be released to the papers. Even in the happier years preceding the kidnaping of his son, he had always found being famous "hateful." Public notice is not, to introverts, necessarily a desirable good.

> *How dreary to be somebody!*
> *How public, like a frog,*
> *To tell your name the livelong day*
> *To an admiring bog.*

Emily Dickinson, who wrote those lines, is, of course, notorious for her introverted seclusion. Carried to an extreme, introversion (like extraversion) can become pathological. It is important for introverts to seek a comfortable balance between needed aloneness and loneliness; between needed stimulation and overstimulation. Extraverts must learn to sustain themselves without constant external reinforcement. They must learn, too, to give introverts room to breathe. One of the problems in friendships or marriages between people with this discrepancy in temporal rhythm is that extraverts tend to take up most of the space. They are so free with the external world that they can deal with more of it at a given time. In consequence, the introverted partner may feel crowded out; there is no room left for him. So when *he* feels like expanding, all the space has already been taken up, leaving him no place to go. This is likely to be even more the case when the extraverted member of the couple is also discontinuous and the introvert, continuous. A marriage between an iFO and an eIA would probably find the introverted feeling type swamped, and great care must be taken to avoid such inequalities of available space. We may not need as much, but each of us should be allowed as much as he or she needs.

There are other factors besides our introversion or extraversion that strongly influence our typological emphases. For one thing, every culture has certain typological sets that it reinforces, and these preferences affect individual members. Our culture happens to be continuous in its attitudes. Most of us probably know more thinking and feeling types than sensation types and intuitives. Does this mean that there actually *are* more of the former than the latter? No systematic study has been made of this subject, nor does it seem likely that a random nose count would yield meaningful percentages of the "forty-seven percent of all Americans with incomes over $20,000 a year are thinking types" variety. First of all, SRs, SVs, IAs, and IOS may have been so successfully trained in continuous-type behavior and may have learned to rely so fully on their access to continuity through their second functions that it becomes difficult to isolate their natural typologies. Secondly, occupational factors will shift such percentages. A professional football player or pilot will probably come across more sensation types in those worlds than intuitives. A university professor may conclude that the world is ninety percent thinking types. And so forth.

Moreover, while there seems to be no tautological relationship between psychetypes and body type, it is probably true that our body type will lead us to draw upon certain trait clusters while neglecting others. For instance, a very mesomorphic (muscular, athletic) aethereal may be more frequently pulled away from imaginative and theoretical concerns and more attracted to physical activities than an ectomorphic (light body build) aethereal. Age and sex differences will also have a bearing.*

Nor has therapeutic experience and personal observation indicated any consistent pattern between psychetypes and our choice of marriage partners. Love is typologically blind. There is one exception: We have found very few successful marriages (though many friendships) between the two discontinuous types, say an IA and a SR or an IO and a SV; on the other hand, there appear to be a great many marriages between feeling and thinking types. As in all relationships, the greater the shared values, the less likelihood of misunderstanding. As we have seen, continuity/discontinuity, aethereal/volcanic, and territorial/oceanic splits represent tremendous divergences in human experience, and when these temporal and spatial barriers are crossed, it is helpful to be aware of the potential problems. One of the benefits of psychetyping is that it allows us to generalize behavior and therefore to be able to predict individual behavior in such circumstances.

We may take it as a general rule that the more typological barriers a marriage attempts to cross, the higher the predictability of an incompatible relationship. Even in such different worlds as those of IOs and TAs (like Victoria and Albert), there is spatial difference but no direct spatial *cross,* and so avenues

*Those interested in astrology may find it significant that a (very cursory) comparison of areas and astrological signs shows certain parallels between aethereals and air signs, and territorials and earth or fire signs. Any generalizations about this subject, however, would require a far more comprehensive and controlled study.

for understanding are left open. But should an SV marry a TA (as the fictional Scarlet O'Hara wished to marry Ashley Wilkes), the chances for successful communication are extremely slim. On top of a continuity/discontinuity split, there is a volcanic/ aethereal discrepancy; the SV's second function is feeling, the TA's is thinking. So, the discontinuous SV (say a male) would be uninterested in his TA wife's idealistic plans for the future and would feel constricted by the intrusions of her past on his present. As a volcanic he would constantly press for engagement; as an aethereal she would frequently pull away. Such seems to have been the typological framework of the marriage between F. Scott and Zelda Fitzgerald. In theory, the only typological advantages to a SV/TA match would be the sheer fascination of complete dissimilarity plus the fact that what one partner valued would be so meaningless to the other that he or she might easily give in to avoid conflicts.

With two people of the same psychetype (say two FVs) or related psychetypes (say a TA and a TR like Pierre and Marie Curie), there is almost no chance of such gross misunderstandings. That their personal values are so close may, on the other hand, make such people stubbornly unwilling to relinquish any given position without a struggle. When the partners are discontinuous (an SV and an SR, like Scarlet O'Hara and Rhett Butler), these disputes will probably occur more often, but last a much shorter time, and be forgotten more quickly. In cases in which the temporal dimension is held constant, but the spatial dimension is crossed, take a TR and an FO, the common assumptions of continuity may be used to help resolve the conflicts that are likely to arise from the territorial's insistence on structure and hierarchies and the oceanic's hatred of structure and his egalitarianism. Moreover, the territorial's resistance to emotional arousal and efforts to close out such situations as quickly and efficiently as possible will clash with the oceanic's need to arouse and sustain intense feelings.

Marriages in which the spatial dimensions are shared, but temporal dimensions crossed, offer the excitement of difference and often seem to run into less difficulty that those that cross spatial lines. Such couples appear to be quite common: SV and FO, FV and SR, TR and IA, TA and IA, SR and TR (like Bogart

and Bacall), or FO and IO (like Louis XVI and Marie Antoinette
—who, irrespective of their many other problems, at least seem
to have been well matched). Here, of course, misunderstandings can derive from very different relationships to time. The
discontinuous partner will be less consistent, more easily bored,
and in more need of changing stimulus than the continuous
one. Typological miscommunications occur because people do
not listen (or rather do not hear) what others are really saying.
For thinking types and feeling types to realize that despite the
great similarities of their continuity they do not mean the same
thing at all when they talk of "the importance of the past" is a
first and necessary step to then hearing what each of them *does*
mean by it.

Similarly, parents can learn that their children may be of
completely different typological makeups than they themselves are, without assuming that their children are therefore
failing to develop in normal and happy ways. Having learned
that, thinking-type parents, for example, will be less likely to
worry about a young feeling type's need to express his or her
emotions so strongly or so often; a young sensation type's insistence on being independent and self-sufficient will not seem
so uncaring to a feeling-type parent, nor will the imaginative
exuberance and lack of social deference in a young intuitive
strike a sensation-type parent as so frivolous or unmannerly. It
is very important to a child's self-development that his or her
typological predisposition be affirmed and new behavioral
skills be praised.

In families in which psychetypes are shared by siblings and
parents, there is likely to be considerable internal harmony, at
least in typological areas. Children then need to be prepared to
deal with the very dissimilar sorts of people they will meet
outside the home; otherwise, going to school, for instance, may
cause what we could call "typological shock." A six-year-old
feeling-type boy who has grown up with feeling-type parents
and two feeling-type sisters may be puzzled or distressed by
the, to him, peculiar behavior of young sensation types, intuitives, and thinking types with whom he is going to have to share
this world.

To discover our own psychetype should enable us to understand the modes through which we can most readily develop our particular potential. We next need to understand that very different modes may be best for other people. Enlightenment comes when we take Proust's voyage of discovery, when we are able to behold the universe though the eyes of another. Then, discovering the strengths of psychetypes unlike our own frees us to appreciate other worlds, while learning their limitations allows us to stop overromanticizing qualities we ourselves find it difficult to acquire. We must at the same time accept the limits of our own psychetype and stop blaming ourselves for not being people we are not. Sometimes we value things less simply because they come to us easily, and desire more what appears unattainable. An oceanic may envy a territorial's aggression and objectivity while the territorial is wishing he or she could be more personal and receptive. The more we do away with blame and envy, the more balanced and fair a view we have of ourselves and others, the more productive energy we can release for living our lives as best we can.

Obviously, those will be happier—and no doubt healthier —who develop the strengths and overcome the weaknesses of their psychetypes. A sensation type who, to the exclusion of other qualities, gives free rein to his or her impulses toward manipulativeness, secrecy, intolerance for others' weaknesses, moral expediency, and disregard for past commitments is less humanly fulfilled (and probably less happy) than one who has chosen to grow in the particular riches of this type: in active energy and skill, in a responsive awareness of other people, and a heightened sensitivity to the world around him or her. The same choice lies open to all psychetypes.

It is through our language that we most immediately sense the differences among us. "I have a dream for this world," says the aethereal. "I have a plan for this world," says the territorial. "Let us act so that this world . . ." the volcanic tells us. "Let us hope and pray that this world . . ." asks the oceanic.

Let us learn to listen to the language of human experience.

SECOND FUNCTION AND SECONDARY AREA

When first learning the characteristics of the basic types, people often find that *two* of the four functions seem to apply to them far more than the other two. This is because of our second functions. Recall that each of the spatial areas is shared by two functions:

Thinking ⎫		Thinking ⎫	
Intuition ⎭	AETHEREALITY	Sensation ⎭	TERRITORIALITY
Feeling ⎫		Sensation ⎫	
Intuition ⎭	OCEANIC	Feeling ⎭	VOLCANIC

While these factors combine, of course, to produce very different individuals—compare Marilyn Monroe, an IO, and Elizabeth Taylor, an FO: Humphrey Bogart, an SR, and Lauren Bacall, a TR; John F. Kennedy, a TA, and Governor Jerry Brown, an IA—such people will nevertheless hold certain common attitudes and display some common behavior. That is because each has the other's first function as his

236 · APPENDIX A

or her second function: in other words, their next available conscious mode of conceptualizing and behaving. Someone's second function will come from the only other type to participate in that person's primary area. Only sensation and thinking participate in territoriality; therefore, an SR's second function is thinking; a TR's second function is sensation. However, a thinking aethereal's second function would be not sensation but intuition, for only thinking and intuition participate in aethereality. So we see in a TA like John F. Kennedy that intuitive ability to "charismize" others with a vision of the future—his dream, for example, of putting a man on the moon (a statement still played over the loud speakers in NASA tour buses). In such moments, Kennedy was drawing not only on his dynamic thinking-type purposefulness but on the wide-sweeping idealism of his second function, intuition. Similarly, IA Napoleon could draw quite effectively on his thinking-type traits.

For a feeling volcanic like Dwight D. Eisenhower, sensation would be the second function, and throughout his life he displayed a number of personality traits that derive from this type: his love of sports, his ability to act quickly and effectively in crises. Conversely, Lyndon B. Johnson's love of telling stories of the past comes out of his secondary feeling function. But a feeling oceanic like Winston Churchill would have his secondary strength in intuition. And again, as with Kennedy, by availing himself of the inspirational facility of this function, Churchill was singularly successful in mesmerizing people into believing in possibilities. By definition, then, the second function of a feeling oceanic is intuition, just as the second function of an intuitive oceanic like Mary of Scotland is feeling.*

The degree to which one is extraverted or introverted seems to affect the pull of the secondary function. In general, we may say that in extraverts the primary area is so dominant that it draws the person over into his or her related (second) function more fully than appears to be the case with introverts. In extraverted continuous types, extraversion pushes the personality toward the second (always discontinuous) function because extraversion always accentuates discontinuity. Thus, in the personality of Elizabeth I, an extraverted TR, territoriality explains more of her behavior (objectivity, competitiveness, organizational ability) than is explained by her aethereality or continuity. As a

*When people are under stress they tend to go deeply into their primary function. When they are very relaxed (say when they have had a few drinks), they often allow their second function more room to express itself. A slightly inebriated TR may start acting like a sensation type, while the SR begans solemnly theorizing in a thinking-type way.

result, she was greatly drawn toward sensation, the second territorial function, and particularly toward those sensation-type characteristics deriving from territoriality (self-control, secrecy, and independence, for instance). Similarly, an extraverted FV like Norman Mailer seems to manifest more volcanic traits than continuous or oceanic ones; he may therefore in some ways more resemble people of his second function (like SV Ernest Hemingway) than those who, while sharing his primary feeling function, are highly oceanic as well as introverted and thus more continuous—like Shubert, for example. In the same way, extraverted thinking aethereals (like Franklin D. Roosevelt) and extraverted feeling oceanics (like Winston Churchill) are so strongly drawn by intuition that they *appear* at times to be intuitives.

When, with sensation types and intuitives, we move in the opposite direction, the gravitational pull of the primary area over into the shared function is mitigated by the counterpressure of heightened discontinuity in extraverted IAs and IOs, SRs and SVs. Nevertheless, a somewhat similar pattern does emerge. Napoleon's intensified aethereality enabled him to draw on a great many of the strengths of his secondary thinking function when organizing and administering his government, and the same is true of extraverted SRs like Julius Caesar or Bismarck—all three of these men acted in ways that, on the surface, are indistinguishable from thinking-type behavior. Likewise, extraverted IOs and SVS, respectively, seem more intensely oceanic and volcanic—and therefore more like volatile and passionate feeling types —than their introverted counterparts.

When we turn to introverts, a different but equally suggestive conformation appears to materialize. Here the personality seems to rely more heavily than do extraverts on the sub-area of the primary function. For Freud, a TR, that would of course be his aethereality, hence his interest in intellectual abstractions and in theories, his generalizing tendency, detachment, and so forth. For Jane Austen, an introverted TA, territorial social order and sexual gamesmanship form the subject matter of her fiction. The introverted FV Judy Garland was drawn constantly into problematic oceanic traits: lack of structure, defenselessness, and difficulty isolating or resolving personal problems. The introverted FO Vincent van Gogh was subject to unmanageable volcanic explosions.

Looking at discontinuous introverts, we see that in them, as in all introverts, the movement toward continuity supports and enhances the pull into the sub-area: Jung, an IO, drawn toward aethereality, resembles, in some regards, a continuous thinking type. SV F. Scott Fitzgerald tried throughout his life to fight off his discontinuity and volcanic involvement and to bring to the fore of his personality his territorial need for order and structure. Introverted SRs (like Lindbergh) are closer to volcanic physicality, and introverted IAs (like Shelley) are closer to oceanic emotionality than their extraverted counterparts. Since the importance of continuity to all introverts blocks off access to the discontinuous functions, this pull of the sub-area toward that area's cross-temporal function is less powerful; in other words, an introverted TA will not be sufficiently drawn to territoriality to give up his continuity and assume discontinuous sensation-type traits. This shift happens occasionally, however. In Judy Garland, for example, we notice how her sub-area oceanic characteristics sometimes click over into intuitive charisma; in fact we can see it happen in her performances.

As always, such comprehensive generalizations will not apply to every individual. There are some people for whom one typological aspect seems to govern behavior more pervasively than all the others: Napoleon is perhaps best studied in terms of his extraordinary extraversion and Emily Dickinson through her introversion *(temporal rhythm)* and Isadora Duncan by her nearly unrelieved discontinuity *(temporal flow)*. The volcanic *sub-area* may be the most salient way to talk about SR Picasso's personality, while *primary area* territoriality seems to have dominated the attitudes and actions of SR Henry Ford. In like manner, the intuitive *second function* of TA Franklin D. Roosevelt often tells us more immediately about his aspirations and impact than do other qualities.

Appendix B

CONTINUOUS

Perception of time evolutional.

   Perceives the past as significant.

   Perceives moments of time and events as recurrent and patterned.

Involvement in the present is guided by a sense of its connection to the past and the future.

   Desire to return to the known, familiar, and loved.

      Reassured by familiar surroundings.

      Values relationships which have a history.

      Loves recurrent celebrations.

      May be at a disadvantage when dealing with the new.

   Likes to familiarize oneself with what might happen so that it will not be too strange or surprising when it occurs.

   Gets pleasure from imagining some event as a future memory.

Consistent and moderate.

   Gets accustomed to things.

      May dislike innovations or have difficulty dealing with them.

Does not like to take too many risks.

Views events apparently underived from past circumstances as disorderly and inexplicable.

Believes in verbal consistency: words must always mean the same things.

Self-sustaining; not easily bored: does not require continuous, varied stimulation from the present.

Patient.

Discomfort with discontinuity.

Strong memories of the past.

Distressed if the past is invalidated.

Desires to relive bits of one's personal past.

Considers one's childhood very important.

May venerate the past.

Believes that past actions should be used to explain the present.

Is likely to continuously apply things learned in the past to the present.

Serious and thoughtful.

Considers plans important.

Takes decision making seriously.

Carefully considers situations before acting.

Thinks one has made use of all available options.

Is concerned about the possibility of negative outcomes.

DISCONTINUOUS

Perception of time existential.

Perceives the past as insignificant.

Perceives moments of time as discrete.

Perceives events as unique.

Involvement in the present and the future is disconnected from the past.

Has an immediate and total response to present situations.

Relies on immediate perceptions.

Is often immoderate because he or she does not compare the importance of the present to the past, does not evaluate the relative significance of events.

Easily gets involved in whatever is presented at the time regardless of prior involvements or long-term situations.

Intensifies the moment.

Seeks out things which would be an "experience."

Sees life as a drama.

Playful.

Impulsive and changeable.

Can throw oneself into current activities without reservation.

Is afraid of missing something.

Believes that something new is desirable, and likely to be available.

Requires continuous stimulation from the present.

Easily bored; dislikes things which go on too long.

Discomfort with continuity.

Weak sense of the past; is unable to remember the past as a continuum; remembers peak experiences.

Relatively unperturbed by past mistakes or failures; may seem relatively untouched by what has happened to him or her.

May be forgetful.

Dislikes the past intruding on the present.

Derives one's feeling of continuity and rootedness from ties with the family.

Has a negative attitude toward "thoughtfulness" and formal learning.

Is impatient with pedantry and with the orderly process of sequential learning.

May take a great dislike to learning traditional things, the things he or she thinks others believe one "ought" to learn.

May be contemptuous of "thinking."

Thinks things can be learned only as they are needed.

Dislikes routine; hates having to repeat tasks or projects.

Believes that words may change their meaning in different situations.

Does not feel bound by past statements.

AETHEREAL

Interested in the possible and the theoretical.

Involved in the future and attracted to the emergent.

May feel the future to be more real than the present.

Has a sense of competence when theorizing about the future, or awkwardness when dealing with the present.

Tends not to be interested in things just for what they are in their present state.

Fascinated with possibilities.

May object to things "as they are."

Goal-proliferates.

    Experiences the self as pulled by multiple possibilities.

    Distrusts skepticism; reluctant to decide something without considering all of the possibilities.

    Strikes others as a "restless searcher."

Believes in the power of ideas.

    Is deeply committed to ideas, theories, or visions.

    Is theoretical and generally interested in scope rather than depth.

    Is impatient with concrete details.

    Acts according to general principles.

    Is idealistic.

        "Aims high," insists on things as they *ought* to be.

        Is concerned with glory.

        Becomes righteously indignant.

Believes in the power of the imagination.

    Loves that which captures the underlying essence of things.

    May seem to others to "leave the ground."

        May use imagery or analogies so complex or idiosyncratic that they interfere with communication.

Intellectual.

    Is knowledgable and careful about that which forms a part of one's theory or vision.

    Is concerned with intellectual achievement.

    Thinking may become an end in itself; may find it hard to turn off mental activity.

    Relies on language to deal with the world.

        Has a strong appetite for conversation.

        Loves verbal elegance; witty; enjoys word play and puns.

Detached.

    Potentially indifferent to things which are not a part of one's mental or imaginative world.

        Intellectual toughness.

    Mistrusts the personal.

        Tends not to value people or things in themselves.

        Sees people as a manifestation of some ideal.

    Mistrusts the corporate existence.

        Individualistic.

        Has a nothing-sacred attitude.

        Arrogant.

        May be unwilling to adapt.

        May be socially insensitive and awkward.

Relatively indifferent to the material world.
  May find the sensual world and natural processes distasteful.
    May prefer the inanimate (e.g., art) to the animate (e.g., nature).
  Needs little from the physical world.
    May be aescetic or spartan in tastes and habits.
    May be unobservant of surroundings.
    Mental world may be damaged by a sudden, hitherto unnoticed
    event in reality which contradicts an essential element in a theory
    or vision.

VOLCANIC

Interested in the actual and the immediate.
  Involved in the present.
    Dislikes not acting in accordance with actual situations.
    Has difficulty assessing things one is not presently experiencing.
    May be unable to anticipate.
    Wants to be in the presence of the person one is involved with.
  Relies on action.
    Prefers a world of finite possibilities.
    Distrusts abstractions and is uncomfortable with theories.
    Sees each human being as unique and special.
    Attentive to concrete details.
Highly engaged with life.
  Adaptable.
    Able to accept life simply, as it is given; strikes others as "natural."
    Can easily integrate oneself into the mores of the age and culture.
    Can be idiosyncratic and still be accepted because of a secure base
    in the corporate structure.
  Is socially and emotionally aware.
    Makes friends easily.
    Is able to assess others accurately.
  Not very goal-oriented; content to putter about.
  Acceptant.
    Good-natured.
    Considers everything going on around one as real and meaningful.
    Is able to endure with dignity whatever life presents.
Highly involved and emotional.
  Unable to be detached from one's own experiences.
    Capable of explosions of strong emotion.
    Tends to scold others.

Responsive to anything that touches one's emotions.
> Protective.

Able to be tough about negative feelings.
> May be willing to manipulate the feelings of others.
> Can be tenacious.

Has a strong sense of personal integrity, and is horrified by a feeling of being unfaithful to the self.
> Deeply moral and capable of being morally indignant.
> Believes in honor.

Is concerned with personal development.
> Is more interested in the depth than the scope of things.
> Attracted to those aspects of life which endure.

Competent in the material world.
> Feels a close relationship to the physical environment, and respects it.
> Loves all living, growing things.
> Acceptant of natural processes.

Is concerned with the body.
> Wants to be fashionable and appropriate.
> Dresses to be pleasing to others and to oneself.
> Worries about aging, and losing one's looks.

TERRITORIAL

Sense of structure to the self highly important.
> Needs to "define" the self and must experience the self as distinct from others.
> Prefers to make one's own structures.
> Desires impersonality and objectivity.
>> Loves and needs privacy.
>> Is unwilling to be in another's debt.
> Desires emotional control and resists emotional arousal.
>> Can treats one's own feelings objectively.
>> Can treat other people's feelings impersonally or see them as irrelevant.
>> Defensive.
>> Dislikes sentimentality.

Sense of structure to the intellect highly important.
> Orderly and habitual.
>> Well-disciplined.
>> Enjoys quantifying: statistics, maps, lists, etc.

Enjoys and is skillful at organization.
   Has great administrative abilities.
   Likes to control and direct things.
   Appreciates organizations.
Considers social structures highly important.
   Is concerned with status and appreciates role and status differences.
      Tends to define people by their function rather than their person-
      hood.
      Needs to have information about people (their background, posi-
      tion, etc.) in order to know how to behave toward them.
   Respects the rules or codes of groups and organizations.
      Attentive to rights and duties.
      Deferential.
   Is concerned about one's respectibility.
   Seeks role models.
   Perceptive about social situations; recognizes the limits of situations
   and does not trangress them.
   Moved by ceremonial displays which give an appropriate form for
   genuine feelings.
Spatial structure highly important.
   Needs to have one's own territory.
      Very sensitive to invasions of territory.
      Needs to defend one's territory; protective; takes care of others.
      Gets homesick.
   Sensitive to spatial needs and creative about the use of space.
Competitive and assertive.
   Desires power.
   Is spurred on by opposition.
   Likes to have worthy adversaries.
      Social gamesmanship valued.
   Likes to face dangers and overcome them; may prefer to see the
   world as an opponent to be overcome.
   Sexually aggressive and attentive to the sexual energy of others.

OCEANIC

Personalness and a sense of freedom to the self highly important.
   Uninterested in self-definitions.
      Unable to assess the self.
   Non-judgmental.
      Readily admits one is in the wrong.

Lacks self-protectiveness, guile, or secretiveness.

Needs to arouse emotions in oneself and in others.

Process more important to intellect than structure.

Flexible.

Has a rippling, flowing quality of mind; mentally joins what appears to be separate.

Dislikes controversy and pitting oneself against others.

Subjective.

Tends to personalize things and to be uncomfortable with things which do not derive from the personal.

Is unable to judge or evaluate one's own ideas objectively.

Social openness highly important.

Uninterested in social structures.

Fears and doesn't like to handle situations involving complex social structures.

Finds it painful to stay in structured situations.

Disregards status distinctions and pays attention to personal qualities.

Unconscious of social roles.

Believes that everyone is entitled to the same rights and considerations.

Often fails to present oneself in the most socially advantageous manner.

Spatial freedom highly important.

Needs free space.

Insensitive to invasions of other people's territory.

Untroubled by intrusions on one's own territory.

Generally unable to deal particularly well with the technical, physical aspects of life.

Unable to plan space.

Receptive.

Reverential.

Goes with the flow.

Unable to maintain a position; appears to drift.

Spirituality.

Seems innocent.

Tends to be less interested in sexuality per se than people of other types.

Often feels as if he or she is not a part of this world; life seems dreamy.

Has difficulty communicating experiences.

Seems whimsical to others.

Passive.

Often feels defenseless and wants to be protected.

Tends to be swayed by others.

May try to control others through passivity or to "engulf" them.

May have trouble isolating and actively dealing with problems, since problems in one area tend to "contaminate" all aspects of life.

Good-hearted and kind.

Is willing to do for others what they will not do for themselves.

Generous.

Looks for and sees the good in other people.

THINKING

(Each trait derives either from one or from some combination of aethereality, territoriality, and continuity)

Temporal continuity highly important.

Structures time; relates the past to the present to the future in a linear progression.

Respects the proper timing of things.

Believes that things will get better with the passage of time.

Becomes discontent if life is not going along at the proper pace.

Has a general interest in time.

Loves history and tends to use historical referents or analogies.

Enjoys following the process of things.

Believes he or she has a significant place or a special function in history.

Considers conceptualization primary basis of life; highly logical.

Finds it important to have ideas, and enjoys having them.

Needs to be alone to think.

Tends to make theories, and takes pleasure in work which entails the synthesis of the logical components of a task.

Needs random input of information.

Lets the head guide the heart; ideas generate feelings, and not the reverse.

Is interested in the problem of when to *stop* thinking.

Needs to know the reason for things.

Fantasizes conversations to work out problems.

Has a strong sense of principles.

Sees any given situation in terms of the principle to be found in it.
Is annoyed when others don't understand one's principles.
Is deeply distressed when two principles are in conflict.
>Defers decisions in the hope that an overriding principle will resolve apparent contradictions, or compromises so as to evolve such a principle.

Has a deep love of justice.
>Has an impersonal system of ethics and compassion for men in general; ethics are divorced from personal emotions.
>Believes in law; may be legalistic.
>Tends to be judgmental and righteously indignant.
>Is angered when people don't follow the rules of justice.

Special vulnerability to emotional arousal.
May be unable to control feelings.
Protects oneself from being hurt by investing energy in many different areas and by creating different channels to express different needs.
Gets disillusioned.
Needs to have feelings activated by others.
>Is able to rule out problematic aspects of one's life from consideration.
>Is often unwilling to sustain a direct expression of feelings.
>Fears that he or she does not have enough feelings.
>Makes mistakes because of a failure to perceive how others feel about things.
>Senses the awkwardness of dealing with others' feelings and so may choose to ignore them.

Tends to be self-critical, and is hard to comfort.

Structure in all areas of life highly important.
Considers it essential to make plans and follow them.
>Is delighted when plans prove effective and infuriated when plans are ruined.
>Is distressed when plans do not go as predicted.
>Annoyed when others fail to understand plans.

Concerned about being on the right path in life and moving in the right direction.
>Deliberates about events before they occur.
>Has stick-to-it-ness.

Wants a structured, well-ordered lifestyle.
>Is sensible about things.
>Is intolerant of chaos, and needs routine.
>Concerned about the careful management of money.

Values proportion and evenness and delights in the proper proportion of things; e.g., in art or architecture.

Desires aesthetic as well as theoretical simplicity.

Constructs systems or principles which contain and resolve at a higher level of abstraction apparent conflicts between other systems or principles.

Is intolerant of ambiguity.

Decisive; seeks and needs early closure on queries or problems.

Is unwilling to be taught isolated skills or random facts.

Excellent organizational ability.

Is responsible about delegating authority.

Maintains a network of communication with those involved in organizations.

Gathers and synthesizes information to use in theories or plans.

Organizes and classifies collections.

Writes, reads, and respects detailed, factual reports.

Likes disentangling mix-ups.

Desires impact.

Needs to be a sapiential authority and cares to give good advice.

Takes oneself quite seriously.

Needs agreement and approval.

Acknowledges the sapiential authority of others.

Considered by others to be a sapiential authority.

Known to give good advice and able to give a sensible answer to any question.

Desires power.

Competitive.

Loves arguing and likes to "score points."

Unwilling to accept failure.

Has a strong reforming drive.

Has the potential for fanaticism, and may wish to see enemies totally annihilated.

Headstrong.

Loves grandness and majesty.

Intellectual quality of personality.

Theoretical and deductive.

Resents being brought down from a level of abstraction.

Analytic and comparative.

Reasons by a process of elimination and is able to screen things out.

Scholarly.

Has pedagogic abilities.

Has the potential for over-intellectualism.
Loves books.
Highly verbal with great capacity for verbal statesmanship.
Believes that words are powerful and may use them as weapons
Loves satire and parody.
Witty and sarcastic.
Reveres language.
May be literalistic.
Fears he or she will be criticized for plainness of writing style.
Delights in discourse in which there is a meeting of minds.
Dynamic and energizing.
Respectful of and insightful about others.
Gives others the sense that they are understood and accepted.

FEELING

(Each of these traits derives from one or some combination of the volcanic, oceanic, and continuous)

Past-maintaining; experiences the emotional impact of past events.
Desires to re-experience the same emotions again.
Loves telling stories of the past.
Emphasizes the significance of childhood.
Has a special sense of those things which will remain important memories.
Is able to maintain feelings when the object of those feelings is no longer present.
May be slow to change or to accept the new.
Sticks to things and may be clinging.
Considers emotions primary basis of life; highly emotional.
Capable of deep, strong emotions and also able to take pleasure in simple emotional responses.
Needs to be experiencing some emotion.
Moody; strikes others as always in some emotional state or another.
Finds it difficult to interrupt an on-going emotion.
May be lost in a strong emotion, and out of a desire to sustain it will allow it to go on longer than is necessary.
May be overwhelmed with emotion.
May be insensitive to others when overwhelmed by his or her own feelings, since the presence of strong emotion tends to obliterate all other considerations.
Desires emotional unity.

Is emotionally aware and versatile.

Able to express feelings accurately (through words, acts, music, etc.).

Has refined taste in delineating subtle shades of emotion and wants to track down each nuance of feeling.

Highly sensitive to emotional climates.

Socially diplomatic and delicate.

Has excellent therapeutic abilities.

Can feel emotions not yet strong enough to be recognized or defined by others.

Is able to master his or her own feelings and to maintain social presence under most circumstances.

Great sensitivity to others.

Perceptive about what others are feeling, even able to perceive others' yet unconscious feelings.

Able to say the right thing to others in emotional situations

Responsive to others' needs.

Wants to avoid hurting others' feelings.

Mortified by misperceiving someone else's feelings.

Easily feels sorry for others.

Sees and rejects self-conscious attempts by others to play on his or her feelings for manipulative purposes.

High potential for negative emotions.

Vulnerable to self-pity.

Tends to complain.

Cannot accept comfort when he or she feels they have done the wrong thing.

Easily gets his or her feelings hurt.

Has a tendency toward self-blame and reproach.

Vulnerable to vindictiveness and may hold grudges.

If hurt, may desire to punish others so deeply they will be permanently incapacitated.

Feels that without human relationships life has no meaning.

Believes that situations gain and grow in the process of interaction with others.

Blossoms within the context of an emotional response from another.

Loves talking about people.

Has a talent for making friends.

Comes alive and sparkles when with friends.

Learns things which would be pleasing to others.

Loves sharing with others.

Inspires loyalty in others.

Places a high value on intimacy.

Is made daring by love.

May leave a love relationship only when it has entirely exhausted its emotional content.

May not be able to leave one relationship until it is supplanted by a greater emotional attachment.

Intolerant of suspense in a love relationship and susceptible to jealousy.

Has a strong desire to belong.

Needs demonstrations of others' affection and susceptible to emotional dependency.

Has difficulty with leave-takings and separations.

Is concerned about his or her appearance and worries about losing looks.

Deep capacity for devotion and loyalty.

Considers faithlessness or falseness a sin.

Ferocious in the defense of loved ones.

When in love, is quite capable of ignoring undesirable personality traits in the loved one.

Trusting.

Nurtures others.

Self-sacrificing.

Tender-hearted and sympathetic.

Feels involved in the eternal life cycles of man and nature.

Enduring and acceptant; is able to keep a simple, unrushed pace.

Is able to cope with death.

Can comfort others by keeping them in touch with the eternal.

Believes in fate.

Is interested in the process of growth.

Has a special relationship to children.

Enjoys hearing others tell stories of their pasts.

Reverence for life and desire not to harm any living thing.

Likes to collect beautiful things.

Engaged quality of personality.

The intellect is guided by the emotions: the heart rules the head.

Tends to lack analytic, detached view of things.

Has a practical, "feet on the ground" attitude.

Finds writing thoughts down easier than articulating them.

Uses irony rather than direct confrontation in arguments; teases people.

Believes intense emotion is the best teacher.
  Learns by empathizing with others.
  Derives the "moral" of any story.
  Personalizes things.
Believes in the private, inner, self-fertilizing aspect of feelings and therefore is rarely bored.
Romantic.
  Has a special relationship to youth as the time of romance and strong emotions.
  Has the potential for disenchantment, the failure of romanticism.
    Sense of the loss of innocence.
  May be sentimental.
Tends to worry and anticipate negatively.
  Pessimistic.
  Likely to think happiness does not enrich one as much as sorrow does.
  Sees the tragic potential in things.
Enchanting and warm.
Responsive and sensitive
  Gives others the sense that they are cared for.

SENSATION

(Each trait derives either from one or from some combination of the volcanic, territorial, and discontinuous)

Present-oriented.
  Focuses entire attention on the present moment.
  Tends not to have future desires or to know what he or she likes until it is experienced.
  Can be completely satisfied in the present, at least for short periods.
  Dislikes the past intruding on the present: "When it's over, it's over."
    Considers looking back morbid.
    "No turning back" attitude.
Has an intense sense of the transitory nature of things.
  Attempts to preserve the present in concrete form (diaries, letters, etc.) as evidence of the past.
  Deep sense of the fragility of life.
    Fascinated with death.
    Sees love-making as a paradigm of the life experience.
    May be depressed on birthdays.

Loves variety and mobility.

 Seeks out new experiences; wanderlust.

 Is surprised to find onself committed to someone, something, someplace.

Physical world the primary basis of the personality.

 Heightened sensory awareness.

  Delights in the sensual world.

  Loves physical comforts and physical tasks.

 Perceives through the senses, and feels most fully alive when engaged in some totally involving sensual experience.

  Communicates by means of the senses, and really only trusts the evidence of the senses.

  Is able to focus total sensory awareness on one immediate experience.

 Has an aesthetic sensibility and sensuality.

  Is perceptive about and concerned with personal aesthetics, including the aesthetics of behavior.

 Sexual prowess.

Negative attitude toward thinking.

 Distrusts abstractions and doesn't like to generalize, so may fail to learn from experience. Learns instead from trial and error.

 Holds facts (data) to be the only basis for action.

  Prefers verbal directness.

  Records things exactly as they are.

 Thinks "seeing is believing" and distrusts words.

 Holds to a situational morality rather than a general theory of ethics.

  Is likely to be motivated by powerful desires rather than logic or plans.

 Life and the life of the body seem synonymous.

  Is likely to remember best what he or she has learned through the senses.

  May be contemptuous of intellectuals.

Strong sense of physical competence.

 Desires to have new skills, enjoys learning and perfecting them— particularly physical, manual tasks and solving technical problems.

  Enjoys sports; high athletic abilities.

  Medical abilities.

 Optimistic because of faith in the body's competence.

  Fearless, cocksure.

 Efficient.

  Has a "be prepared" attitude.

Feels close to and respects the physical environment.
Is careful, willing to take risks but not foolhearty.
Senses a pattern of extrapersonal forces in nature.
Observant.
Utilizes whatever is provided by the environment.
Delights in creating a pleasing physical environment, but willing to tolerate physical discomfort.

Insists on self-sufficiency.
Insists on order.
Precise; allows no substitutes: "right tool for the right job."
Fussy.
Likes to take charge and give orders.
Nags others.
Tactical; draws up "battle plans."
Practical and expedient.
Immediately recognizes what is necessary and works with speed and economy of effort.

Insists on control in oneself and in others.
Angered by revelatory impulses in the self or others; tends to be secretive.
Independent; has a "don't fence me in" attitude.
Enraged when others get in his or her way.
Defends one's own and others' territory.
Appreciates those who meet one's needs.
Remembers what has threatened one, can be vengeful.
Intolerant of "weakness" in the self or others.
Self-confident; finds it hard to quit until one has total victory.

Considers social structures very important; understands how they work and respects them.
Values good manners and is respectful of elders.
Resistant to change.
Needs to bond with others.

Manipulative in interpersonal relations; may find it difficult to restrain oneself from manipulating those considered weak.
Likes to create and control situations and enjoys power manipulations and intrigues.

Desires peak experiences.
Action-oriented; finds it difficult not to act or to delay acting.
Assertive, takes control of situations.
Crisis-oriented.
Loves challenges and appreciates crises because they are ex-

hilarating peak experiences which call for bold, decisive action.
Loves crises-filled worlds like politics, surgery, courtroom law.
Able to deal well with crises.
Tries to turn all situations into peak experiences and may be willing to manipulate others in order to do so.
May be cautious in response to the sense that an up-coming situation could be a crises.

Views life as a game and likes playing roles; may be willing to take on different roles to fulfill different situations.
Likes uniforms.
Likes practical jokes and playing games devised by others.

Mythologizes experiences since people, places, and events gain an increasingly significant meaning if overlaid with a mythological veneer.
Loves mysteries and is susceptible to magic.
Interested in conjuring and magicians; facility with sorcery.
Communicates with objects and keeps totem objects which symbolize territory.
Superstitious; believes in signs and synchronicities; waits for the inner moment to signal one to begin something.

Reactive quality of the personality.
Needs immediate impact and may be reluctant to go on unless a definite response is forthcoming.
Needs to know quickly whether one has "gotten through" to others and how they are responding.
"Negative capability": responsiveness to what is outside oneself; sees self as the result of experiences rather than the cause.

Magnetic and vital.

Knows what will please others.
Gives others a heightened sense of their beauty, intelligence, charm, etc.

INTUITIVE

(Each trait derives from one or some combination of the aethereal, oceanic, and discontinuous)

Future-oriented.
Believes that the future can't come fast enough and so tries to draw the present into the future.
Sees the relevant future as a far, far-reaching one; things go on endlessly, even death is not an end.

Fascination with suicide.

Prophesies.

Is concerned about safe-guarding the future and attempts to control it.

Optimistic, even unstumpable, because of faith in the future.

Fears being pinned down and hates closure.

The vision is the primary basis of the personality.

Tends to have a far-reaching vision (of man, God, art, progress, etc.).

Prefers dealing with the cosmic; expands things to cosmic dimensions.

Is completely involved in the vision and totally committed to it.

Feels that until one has a vision, life has no center.

Finds it hard to remember things which are not a part of one's vision, though he or she has an excellent memory of things which are connected to it.

Is horrified by the failure of a vision.

Relatively indifferent to the "real," utilitarian world.

Unrealistic; believes that "reality" does not reside in the tangible, material world.

Sees reality as oppressive.

May be uncritically acceptant of various aspects of the outside world because they are not empirically tested.

Impractical.

Indifferent to the practical aspects of tasks.

Unobservant of surroundings.

Tends not to be *au courant* with what is going on in the world.

May be clumsy.

Social roles and status differences do not seem meaningful, and may not be noticed.

May fail to perceive when one has violated a social norm and so may be tactless or socially awkward.

May suspect the motives of others.

May find it hard to believe that people cannot be strongly motivated by sexual desire per se.

Highly imaginative quality of the personality.

Puts great trust in the imagintion and is indifferent to the factual and literal.

May seem to be operating directly out of the unconscious.

Contemptuous of unimaginativeness.

Snobbish.

May be controlled by his or her imagination.

Strikes others as extraordinarily, perhaps excessively imaginative.

Lives in a radical, whirling mental world.

Rapidly inspired: one thought, image, or idea immediately suggests another.

May mix-up quotations, metaphors, and references.

Likes neologisms.

Believes in destiny and in forces beyond man's purview.

Is interested in religion and spiritual matters.

Has imaginative rather than active energy, and will shun or delay action which does not activate imagination.

Tends to let things happen.

Leaps into action exuberantly once imaginative energy has been activated and can then keep on acting since energy set in motion in one area spills over into others.

Handles conflicts by removing oneself from the situation or by threatening to leave.

Hates change around one.

Charismatic quality.

Inspires others; acts as a catalyst in whose presence others change.

Tends to have a meteoric career: rapid rise and swift fall.

Places a high value on one's charismatic ability.

Feels fully alive only when inspiring others.

If he or she does not have an effective vision, they will try to inspire others with their own lives.

Plays God.

Dislikes teaching because he or she prefers inspiring people.

Cannot tolerate a denial of one's charisma.

Moves to make sure charismatic potential is not diminished.

Responds to stress situations by turning on more charisma.

Has a sense of competition with others over who's got more charisma.

Hates showiness or strong emotionalism in others.

Cannot listen to others.

Hates exaggeration in others; especially about non-imaginary things.

Concern about whether or not inspirations will be responded to can make him or her shy.

May become vicious if charisma is denied.

Excessive quality; gets carried away.

Disregards consequences.

Cannot structure time.

Has swift, strong reactions to people and things.

Drowns people in communications.

Irrepressible; talkative and playful.

    Enjoys costumes.

    As an adult, he or she may strike others as an overgrown child.

Seeks a high level of excitement.

    Fun-loving.

    Fascination with cruelty.

    Loves to cheer people up and likes giving them presents.

    Exaggerative.

        Tends to boast.

Eccentric.

    Wants to be different.

        Is drawn to improbable people.

    Worries if he or she is normal.

        May be thought mad by others.

Changeable.

    Has rapid fluctuations of mood from one extreme to another.

    Is always turning over a new leaf and is easily converted.

    Sees the world as in constant change and perpetual motion, and as therefore unpredictable; adopts a "you never can tell" attitude.

Inspirational.

Charms and moves others.

EXTRAVERT

Gains primary pleasure from interactions with the external world.

Learns things by observation of the external world.

Has much energy available to deal with the external world.

Seeks new situations for stimulation.

Under most circumstances, values interactions with others over solitude.

Is not especially comfortable with introspection.

Tends to find solitude and quietude boring.

May easily experience solitude as loneliness.

Feels that things are not completely real unless externalized.

INTROVERT

Feels that things actually are very different when externalized than when they remain internal.

Desires periods of solitude; for example, enjoys being alone with nature.

Must seek a comfortable balance between needed aloneness and loneliness; between stimulation and overstimulation.

Tends to feel shy and inhibited in new situations.

Has a tendency to dislike large gatherings and public notice.

Fears being invaded, bombarded by the outside world.

Has an outer life less "dramatic" than that of an extrovert.

Gains the greatest pleasure from the inner life.

Learns things from inside the self, from exploration of his or her own heart or mind.